THE SWIMMING TRIANGLE

A Holistic Approach to Competitive Swimming

NICK BAKER

Former Olympic Coach and Founder of Peak Performance Swim Camp

Positive Swimming

i

For more information: www.theswimmingtriangle.com

Cover photos and design by:
Brian Adams PhotoGraphics, Inc.
www.brianadamsphoto.com

Book design by:
Arbor Books, Inc.
www.arborbooks.com

Printed in the United States of America

The Swimming Triangle: A Holistic Approach to Competitive Swimming
Nick Baker

1. Title 2. Author 3. Swimming

Library of Congress Control Number: 2011911381
ISBN 13: 978-0-615-50813-9

TABLE OF CONTENTS

—

"EMPTY YOUR CUP. A FULL CUP CANNOT ACCEPT ANYTHING MORE. SIMILARLY, A PERSON WHO BELIEVES THAT HE CANNOT LEARN ANTHING ELSE WILL STAGNATE QUICKLY AND NOT MOVE TO HIGHER LEVELS. A TRUE SIGN OF A MATURE INDIVIDUAL IS SOMEONE WHO SEES EVERY OPPORTUNITY AS A CHANCE TO LEARN. EVEN THE TEACHERS HAVE TEACHERS."

—

—Robert S. Sharma, *The Top 200 Secrets of Success*

ABOUT THE AUTHOR

Nick Baker has been involved in the great sport of competitive swimming since 1961. He swam competitively for eleven years, coached club for twenty-one years, and has coached swim camps exclusively for the past eighteen years. He started his coaching career in Canada in 1972, then moved to Ft. Lauderdale, Florida, in 1993 to operate a swim camp there. In 1995 Nick published *101 Winning Ways*, a motivational book for competitive swimmers. The material for the book came from observing the *winning ways* of successful swimmers he coached.

Nick cofounded the original Peak Performance Swim Camp in 1996. In 2005 he branched out on his own and founded the present-day version. Since then Nick has traveled throughout the United States and abroad, conducting his holistic camps and clinics. Past international locations include: Antigua, Aruba, Bermuda, Brazil, Canada, China, Curacao, England, Hong Kong, Jamaica, Singapore, Spain, Turkey, and Venezuela. Past US locations include: Alabama, Alaska, California, Connecticut, Florida, Georgia, Illinois, Indiana, Kansas, Kentucky, Maine, Maryland, Massachusetts, Michigan, New Mexico, New York, North Carolina, Oregon, Pennsylvania, Texas, Utah, Virginia, Washington, Wisconsin, and Wyoming.

Peak Performance Swim Camp currently offers more than two dozen swim camps and clinics annually including clinics for triathletes and master swimmers. More than 800 swimmers from over 30 countries participated in 2011. Private coaching as well as start, stroke, and turn video analysis are also available throughout the year.

In 2007 Nick formed a dynamic partnership with US Sports/Nike Camps, America's largest sports camp network and official operator of Nike Sports Camps worldwide. Over the past thirty-nine years Nick has coached swimmers of all ages and abilities, including Olympic finalists, Olympic trial qualifiers, NCAA champions, senior national champions, junior national champions, state champions, national qualifiers, junior national qualifiers, zone champions, and junior Olympic champions. In 1992 one of Nick's former swimmers, Lisa Flood, qualified for the 1992 Canadian Olympic team in the 100 BR, placing fourteenth overall. Nick attended the Olympics with Lisa as her personal coach. Lisa also won the 200 BR at the NCAA Division 1 Championships, medaled at the Pan American Games, and competed in her second Olympics in 1996, placing twelfth in the 100 BR.

Nick has been a featured writer in *Swimming World* magazine and presented at numerous coaching clinics throughout the world. He also acts as a consultant to various swim teams including the Greenwich YMCA in Greenwich, Connecticut.

FROM THE HEART

Swimming is my passion in life and I am truly blessed. Even though I have coached for almost four decades, I still wake up every morning eager to learn more about the sport I love. I have countless books and DVDs on the subject and surf the web daily in my quest to expand my swimming knowledge. My thirst for knowledge is greater today than yesterday and my passion for swimming grows by the hour. I coach virtually every day of the year with the exceptions of Thanksgiving, Christmas, and Easter.

My number one coaching goal is to provide swimmers with the mental, technical, and physical skills necessary to maximize their true potential. I also strive to enhance their self-worth and confidence levels so they may soar in both swimming and life.

I believe my gift for coaching came from God and endeavor to use it as intended. Coaching has never been about me but rather those I coach. I have no desire to be the center of attention; I reserve that for others. I choose to lead from behind the scenes, empowering swimmers to excel on their own merit. Lao Tzu, the mystic philosopher of ancient China, once said, "A leader is best when people barely knows he exists; when his work is done, his aim fulfilled, they say, "We did this ourselves." His words ring clear each day I step upon the pool deck.

I chose to write *The Swimming Triangle* because I have a deep desire to share my passion with the competitive swimming community, and to offer an alternative approach to coaching swimmers. I believe the focus in swimming should be as much on the journey as the final destination. In other words the day-to-day competitive swimming experience should be as important as the ultimate goal. A holistic approach fulfills this objective and is far more effective in maximizing individual potential due to its focus on the whole swimmer (mental, technical, and physical). It also meets many of the desired objectives of youth sport, including self-image enhancement, character development, teaching of life skills, improvements to health and fitness, and providing a positive place for children/young adults to channel their energies.

A TIMELY ALTERNATIVE

Contrary to popular belief, swimmers can never realize their true swimming potential based on physical conditioning alone. Unfortunately many coaches over-train and under-teach their swimmers, cramming every last yard into practice as opposed to creating practices that fully prepare swimmers for the demands of competition. As a result swimmers become experts at practicing rather than experts at performing. Over the years I have observed countless numbers of swimmers able to endure 10,000-yard practices but unable to achieve best times in competition due to a lopsided training approach. While optimal physical conditioning is a key to peak performance, so too is optimal mental and technical conditioning.

From a mental standpoint, swimmers' thoughts, both in and out of the pool, act like internal guidance systems directing them toward or away from their desired goals. Positive, focused, and determined minds brimming with self-confidence will no doubt lead to victory while minds that are lacking lead only to defeat. Therefore an ongoing mental conditioning curriculum geared toward developing essential mental skills must be a part of everyday practice.

From a technical standpoint, swimmers' skill levels ultimately determine the degree of success. Highly skilled swimmers work with the water, maximizing propulsion and minimizing drag, while poorly skilled swimmers fight the water, spinning their wheels down the pool. Therefore an ongoing technical-conditioning curriculum geared toward developing essential technical skills must be part of everyday practice.

> **Note:** *Research indicates elite-level swimmers enjoy up to a seventy-percent technical advantage over the competition—an astounding amount!*

Developing an approach that conditions swimmers on all three fronts has been my goal since day one, and *The Swimming Triangle* represents my goal brought to life. My hope is to inspire other coaches to follow suit so a greater number of swimmers develop their God-given talents to the fullest.

A LEAP OF FAITH

The majority of coaches tend to coach the way they were coached with minor adjustments or updates here and there. The two most common reasons given include familiarity with an existing approach and a proven track record. In other words they find it easy to implement and know it works.

A holistic approach, on the other hand, is out of the box in terms of philosophy, structure, demands, and expectations. Therefore its appeal may be limited to open-minded, hard working, and courageous coaches seeking a fresh alternative. I have practiced holistic coaching my entire career and have found it to be a tremendously rewarding decision with countless success stories to share.

CHAPTER ORDER

The three main chapters of The Swimming Triangle (The Mental Conditioning Curriculum, The Technical Conditioning Curriculum, and The Physical Conditioning Curriculum) were placed in their respective order for a specific reason, as if swimmers were being developed from scratch. In order to maximize their potential to the fullest, the holistic coach must begin the process of mental conditioning from day one. In other words, get them thinking in the right way to insure that the technical and physical curriculums are fully understood, appreciated, and realized. That is not to say that the other two curriculums must wait on the sidelines until the mental curriculum is in full swing. It just means that mental conditioning should be seen as a precursor to technical and physical conditioning. Think of it as tilling the soil before planting the seed.

CHAPTER 1

Introducing the Holistic Approach

Goal setting is a competitive swimming ritual, with swimmers setting short- and long-term goals season after season. The two most popular forms of swimming goals include the achievement of best times and qualifying for higher levels of competition. In a holistic approach, swimmers are also expected to add the goal of personal excellence to the mix. Striving for personal excellence permeates every aspect of life. As a result swimmers soar in the pool, in school, and in life in general.

To a large extent, the successful completion of any swimming goal depends upon the coach's approach. Unfortunately many coaches employ a one- or two-sided approach, ignoring critical conditioning needs from a holistic point of view. An approach that fails to address the full spectrum of mental needs ultimately produces swimmers who lack vital mental skills and character traits. An approach that fails to address the full spectrum of technical needs ultimately produces swimmers who lack necessary technical expertise. An approach that fails to address the full spectrum of physical needs ultimately produces swimmers who lack essential physical qualities. With that said, a holistic approach seems the most logical.

The vast majority of competitive swimming programs subscribe to a conventional approach, where the amount of time dedicated to essential mental and technical conditioning is considerably less than the amount of time dedicated to physical conditioning. Typically seventy-five to ninety percent of weekly practice time is dedicated to physical conditioning with the remaining time dedicated to mental and/or technical conditioning. In some cases competitive swimming programs go to the extreme, resulting in an approach known as *garbage yardage*, where physical conditioning reigns supreme, leaving little time for essential mental and technical needs.

On the contrary a holistic approach offers mental, technical, and physical curricula rolled into one, with each curriculum designed to complement and optimize the other two. Although the time allocated to each is different, all three curricula are considered equal in importance and one can never supersede another. The holistic coach strives to make every set in practice a mental, technical, and physical experience.

Another unique characteristic of a holistic approach is the time line, where achieving the goal of best times, higher and higher levels of competition, and personal excellence is a long-term proposition. While a noticeable improvement is expected year to year, swimmers are not expected to reach peak levels until their latter years of swimming. This all-important perspective provides coaches with opportunities to develop swimmers at a sensible pace, creating an environment free of the many pitfalls associated with having to be the best at a young age.

In addition the degree of conditioning must be age/ability friendly and goal-specific. A holistic approach encourages a thoughtful, organized progression with swimmers' goals and best interests as the guiding lights. Training swimmers in this manner no doubt takes longer than other approaches, but the resultant benefits and rewards are far greater. In the short term, it is much easier to improve performance by increasing yardage as opposed to laying down a solid mental, technical, and physical foundation. However a short-term solution will never lead to sustainable growth and long-term success.

Some coaches may find the holistic practices (outlined in Chapter 6) much easier than the ones they offer, but two important factors must be considered. In a holistic approach, best-form stroke and turn technique are required throughout every practice, initially reducing the total number of yards/meters performed. In addition the average speeds per twenty-five are typically faster than those achieved in other approaches due in part to six-speed training and touch time training as outlined in Chapter 4. A holistic approach begins with a quality over quantity perspective, progressing to a quality and quantity perspective over time. Peak Performance Swim Camp uses an abbreviated version of holistic training (due to the duration of camp) and swimmers find it very challenging.

> **Note:** *Typically coaches who employ a garbage yardage approach develop successful age-group swimmers due to physical superiority alone. Sadly, naïve parents jump on the bandwagon, believing their children are the next swimming superstars. All too often swimmers who are exposed to this approach end up injured, burned out, or, ill prepared to compete at the elite level later in their careers. While there are always exceptions to the rule, a holistic approach is by far the better choice.*

A POSITIVE COACHING STYLE

The coach is the captain of the ship and ultimately responsible for the full implementation of a holistic approach. While the mental, technical, and physical curricula are in place, the overall look and feel lies with the coach. Therefore the need for a positive coaching style is absolutely essential. I believe Norman Vincent Peale said it best: "The person who sends out positive thoughts activates the world around him positively and draws back to himself positive results."

Coaches who adopt a positive coaching style will undoubtedly be in the best positions to optimize the many benefits inherent in a holistic approach. Characteristics of a positive coaching style include:
- Coaching every minute of practice

- Emphasizing the positive wherever and whenever possible
- Providing ongoing constructive feedback throughout practice
- Seeking to engage swimmers in warm and honest dialogue
- Applying a patient approach
- Providing unconditional support
- Rewarding effort as well as outcome
- Treating swimmers with respect regardless of their abilities
- Enhancing self-esteem wherever and whenever possible
- Encouraging personal excellence both in and out of the pool
- Maintaining an open and objective mind
- Providing swimmers with opportunities deserving of their effort
- Using sound coaching principles to engage and inspire
- Respecting the authority and status of their position as coach
- Understanding that swimmers have unique strengths and weaknesses
- Making time for all swimmers
- Leading by example
- Encouraging swimmers to take responsibility for their actions and results
- Recognizing achievements no matter how small
- Seizing teachable moments to build positive character traits such as confidence, self-motivation, and a passion for life
- Setting positive expectations for training, skill acquisition, and personal behavior
- Passing their passion for the sport on to others

- Creating conditions where success is the rule rather than the exception

Note: *The expression, "Kids don't care how much you know until they know how much you care," is well-known within the coaching and teaching community. A positive coaching style is caring personified.*

In addition the holistic coach is well versed in the many reasons why swimmers retire from the sport prematurely. Knowing in advance keeps them in tune with the needs of swimmers. Common reasons for early retirement include:

- Loss of interest
- Finding the sport unrewarding
- Lack of fun
- Too much pressure and worry
- Finding it boring
- Dysfunctional swimmer-coach relationship
- Lack of time for study
- Desire to participate in a non-sport activity
- Lack of inspiration
- Too time consuming

CHAPTER 2

The Mental Conditioning Curriculum

The mental conditioning curriculum constitutes the first side of the swimming triangle. The material presented here is blended with the content of the technical and physical curricula to create a holistic effect. Optimal mental conditioning is a prerequisite to achieving the ultimate swimming goal and the primary purpose of the mental conditioning curriculum. Mahatma Gandhi, the prominent Indian political and spiritual leader, once said, "A man is but a product of his thoughts; what he thinks, he becomes."

> **Note:** *The mind is the center of all thought and therefore all action. Without thought, there can be no action. Therefore, swimmers' thoughts—more than any other single factor—determine the level of performance in both practice and competition. Without question, high-quality thoughts produce high-quality results; while low-quality thoughts produce low-quality results. With that said, I have never understood why so many coaches resist adding a structured mental conditioning curriculum to their programs. Perhaps they see it as diverting valuable time away from physical conditioning, or because they believe the reported benefits are more fluff than fact. Whatever the reason, I happen to believe that swimmers achieve far more when the mind is fully engaged.*

The information contained in this chapter and presented in the form of concepts constitutes the mental conditioning curriculum. Each concept is intended to provoke thought encouraging swimmers to think and act in ways they have never thought or acted before. Some are intended to broaden their overall knowledge base while others are intended to foster essential mental skills and key character traits.

In a holistic approach, the coach is charged with introducing, extrapolating, and integrating the various mental concepts into practice via pre-practice chalk talks or practice themes. No practice is complete without one or more concepts being added. From a holistic point of view, a practice that conditions swimmers technically and physically but fails to do so mentally is considered a wasted practice.

> **Note:** *The degree of mental conditioning also affects the degree of technical and physical conditioning. From a technical standpoint, mentally fit swimmers maintain a higher quality of technique throughout practice due to enhanced focus abilities. From a physical standpoint, mentally fit swimmers work harder in practice due to higher degrees of mental toughness.*

MENTAL CONCEPTS

For brevity's sake and my desire to keep the mental, technical, and physical chapters somewhat balanced, I have chosen to limit the number of mental concepts to seventy-five, although many more could have been added. Additional concepts are posted on The Swimming Triangle website at www.theswimmingtriangle. com. Each concept is intended to highlight a core consideration making the all-important mental side of swimming more easily understood and applied.

1. Word Power

When swimmers state they "will try" to accomplish a specific task or goal, it means they will make an attempt to achieve it. When swimmers state they "will" accomplish a specific task or goal, it means they will achieve it. All too often swimmers spend their time trying to achieve rather than achieving. Choosing the right words and train of thought is a powerful beginning that makes all the difference in the final result. In a holistic approach, the use of the word "will" is much preferred over "try."

2. 10,000 Hours

The basic premise behind this idea is that it takes approximately 10,000 hours of deliberate practice to become a master at a chosen pursuit. This finding is attributed to Anders Ericsson, widely regarded as one of the world's leading theoretical and experimental researchers on expertise. His discovery stems from an experiment conducted at the Berlin School of Music, where students were divided into three groups based on levels of achievement. Those considered elite put in approximately 10,000 hours of deliberate practice while those considered good or average put in 8,000 and 4,000 hours respectively.

The same concept can be applied to the world of competitive swimming, where elite-level swimmers (mid-twenties or older) can safely claim the same amassing of hours. The holistic coach stresses the value of a long-term commitment, the need for perfect or near-perfect attendance, and the importance of deliberate practice in the pursuit of swimming excellence.

3. Role Models

The world of competitive swimming has many role models, but what good are they if swimmers choose not to follow them? For example swimmers who choose Missy Franklin as a role model must do their utmost to mirror her mental outlook, technique, and work ethic. Having role models in name only is an exercise in futility. The holistic coach encourages swimmers to adopt role models to enhance performance. Swimmers are also encouraged to learn all they can about their role model's positive character traits.

4.   In the Blink of an Eye

Improving swimming endurance can take weeks to months. Improving a start, stroke, or turn technique can take days to weeks. Improving an attitude can take the blink of an eye. Allow me to explain. Imagine a swimmer lying in bed on a cold winter night. As 5:00 a.m. nears, Mom walks into the room, announcing it's time to wake up. The swimmer replies, "I'm too tired and not feeling well." Mom replies, "That's too bad, as I had planned on taking you out for your favorite pancakes after practice." At which point the swimmer jumps out of bed and dresses quickly. Without question, changing an attitude is the fastest way to make a change for the better. Swimmers should never underestimate the power of the mind. In a holistic approach, choosing and maintaining the right attitude is an everyday challenge.

5.   Tenacity Can Trump Talent

Talent alone cannot guarantee success in the pool. The need to be tenacious, or unwilling to let go of a dream, regardless of the degree of difficulty is absolutely essential in a sport filled with so many ups and downs. Over the years I have observed many super-talented swimmers struggle due to a lack of tenacity while other less talented swimmers thrived because of it. The holistic coach cites examples of successful people from the swimming world and beyond who exhibited tenacity in attaining their goals.

6.   The Story of Abraham Lincoln

Abraham Lincoln was one of the greatest presidents in the history of the United States. He experienced more failure than success, but that did not make him a failure. Failures become permanent only when one stops trying. Hopefully Lincoln's struggles can serve as an inspiration to all:

1832: Defeated for Legislature

1833: Failed in business and spent the next seventeen years of his life paying off his debt

1834: Elected to Legislature

1835: His sweetheart, Anne Rutledge, died

1836: Suffered a nervous breakdown

1838: Defeated for speaker

1840: Reelected to Legislature

1843: Defeated for Congress

1846: Elected to Congress

1849: Defeated for land officer

1854: Defeated for Senate

1856: Defeated for vice president

1858: Defeated for Senate

1860: Elected president of the United States

1863: Abolished slavery through the Emancipation Proclamation

7. Power of Purpose

Swimmers with purpose chart a straight line to success, avoiding many of the detours and pitfalls others fall victim to including petty worries, self-doubt, indecision, fear, and self-pity. By avoiding these detours and pitfalls, they achieve far more in a shorter period of time. Without question, defining one's purpose is key to long-term swimming success. In a holistic approach, purposeful practice is the rule rather than the exception.

8. External Versus Internal Opposition

There are two forms of opposition: external and internal. External opposition comes in the form of opposing swimmers while internal comes in the form of personal fears, doubts, and/or lack of confidence. To excel at the highest level, swimmers must be able to defeat both. The holistic coach assists swimmers in identifying and rectifying forms of internal opposition knowing that those who fail to address it can never realize their full potential. **Note:** *Overcoming internal opposition is one of the biggest challenges both in the pool and in life in general.*

9. The Coach's Expectations

Ideally swimmers should view the coach's expectations as a set of guidelines intended to assist them in achieving their ultimate goals rather than obstruct them. In a holistic approach, expectations remain somewhat flexible to allow for personality differences and/or extenuating circumstances. A partial list includes:

- Treat the coach with the utmost respect at all times
- Treat fellow teammates with the utmost respect at all times
- Behave like ladies and gentlemen at all times
- Strive for 100 percent attendance
- Live a positive lifestyle away from the pool
- Refrain from whining in practice
- Refrain from cheating in practice
- Be a good sport and a team player at all times
- Strive for personal excellence in the pool and at school
- Attend all designated swim meets
- Support all team functions
- Arrive on time for practice and swim meets
- Bring all necessary equipment to practice in good working order
- Refrain from talking when the coach is talking
- Be open-minded
- Support the team philosophy
- Be a problem solver, not a problem maker

10. Value Added

Peak performance in any pursuit is ultimately tied to one's feeling of value, and the greater value felt the greater the performance potential. The holistic coach adds value to swimmers by accepting them for who they are; providing ongoing constructive feedback; offering sets within practice that challenge, yet provide a sense of accomplishment, and addressing individual needs. Ideally swimmers should leave practice feeling more valuable then when they arrived.

11. Think Positive

From time to time, I will ask swimmers to list all of the positive things that can be achieved with a negative attitude. Needless to say, there is no list. The need to think positive is paramount both in swimming and life, as nothing of significance or value can be achieved without doing so. Over time swimmers who choose to think positive experience far greater success than those who do not. Thinking positive has many applications in the world of competitive swimming. For example it can build self-esteem, increase optimism, reduce stress, enhance sleep, and heighten enthusiasm. In a holistic approach, thinking positive is a minute-by-minute expectation.

> **Note:** *The holistic coach is also realistic, understanding that the development of a positive attitude can be a long-term proposition.*

> **Note:** *Swimmers who attend Peak Performance Swim Camp receive a Swim Positive wristband upon arrival to camp. The band serves as a reminder to think positive no matter the circumstances.*

12. Enrich and Enlighten

Competitive swimming has a unique history and culture dating back more than 100 years. It is one of the most popular sports in the world and considered a premier Olympic event. Its most famous participant, Michael Phelps, is viewed as one of the greatest Olympians of all time, having won eight gold medals and breaking seven world records in a single Olympics. The holistic coach takes time to educate swimmers on great performances past and present, the latest trends in swimming, international meet results, and more. As swimmers learn more, their pride in and commitment to the sport grows.

13. The Confidence Bank

In swimming, confidence is worth its weight in gold. However, attaining the level of confidence needed to excel in the pool is not automatic. Swimmers must actively work at improving confidence levels, similar to improving fitness levels. One such method involves a concept called the confidence bank, where a swimmer makes a daily deposit into an imaginary bank account based on various positive experiences and accomplishments. Examples include performing well in practice, receiving praise from the coach or fellow teammates, posting a best time in competition, making finals, or winning an event. Each time a positive experience or accomplishment occurs, the swimmer symbolically makes a deposit. As time passes the bank account swells to the point where confidence abounds and the swimmer feels like a millionaire.

14. *101 Winning Ways*

In 1995 I published a book entitled *101 Winning Ways*, containing 101 winning attitudes and behaviors key to victory in swimming and life in general. Cartoons are used throughout the book to further underscore its vital message. The book's simple format provides the holistic coach with a ready-made opportunity to incorporate winning ways into daily practice. Three of my favorites include:

- Winners know if it's worth having, it's worth waiting for. *They know it takes time to be first in line.*
- Winners are more like elephants and less like

alligators. *They have big ears and small mouths, not big mouths and small ears.*

- Winners see success in 3-D. *They see desire, dedication, and determination as keys to success.*

Note: *To purchase a copy of* 101 *Winning Ways, visit the Peak Performance Swim Camp website at www.swimcamp.com.*

15. The Benefits of Competitive Swimming

Swimmers give up so much to pursue the sport they love, but they also receive a lot in return. Mental benefits include increased discipline, focus, and mental toughness—qualities of successful people in all walks of life. Physical benefits include better health, improved fitness, and enhanced appearance. Other significant benefits include participation in one of the greatest sports of all, peer and public recognition, college scholarship opportunities, and the possibility to compete at an elite level. Unfortunately many swimmers lose sight of the benefits due to the rigorous demands of the sport. To keep things in perspective, the holistic coach makes a point of stressing swimming's many benefits whenever the opportunity presents itself.

16. Get Real

What swimmers say and do can often differ. They may say, "I want to be the best" but consistently fail to give their best. Getting real or honest with oneself is an important step in the achievement of any goal. Swimmers who decide they want to be the best must accept all of the consequences that go with their decision, just like ambivalent swimmers must accept the consequences that go with their indecision. No swimmer can have it both ways. By saying one thing and doing another, they remain in a constant state of limbo.

17. Challenging Versus Hard

Those in search of adventure may dream about climbing Mount Everest not because it's hard, but because it's challenging. They climb not because of the guarantee of success but for the thrill. Reaching the peak is the added bonus. Applying this concept to the world of swimming is a perfect fit, as it provides swimmers with an alternative way of thinking. For example rather than view a practice as hard or grueling, it should be viewed as a challenge waiting to be conquered.

18. Risk Versus Reward

A turtle can only make progress by sticking its neck out. The same holds true for swimmers. To cultivate a willingness to risk, the holistic coach provides swimmers with unconditional support, creating an environment where risking is the rule rather than the exception.

19. Advance Swimming IQ

It is a well-known fact that knowledge equals power. Swimming is a knowledge- based sport, and the more knowledgeable swimmers become the greater their chances of success. I am often amazed by how little knowledge most swimmers possess regarding general stroke concepts, and they know even less when it comes to their own starts, strokes, and turns. They also lack essential knowledge of sports nutrition, racing strategies, stress alleviation, the purpose of drills, and how to train. In a holistic approach, educating swimmers is a top priority. While taking the time to educate demands a greater effort on the coach's part, it also pays bigger dividends.

20. Anxiety Control

Anxiety is defined as an uneasiness of mind caused by fear or misfortune. Unfortunately, feelings such as these are a natural part of sports. Swimmers can easily experience fear or misfortune in practice or competition. Although the risk of anxiety exists, it must never develop to the point where it impedes or immobilizes. All too often I encounter swimmers who are well-conditioned technically and physically but unable to perform to expectations due to high levels of anxiety. While removing anxiety entirely is not possible, the holistic coach avoids adding additional amounts through unrealistic demands, threats, or ultimatums. In addition various anxiety-reducing techniques are taught and rehearsed frequently in practice. Reducing anxiety levels to a manageable amount eliminates many of the roadblocks swimmers encounter in pursuit of their dreams.

Note: *The inability to deal effectively with anxiety is a leading cause of early retirement from the sport. Parents should also refrain from adding additional amounts of anxiety through unrealistic demands, threats, or ultimatums.*

21. The Power of Passion

Passion is defined as a powerful feeling or compelling emotion. Darrell Andrews's best-selling book, *How to Find Your Passion and Make a Living at It,* makes a point I strongly believe in. It implies that when people make careers out of something they are most passionate about, work becomes more enjoyable, fulfilling, and ultimately more rewarding. Unlocking this all-powerful emotion is key to maximizing one's potential in any endeavor. More in life can be accomplished through the power of passion than through any other human emotion. This important obser-vation holds true for swimming as well. To maximize potential, swimmers must add passion to the mix.

Note: *While some may disagree, I believe passion can be developed through sound coaching principles. One of* *my favorite sayings comes from the late Cus D'Amato, mentor and coach of Mike Tyson, former heavyweight boxing champion of the world. In describing his many years of coaching and mentoring Mike, Cus stated: "A boy comes to me with a spark of interest. I fed the spark and it became a flame. I fed the flame and it became a fire. I fed the fire and it became a roaring blaze." Coaching is an art, and great coaches know how to instill passion in their athletes.*

22. The Ten Keys

Most coaches and swimmers believe hard work is the key to swimming success. While hard work is a key, it is not the only one. In fact there are at least ten keys, each with the potential to impact success in a significant way. To reinforce this all-important concept, the holistic coach offers the following self-test at least once every six weeks. Swimmers are encouraged to answer the questions honestly, resisting the urge to give an undeserving score, whether too high or too low. A score of ten is most desired. In addition swimmers should refrain from making their answers public.

 1.   On a scale from one to ten, how good is your technique?

Note: *Technique includes starts, strokes, turns, and finishes. You may choose to evaluate your best stroke and its relative start, turn, and finish or all starts, strokes, turns, and finishes. If you choose the latter, score yourself out of ten on each item separately and then calculate the average.*

 2.   On a scale from one to ten, how self-motivated are you?

 3.   On a scale from one to ten, how physically fit are you?

Note: *Fitness is defined as endurance, strength, and flexibility. Score yourself out of ten on each item separately and then calculate the average.*

4. On a scale from one to ten, how mentally tough are you?

5. On a scale from one to ten, how healthy is your lifestyle?

Note: *Lifestyle includes such things as sleep, use of spare time, homework, the types of friends you hang out with, etc.*

6. On a scale from one to ten, how well do you handle the expectations associated with competition?

Note: *Expectations include personal, coach-related, and parent-related.*

7. On a scale from one to ten, how hard do you work in practice?

8. On a scale from one to ten, how passionate are you about swimming?

Note: *Passion is defined as an intense desire or enthusiasm for something.*

9. On a scale from one to ten, how healthy are your eating habits?

10. On a scale from one to ten, how positive is your attitude?

Upon completion, total your scores, circling your lowest score(s) to identify the area(s) most in need of improvement. Ideally your overall score should improve test to test.

Note: *In my experience successful swimmers at the international level score ninety-five or higher; successful swimmers at the national level score ninety or higher; successful swimmers at the state level score eighty-five or higher.*

23. Fortune Favors the Brave

To reap reward, swimmers must be willing to endure or face unpleasant challenges even though they may fear them. Moving forward in the face of fear is the only way to achieve things truly desired. All too often swimmers make the mistake of avoiding fear by choosing the easy way out. For example choosing not to push hard in practice or scratching out of a super-challenging event like the 200 butterfly. From their perspective they made the right choice, but in reality the challenges that generate the most fear typically deliver the greatest rewards. In a holistic approach, facing and overcoming fear wherever it exists is a top priority.

24. Focus

Focus is the ability to gather scattered thoughts and narrow them to a thought most beneficial to the task at hand. Offering focus drills within the practice setting is most important, especially in a sport with such high performance demands. One such drill begins with swimmers performing a series of five deep inhales followed by five slow exhales at the edge of the pool. Each exhale is intended to remove scattered thoughts, bringing greater focus and clarity to the task at hand. Once complete, a 25 freestyle is performed with the goal of maintaining a tight, symmetrical, continuous kick for the entire twenty-five. Should the kicking pattern change, swimmers must stop immediately. At first they may lack the focus skills necessary to detect a change and require the coach's assistance. Given time they should improve to the point where they can detect even the smallest change.

Note: *This concept can be used to enhance other key factors relative to peak performance in the pool, including increasing training intensity in practice, enhancing essential racing skills, and developing the ideal racing focus.*

25. Apples on a Tree

Apples ripen at different times—some early, some late, and some in between. The same scenario holds true in the world of swimming, where swimmers ripen at different times—some as young-age groupers, others during puberty or their teenage years. Many coaches and parents alike mistakenly believe swimmers must ripen early (ten and under) to reach the elite level. On the contrary, research indicates the vast majority of elite-level swimmers ripen during puberty and beyond.

Note: *Over the years I have witnessed numerous cases where swimmers were forced to ripen prematurely, leading to disastrous results. In most cases the motivation behind this behavior was ego-driven, where coaches and/or parents pushed swimmers for personal gain or self-glorification. In a holistic approach, swimmers ripen when ready.*

26. Confidence

Henry David Thoreau, the famous American author, once said, "If one advances confidently in the direction of his dreams and endeavors to live the life he has imagined, he will meet with success unexpected in common hours." As mentioned previously (in The Confidence Bank), confidence plays an enormous role in the degree of success swimmers experience. Confident swimmers embrace challenge while those who lack it retreat to the shadows. The following suggestions can significantly enhance confidence levels:

- Train your hardest on the hardest sets.
- Recognize your success, no matter how small.
- Avoid people who belittle you.
- Erase confidence-destroying words from your vocabulary such as *can't*, *won't*, and *never*.
- Set realistic mini-goals that can be accomplished in a matter of days or weeks.
- Erase confidence-destroying thoughts from your mind such as *I lack talent*, *I'm too small to be fast*, or *I started swimming too late*.
- Learn from your failures, then move on.
- Face up to your fears, starting with the smallest ones.

27. Near Perfection

Perfectionism is the belief that anything less than perfect is unacceptable. While perfectionism is a noble goal, it is fraught with danger and against all odds. Swimmers who adopt the goal of perfection may find it does more harm than good, leading to feelings of anxiety and fear and a lack of fulfillment. As an alternative the holistic coach promotes the concept of near perfection, where swimmers pursue perfection but with the understanding that absolute perfection is not obtainable. By embracing this concept, swimmers are free to enjoy the many benefits without the unwanted baggage.

> **Note:** *Vince Lombardi, one of the most successful American football coaches of all time, once said, "Perfection is not attainable, but if we chase perfection we can catch excellence."*

28. Resist the Urge to Be Average

"How many of you want to be average?" is a question I often pose to swimmers who attend my camps. As one might expect, no one ever raises a hand. While being average demands less, it also delivers less. Over the span of time, individuals who have refused to settle for average have accomplished the world's greatest feats. Without question swimmers must strive to think and act in above-average ways to be above average.

29. Self-Concept

Swimmers tend to view themselves based solely on how well they performed in the latest competition. If they're successful their self-concept shoots sky high; if not, it plummets to the ground. All too often this approach leads to inconsistencies in performance, with swimmers up one day and down the next. Ideally, self-concept should reflect swimmers' overall accomplishments achieved over the course of time.

> **Note:** *The following quote is from Dr. Ralph Richards, a leading swimming authority from the Western Australian Institute of Sport: "Elite level swimmers have a well-balanced sense of self. That is, they have a healthy self-concept and a deep rooted belief in their ability."*

30. Work Ethic

Thomas Jefferson, the third president of the United States, once said, "I'm a great believer in luck, and the harder I work, the more I have of it." Work ethic is defined as a moral belief in the benefit and importance of hard work. Motivating swimmers to work hard can go a long way in instilling a solid work ethic, but educating swimmers on the values and importance of hard work is also an essential part. Characteristics of a solid work ethic include a willingness to work hard without guarantee of success, a willingness to work day in and day out without immediate reward, and the ability to persevere regardless of obstacles. In a holistic approach, ongoing motivation and education go hand in hand.

31. Train Smart—Race Stupid

While the title for this mental component may seem out of place, there is a great deal of truth to it. Elite-level swimmers compete with few thoughts in mind. They race on autopilot, their starts, strokes, turns, finishes, and racing strategies preplanned and automated through thoughtful and repetitive practice. By the time the race rolls around, thinking narrows to a few thoughts. The holistic coach provides swimmers with unlimited opportunities to automate every mental, technical, and physical aspect of a race.

32. Competitiveness

Swimmers who possess a high degree of competitiveness have a strong desire to compete. Whether the result of nature or nurture, some have more than others. If I had to choose between a swimmer who possessed a high degree of physical fitness, a swimmer who possessed a high degree of technical expertise, and a swimmer who possessed a strong desire to compete, I would chose the last one every time. My decision is based on the fact that swimming is an extremely competitive sport and swimmers who possess a strong desire to compete will find a way to win regardless of the circumstances. The holistic coach positively promotes the spirit of competitiveness at every juncture.

33. Mental Toughness

Competitive swimming is one of the toughest sports of all—its demands are legendary. Swimmers take great pride in their ability to wake up for practice at ungodly hours, train thousands upon thousands of yards/meters in less than ideal conditions, and compete in one grueling event after another. A high degree of mental toughness is vital in such a demanding environment. As one might expect, no two swimmers possess the same amount. To bridge the gap, the holistic coach offers a graduated series of mental toughness experiences within practice and competition to develop this all-important mental concept.

34. Rewards That Fit

Research indicates the perceived reward is the single most important factor in predicting one's dedication and willingness to work toward any goal. Swimmers willing to work hard do so in part because the resultant reward is well-defined and desired, while swimmers who are unwilling to work hard do so in part because the resultant reward is ill-defined or has little meaning to them. The holistic coach assists swimmers in identifying clear and meaningful short-term and long-term goals. Swimmers who lack such goals are like ships adrift at sea.

35. Commitment

It takes more than natural ability to be a success in the pool. Over the years I have had the good fortune to coach a number of swimmers with amazing natural ability. Unfortunately, few realized their true swimming potential due to a lack of commitment on their part. All too often I found myself having to sell them on swimming. Over the short term it worked, as they responded by attending more practices and working harder, but in the end most slid backward or quit. This lack of commitment is epidemic in swimming today, due partially to how lax our society has become in honoring commitments and the fact that most swimmers have far too many options to choose from. The degree of commitment required to achieve success is substantial, and swimmers must be willing to accept this reality or face the unfortunate consequences.

36. Coping

The German philosopher Friedrich Nietzsche once said, "That which does not kill us makes us stronger." This famous quote seems most appropriate in the world of competitive swimming, as swimmers are subjected to a multitude of physical and mental adversities on a regular basis. Unfortunately many are left to fend for themselves. If they cope, they survive; if not, they die (relatively speaking, of course). In a holistic approach, teaching coping skills is a never-ending process beginning at the novice level. Examples include reframing situations in a positive light, learning how to calm the mind through positive self-talk, meditative breathing, and dividing challenges into bite-size pieces.

37. The Five Ps

Conveying complex concepts in a simple manner is a true art form. One such concept is known as the five Ps, which stands for: proper planning prevents poor performance. Swimmers who embrace this concept use their time and energy wisely to gain the competitive edge. Examples include attending all or most practices, addressing individual training or race-related weaknesses once identified, incorporating whatever feedback is given by the coach, changing wasteful scheduling practices such as setting appointments during practice time, and participating in key competitions throughout the year.

38. Self-Evaluation

The quality and effectiveness of my coaching is constantly on my mind, and at the end of each day I automatically grade myself on my performance. Was I engaging? Did I inspire? Were my explanations clear and concise? This automatic self-evaluation process has been a part of my daily coaching routine from the beginning, stemming from my desire to be a better coach. While I don't always succeed, I do try. Whenever I conduct myself in a manner that reflects poorly on me, I make the necessary corrections. In a holistic approach, swimmers are instructed to score themselves out of ten at the end of each practice with ten being most desired. The score is based on how well they applied themselves mentally, technically, and physically throughout the entire practice. The need to be totally honest with oneself is paramount, even if the truth hurts.

39. Empowerment

The Chinese proverb "give a man a fish, feed him for a day; teach a man to fish, feed him for a lifetime" fits perfectly within a holistic approach. The holistic coach is committed to teaching swimmers how to fish on their own by providing the necessary mental, technical, and physical skills. While this approach requires a greater degree of effort on the coach's part, the return on investment is well worth it.

40. Self-Belief

If eight swimmers with identical times raced, who would win? The one who believed most in himself or herself and his or her abilities. Self-belief acts like a catalyst, heightening the degree and rate of success. Unfortunately many swimmers lack the self-belief necessary to realize the success they desire and deserve. Self-belief can be easily influenced in a positive or negative light via personal thoughts, internal dialogue, competency levels, outward appearance, overall level of success, and acceptance by fellow teammates. Persons of authority or stature can also have a significant impact on swimmers' self-belief. The holistic coach is ever mindful of the vital role it plays in the pursuit of goals and does his utmost to nurture it.

41. Three Types of Swimmers

While no two swimmers are alike, they generally fall into one of three categories: 1) workhorse swimmers, 2) racehorse swimmers, or 3) workhorse/racehorse swimmers. Workhorse swimmers work hard in practice but typically fail to swim up to expectations in competition. Racehorse swimmers soar in competition but typically fail to work up to their potential in practice. Workhorse/racehorse swimmers represent the best of both, working hard in practice and soaring in competition. The holistic coach has a ready-made plan in place to address swimmers' individual shortcomings. In the case of workhorse swimmers, stress reduction techniques are rehearsed frequently in practice. In the case of racehorse swimmers, practices are structured in a manner designed to encourage greater effort.

42. Open Communication

An open line of communication must exist between swimmer and coach to maximize a swimmer's true potential. Both parties must feel free to discuss any matter that falls within the swimming domain. If two-way communication is lacking, the swimmer-coach relationship becomes dysfunctional and impacts performance in a negative way. The holistic coach works diligently at establishing and maintaining an open line of communication by listening, not lecturing, reserving judgment, and placing swimmers' needs first.

Note: *Unfortunately parents, including well-meaning ones, can often interfere and damage the open line of communication that must exist between swimmer and coach.*

43. Keep It Simple

Hans Hofmann, the abstract expressionist painter, once said, "The ability to simplify means to eliminate the unnecessary so that the necessary may speak." All too often swimmers waste valuable time by engaging in the unnecessary. Examples include fooling around during Dry Land training, talking when the coach is talking, wasting time in the locker room, daydreaming through a stroke or turn progression, or taking extra-long washroom breaks. Unfortunately these unnecessary behaviors detract from the task at hand, watering down the practice experience and potential benefits. To maximize time spent, swimmers must simplify the process by eliminating behaviors that offer the least value and impede progress.

44. Patience

Wouldn't it be nice if swimmers could prepare rigorously for competition throughout the week and be guaranteed success on the weekend? If this unrealistic scenario were true, there would be no need for patience; unfortunately, this is not the case. Swimmers must have the ability to put off success for long periods of time while subjecting themselves to the rigors of training. The holistic coach cites examples of successful people from the swimming world and beyond who exhibited great patience in attaining their goals.

Note: *See the story of Abraham Lincoln.*

45. The Value of an Open Mind

The science of swimming is ever changing. To accommodate

change swimmers must be open-minded and willing to try new things. Over the years I have encountered many closed-minded swimmers who preferred to stick with outdated techniques or training methods simply out of habit. Their reluctance to be open-minded was extremely counterproductive and a roadblock to success. The holistic coach encourages this all-important mental quality and makes a conscious effort to recognize those who embrace it.

46. Good Pain Versus Bad Pain

There are two kinds of physical pain: good and bad. Examples of good pain include sore muscles and what is commonly referred to as a stitch (a sharp pain in the lower abdomen). Examples of bad pain include a pain in the shoulder, knee, or lower back. Good pain leads to improved fitness and enhanced performance while bad pain leads to injury and has the potential to end a career. To excel, swimmers must be willing to endure as much good pain as possible. At first glance some may find this concept difficult to accept, but it is the only way to prepare for the challenge of competition successfully. The holistic coach employs a graduated approach, allowing swimmers to experience good pain in a progressive manner. Exposing swimmers to excessive good pain before they are mentally prepared to do so can do more harm than good, leaving them fearful and reluctant to embrace this all-important mental concept.

47. Self-Leadership

Harold R. McAlindon, author of *The Little Book of Big Ideas*, once said, "Do not follow where the path may lead. Go instead where there is no path and leave a trail." To be a success in the pool, swimmers must be willing to take the lead and go where they have never gone before. While often scary at first, taking the lead becomes easier with practice. Examples include swimming to win the heat, leading the lane in practice, moving to a faster lane or a more competitive group, and competing in more-demanding events. The holistic coach encourages swimmers to take the lead wherever and whenever possible.

48. A Winning Formula

No two swimmers win a race in the same manner. One may win due to physical superiority and a pit bull mentality while another may win due to greater technical skills and a superior racing strategy. The point I wish to make is that swimmers have the capacity to win based on their own unique blends of mental, technical, and physical abilities. In a holistic approach, identifying and nurturing a swimmer's individual winning formula is a top priority.

49. Shared Responsibility

In general, competitive swimming is a coach-centered discipline where the coach leads and the swimmer follows. While this model no doubt works, I believe a model that allows both coach and swimmer to share responsibility works best of all. By sharing responsibility the swimmer becomes more engaged in the process and gives more of himself or herself. Obviously the degree of responsibility is dependent upon the swimmer's maturity level and track record. In a holistic approach, swimmers are provided frequent opportunities to assume greater responsibility for their swimming. Examples include choosing what stroke(s) to train in a stroke set, choosing what events to swim in competition (starting with less-important meets), and designing a swim-meet warm up.

> **Note:** *In all cases the amount of responsibility given is dependent upon results. Swimmers who perform better are given even more while those who perform worse are given less.*

50. Overthink, Underperform

Swimming is a thinking sport, with the need to excel a constant theme. While a thoughtful approach is essential, too much thought can lead to doubt and indecision. It is not uncommon to find swimmers frozen in thought and unable to access their true mental, technical, and physical abilities. Overthinking is epidemic in swimming and a major performance inhibitor. In light of this unfortunate truth, the holistic coach introduces various mind-clearing techniques (such as meditative breathing) to assist swimmers in reducing the amount of unwanted thought prior to competing.

> **Note:** *Coaches and parents alike are responsible for causing swimmers to overthink in competition. Therefore they should refrain from adding any last-minute thoughts. All desired racing skills and attitudes must be automated within the practice environment and prior to competition. Once swimmers arrive in the competitive*

arena their minds must remain free and clear.

51. Highs, Lows, and Plateaus

If one were to track the yearly progress of elite-level swimmers they would discover periods where performance improved, stayed the same, or declined. Reasons for fluctuations in performance vary, including adjustments to the training regime, lack of motivation, overtraining, illness, or a combination. Whatever the reason, elite-level swimmers continue to strive no matter what, knowing better days will eventually return. Case in point: in the two years leading up to his phenomenal performance at the Beijing Olympics, Michael Phelps did not post a best time in his signature event, the 200 butterfly.

52. Process Over Results

Waiting for specific results to occur can be like waiting for water to boil—seeming to take forever. Impatient swimmers can easily become consumed by their apparent lack of progress, leading to increased levels of frustration, anxiety, self-doubt, and inconsistencies in performance. To rectify the problem, a change of focus is required. For example rather than focus on best times, the process involved in achieving best times becomes the primary point of focus.

53. God's Cake (Author Unknown)

A daughter is telling her mother how everything is going wrong. She's failing algebra, her boyfriend broke up with her, and her best friend is moving away. Meanwhile her mother is baking a cake and asks her daughter if she would like a snack. The daughter replies, "Absolutely! I love cake!" At that point the mother offers her daughter some cooking oil. "Yuck," replies the daughter.

The mother responds by asking, "How about a couple of raw eggs?"

"Gross," the daughter replies.

"Would you like some flour or baking soda?"

The daughter replies, "Those are yucky."

To which the mother replies, "Yes, all those things seem bad all by themselves, but when they are put together in the right way, they make a delicious cake."

God works the same way. Many times we wonder why He would let us go through bad and difficult times, but God knows when He puts all of these things together in His order and time, they always work out for the best! All we need to do is to trust Him and realize that in time He will make something wonderful.

> **Note:** *At first I was hesitant to place the above mental concept in my book, so as not to offend people of alternate views. However, after much thought, I decided to proceed knowing many swimmers look to God for strength.*

54. Fear of Failure

The fear of failure can imprison swimmers, severely limiting their willingness to try. But failure is a natural part of the success process and must be experienced to achieve any meaningful goal. Michael Jordan, perhaps the greatest basketball player of all time, once said, "I have missed more than nine hundred shots in my career. I have lost almost three hundred games. On twenty-six occasions I have been entrusted to take the game winning shot and missed. I have failed over and over again in my life, and that is why I succeed." Swimmers who never risk failure never truly succeed.

> **Note:** *Wayne Gretzky, perhaps the greatest hockey player of all time, once said, "You miss one hundred percent of the shots you don't take." Fear of failure has no place in hockey or swimming.*

55. Change for the Better
Swimmers must constantly evaluate the effectiveness of their practice habits and make the necessary changes where and when needed. Practice habits that deliver the desired result should be repeated while those that do not should be replaced. Unfortunately many swimmers fall victim to unproductive habits, choosing to repeat them time and time again and allowing them to have a detrimental effect on their swim-meet performance. Case in point: floating into the walls when executing freestyle turns in practice and then repeating the same faulty behavior in competition. The ability to change for the better regardless of degree of difficulty is a key ingredient to achieving any goal. In a holistic approach, eliminating unproductive habits is a daily ritual.

56. Magic Pill
If only I had the genius to create a magic pill that produced amazing results with little effort on swimmers' parts. I would be the most successful swim coach on the planet! Unfortunately no such pill exists (at least to my knowledge), but all is not lost. Swimmers can still achieve amazing results through the power of positivity, passion, dedication, focus, hard work, and self-belief.

57. Consistency Is Key
Swimmers who put forth a consistent effort practice after practice reap the greatest rewards. To track consistency levels, the holistic coach concludes each practice by having swimmers grade the amounts of technical and physical effort they put forth. A score of ten is excellent; nine is very, very good; eight is very good; seven is good; and six or below needs improvement. Honest appraisals are essential in order for this concept to work as intended. To further this concept, swimmers are encouraged to record scores at home on a large poster hung on their bedroom wall. The poster is extremely effective in identifying consistency trends from week to week.

58. One Step at a Time

Self-improvement is best achieved by taking small steps. John Wooden, one of the most successful coaches in the history of college basketball, once said, "When you improve a little bit each day, eventually big things occur. Not tomorrow, not the next day, but eventually a big gain is made. Don't look for the big, quick improvement. Seek the small improvement one day at a time. That's the only way it happens—and when it happens, it lasts." The holistic coach assists swimmers in identifying the small steps necessary for big improvement.

59. Pit Bull Mentality

The Mark Twain quote "it's not the size of the dog in the fight that counts, but the size of the fight in the dog" is one of my all-time favorites. It conveys so much. Small swimmers with big hearts, a desire to fight, and a willingness to go the distance can be victorious over much larger opponents.

60. Need Versus Like

Swimmers often make decision based on like rather than necessity. For example some choose to miss morning practice because they like to sleep in while others resist changing their strokes for the better because they like how the old ones feel. To achieve the ultimate swimming goal, swimmers must choose what they need to do over what they like to do. In a holistic approach, "need" is seen as a necessity where "like" is seen as a luxury.

61. Nervousness

There are two kinds of pre-performance nervousness: negative and positive. Negative nervousness stems from the belief that something bad is about to occur while positive nervousness stems from the belief that something good is about to occur. Typically the nervousness felt is dependent upon the swimmers' levels of preparedness. Well-prepared swimmers are far more likely to experience positive nervousness while ill-prepared swimmers are far more likely to experience negative nervousness. Understanding the difference can make all the difference.

Note: *Over the past eighteen years I have conducted more than 300 swim camps and clinics. Experience has taught me that the better I plan and prepare beforehand, the less negative nervousness I feel prior to and during my performance.*

62. The Coach-Swimmer Relationship

The competitive swimming experience is a *we* thing, not a *me* thing. Mutual respect, appreciation, and cooperation must exist between coach and swimmers in order for all to benefit. Coaches who receive the respect, appreciation, and cooperation they deserve are far more likely to treat swimmers in a similar manner and vice versa. Both parties must do their utmost to foster a winning relationship. For example in a holistic approach the coach makes a point of greeting swimmers by name upon arrival to practice each day. In return swimmers greet the coach in a similar manner. This simple gesture may seem trivial to some, but it goes a long way in strengthening the bond between them.

63. Affirmations

Research indicates a person thinks between 45,000 and 50,000 conscious and subconscious thoughts per day, or approximately 150 to 300 per minute. Research also indicates up to eighty percent of these thoughts have the potential to be negative in nature. Combating negative thoughts is never easy, but there are a number of psychological techniques available to overcome them. One involves the use of affirmations (positive programming), where swimmers repeat positive comments about themselves throughout the day. In time these positive affirmations become a regular part of their day-to-day thinking. Examples include:

- "I feel great."
- "The better the competition, the better I swim."
- "I fear nothing."
- "If they can, I can."
- "I'm up for any challenge that comes my way."
- "The tougher the race, the better I swim."
- "I can achieve anything I put my mind to."
- "I'm getting better day by day."
- "The tougher the set, the better I do."
- "I have all I need to succeed."
- "I am invincible."
- "I'm a winner."
- "Nothing can stop me from achieving my goal."

In a holistic approach, swimmers are instructed to create three to five applicable affirmations at the beginning of each short course and long course season. Affirmations must be repeated with clarity, enthusiasm, and meaning at least five times each. Swimmers have the option of repeating affirmations silently or out loud. For greater effectiveness affirmations should be repeated first thing in the morning, last thing at night, and throughout the day when possible.

> **Note:** *Visualizing affirmations can dramatically increase their effectiveness.*

64. Adaptability

The competitive swimming experience involves one change after another. Examples include aging up, changes in the practice schedule, unfavorable race conditions, changes in coaches, slumps in performance, and advancement from one training group to the next. Over the years I have witnessed countless examples of swimmers who struggled due to an inability to adapt. I once saw a swimmer put his fist through a bathroom wall because he couldn't find his favorite goggles! As a result he injured his hand and was unable to compete in the 100 backstroke—an event in which he was ranked first. The only permanent thing in life is change, and swimmers must adapt or face the unfortunate consequences. The holistic coach intentionally creates scenarios within practice and competition where swimmers must either adapt or fail.

65. Delayed Gratification

There is no express lane to success. In the quest for success, swimmers must be willing to endure a great deal of pain and sacrifice with little reward. Unfortunately many choose the opposite response and withdraw during difficult times. While completely understandable, this response is totally counterproductive. Experience has shown that success favors those who continue to strive no matter how unrewarding it is.

66. Embrace Challenge

The path of most resistance pays bigger dividends than the path of least resistance. All too often swimmers look for ways to minimize whatever challenges they face. In addition many see challenge as something to be avoided rather than embraced. In a holistic approach, challenges are initially introduced in bite-size pieces to make them more appealing, manageable, and achievable. As swimmers' enthusiasm and confidence grow greater, challenges are added.

67. An Army of One

The popular recruiting slogan "An Army of One" underscores one of the overriding tenets of a holistic approach: swimmers must be their own forces, relying upon their mental, technical, and physical capabilities to succeed.

Unfortunately a lack of self-reliance is commonplace in swimming. For example swimmers will often wait for the coach to tell them what to do even though they already know what to do. As a result valuable time, energy, and resources are wasted.

This type of behavior not only reflects poorly on the swimmers involved but also suggests an inability to succeed on their own. Without question the reluctance to rely upon oneself diminishes long-term growth and the overall degree of success.

> **Note:** *Elite-level swimmers virtually coach themselves, reducing the hands-on involvement of the coach. In a perfect world, every coach should have the opportunity to coach at least one elite-level swimmer. The experience is one of a kind and memorable.*

68. Maximize the Moment

One of the most effective ways to enhance swimming performance is to maximize the moment or make the most of the moment at hand. Sadly many swimmers take each day for granted, failing to see it as a precious gift and a once in a lifetime opportunity. They act as if they have all the time in the world. Perhaps Nigerian-born artist Babatunde Olatunji said it best: "Yesterday is history. Tomorrow is a mystery. And today? Today is a gift. That's way it's called the present."

69. Work—The Great Equalizer

The world is filled with people who owe their success to one simple fact: a willingness to work harder than those around them. They were not fortunate enough to have been born into the right family or to have graduated from an Ivy League school. They simply worked their butts off. Swimmers who feel disadvantaged (due to a late start, size disparity, or whatever else) can excel far beyond expectations simply by getting their rears in gear!

> **Note:** *Two-time Olympic Gold Medalist Kosuke Kitajima of Japan is only 5 feet, 9 inches tall and weighs 140 pounds!*

70. Fool's Gold

The term *fool's gold* refers to a type of mineral known as iron pyrite, which resembles gold but is worth far less. Gold-rush prospectors were often fooled by its appearance and believed they had struck the mother lode. Swimmers are often fooled in similar ways by believing that certain attitudes, behaviors, or fads have great value when in fact they have little. For example many swimmers mistakenly believe that physical fitness is far more important than mental or technical fitness, that a lack of sleep has little impact on meet performance, or that high-caffeine drinks or magical food supplements can take the place of hard work.

71. Using the Imagination for Good

The imagination is a wonderful gift and a powerful tool that allows us to envision whatever we choose. While responsible for tremendous good, it can also produce a great deal of fear, anxiety, and negativity when used to imagine the worst. Unfortunately swimmers are notorious for this, especially prior to competition. Rather than imagine race-winning performances, they imagine all sorts of worst-case scenarios, including false starts, missed turns, losing count, getting disqualified, or dying on the final fifty. Keeping the imagination in check is key to great swimming performances. Albert Einstein, the father of modern physics and one of the most prolific intellects in human history, once said: "Imagination is everything. It is the preview of things to come."

72. Trying Hard Versus Trying Easy

One would think trying hard would be the best way to achieve any goal. But at times it can actually make things more difficult. For example swimmers who try hard to make a certain time may find the time more elusive than ever. At times like this, a better alternative would be trying easy, where swimmers put forth their best effort in a more relaxed manner and with little expectation or self-imposed pressure. Removing these mental hindrances allows effort to flow freely, making the achievement of the goal far more likely. In a holistic approach, the concept of trying easy is used frequently within practice to demonstrate its effectiveness.

73. Letting Go
To excel in competition, swimmers must let go or stop stressing over the things that are beyond their control. Examples include overcrowded warm ups, heat assignments, lane assignments, other swimmers in the heat, pool conditions, and weather conditions. Instead they should focus on the things within their control. Examples include attitude and outlook, race prep, racing strategies, and the amount of effort put forth. Letting go allows swimmers to channel their energies into the things they have control over, thus improving the chances of a better outcome.

74. Practice Is Where Hard Things Become Easy
Performing elite-level racing skills can be extremely challenging, to say the least. Examples include breathing every other stroke in a 200 butterfly, splitting a near-best time on the first 50 of a 100 backstroke, eliminating the glide phase in breaststroke, maintaining a six-beat kick for freestyle, and traveling fifteen meters underwater off a start or turn. To execute these elite racing skills in competition, swimmers must have the discipline and drive to execute them in practice. Those who choose to avoid them never truly excel.

75. Overcoming Obstacles
There are two kinds of obstacles: those within us and those that others put in front of us. To achieve their most-desired goals, swimmers must develop a mind-set that any obstacle, large or small, can be overcome. Michael Jordan, perhaps the greatest basketball player of all time, once said, "Obstacles don't have to

stop you. If you run into a wall, don't turn around and give up. Figure out how to climb it, go through it, or work around it." In a holistic approach, overcoming obstacles is the rule rather than the exception.

> **Note:** *The seventy-five mental concepts outline above represent less than half of the total number of concepts used in a holistic approach. Additional concepts are posted on The Swimming Triangle website at www. theswimmingtriangle.com.*

ACHIEVING THE MENTAL EDGE IN COMPETITION

Swimmers who possess the mental edge reign supreme in competition. Some instinctively have it, but most need help to acquire it. There are numerous mental edge strategies, but many fail in the real world of swimming due to the degree of complexity relative to swimmers' ages and experience. The following five examples are swimmer-friendly, highly effective, and easily implemented in a competitive setting:

1. Respond to Doubts Immediately

It's natural for doubts to pop up prior to competition. Responding immediately with truthful opposites can go a long way in counteracting negative effects. For example swimmers who doubt their ability to finish a 100 butterfly race successfully should respond immediately by reminding themselves how much butterfly they

performed over the past thirty days. In addition swimmers should take the opportunity to list common doubts along with truthful opposites beforehand. That way they are prepared to respond should the need arise.

2.   Space Out

This effective strategy involves turning down all external stimuli to a minimum. In doing this swimmers still operate at a level where they are fully aware of time or the next scheduled event, yet they float above all the unwanted distractions, pressures, and potential negativity that typically exist within a competitive setting. The holistic coach simulates race conditions in practice to provide swimmers with opportunities to space out on demand. Swimmers are also encouraged to use this technique at times of stress throughout the day.

> **Note:** *I often use this strategy in pressure-filled or negative settings.*

3.   Breathe In, Breathe Out

Deep breathing is nature's way of calming the mind and body, making it extremely useful in high-stress, competitive settings. Swimmers are instructed to perform a series of deep inhales and deep exhales to the count of five whenever or wherever stress mounts prior to competition. Examples include on the way to the pool, during the swim-meet warm up, while sitting in the stands, and while standing behind the block. In addition swimmers are encouraged to practice deep breathing at bedtime or at times of stress throughout the day.

4.   The Ideal Mental State

In this strategy swimmers are instructed to identify their ideal mental state prior to a successful performance. Some may prefer a highly energized state while others a more relaxed one. Once the mental state is identified, the holistic coach provides swimmers with numerous rehearsal opportunities in practice. From here swimmers are challenged to recreate the ideal mental state in competition. Activities that interfere with this process, such as excessive socializing or video-game playing, are discouraged.

Note: *At the 2008 Olympics, Michael Phelps competed in seventeen races over nine days, breaking seven world records and winning eight gold medals! How's that for a mental edge?*

5. Visualize

To visualize is to focus on positive mental images in order to achieve a desired goal. It works by creating neural patterns in the brain as if the person had already achieved it. Over time these patterns etch small tracks in the brain cells directing the person seamlessly to the desired goal. There are various forms of visualizing that can be used in competitive swimming. One involves visualizing a positive outcome in a variety of unfavorable conditions. For example, winning from behind, coming off a poor start to win, winning with goggles full of water, or winning from the outside lane. Swimmers who visualize winning in these unfavorable conditions are more likely to remain calm, focused, and confident should they arise in competition.

CHAPTER 3

The Technical Conditioning Curriculum

The technical conditioning curriculum constitutes the second side of the swimming triangle. The material presented here is blended with the content of the mental and physical curricula to create a holistic effect. Optimal technical conditioning is a prerequisite to achieving the ultimate swimming goal and the primary purpose of the technical conditioning curriculum.

> **Note:** *"Technique, technique, and technique at a young age overrides all other aspects of preparation. If a swimmer can arrive at 16 years of age with great technique, and has done speed training early in their life, you have a great opportunity to produce results."*
> —*Bill Sweetenham, 5-time Olympic Head Coach, 8-time Commonwealth Games Coach, 9-time World Championships Coach*

The expression *ten coaches, ten approaches* says it best when it comes to teaching competitive swimming technique. In my experience swimming coaches fall into one of three categories: 1) those who teach and reinforce basic technical principles, 2) those who combine the basics with the latest trends, or 3) those who pay lip service to technique. In other words they say it's important but spend little or no time teaching or reinforcing it. On occasion, I encounter coaches who prefer to teach only one style of technique. While simple in approach and application, it makes little sense to me. How can one style of technique be suitable for every swimmer on a team? Teaching only one style is similar to a clothing store offering only one size pants! One size does not fit all in clothing or swimming technique. In a holistic approach, technique is divided into three groups: 1) basic, 2) advanced, and 3) individual. Examples of basic technique include the track start, an open back to breast turn, or single-sided breathing in freestyle. Examples of advanced technique include the slingshot start, the back to breast somersault turn, or bilateral breathing in freestyle. Examples of individual technique include straight-arm freestyle recovery, side breathing in butterfly, or undulating breaststroke. Swimmers are introduced to basic technique first, like breathing to only one side in freestyle. From here the advanced technique of bilateral breathing is taught. In the event swimmers find bilateral breathing awkward or less efficient, the individual technique of single-sided breathing with an occasional breath on the opposite side is introduced.

The technical conditioning curriculum chapter consists of a series of technical concepts followed by a brief description of each start, stroke, turn, and finish. Stroke technique is constantly evolving. By the time *The Swimming Triangle* is published many new technical concepts will have been introduced to the world of competitive swimming. As mentioned previously, research indicates elite-level swimmers enjoy up to a seventy-percent technical advantage over the competition; therefore coaches who ignore the technical side of swimming (or play lip service to it) place swimmers at a huge disadvantage. The need for best-form start, stroke, and turn technique cannot be denied and is vital to peak performance in the pool.

Note: *The degree of technical conditioning also affects the degree of mental and physical conditioning. From a mental standpoint, technically fit swimmers experience greater confidence and pride due to enhanced technical skills. From a physical standpoint, technically fit swimmers develop greater physical fitness due to the* *increased demands of superior technique.*

TO EACH HIS OWN

Over the years I have read countless articles on competitive swimming technique written by the top coaches and swimming scientists in the world. One obvious conclusion is that no two swimming authorities view or teach technique in the same manner—a point I truly respect, value, and understand. Whatever position is being proposed, the bottom line remains: does it enhance swimming performance? At various times throughout my coaching career, coaches have disagreed or criticized my methods of teaching even though swimmers experienced significant to dramatic improvement. At this point in my coaching career, I really don't care what others think, provided the swimmers benefit in the end.

In addition I find much of the technical material available to be cumbersome and difficult for swimmers to comprehend and apply. Therefore I prefer to stick with my simple methods of teaching and the technical tricks I employ to enhance performance. I'll let the results speak for themselves.

AN UNEQUALLED OPPORTUNITY

Each year I review over 100 above and below water videos of swimmers who attend my swim camps and clinics. They come from all corners of the globe and range in ability, from novice to national level. The in-depth reviews typically take more than two hours to complete. Needless to say it provides me with an unequalled opportunity to view the quality of swimmer's starts, strokes, and turns. On average I would rate them a five out of ten in terms of technical competency. I see this as a reflection of the type of training they are subjected too with a greater emphasis placed on the quantity of yards versus the quality of yards. Swimmers who fail to develop the correct start, stroke, and turn technique during their formative years can never truly realize their full potential in their senior years.

TECHNICAL CONCEPTS

For the sake of brevity and my desire to keep the mental, technical, and physical chapters somewhat balanced, I have chosen to limit the number of technical concepts to seventy-five, although many more could have been added. Additional concepts are posted on The Swimming Triangle website at www.theswimmingtriangle. com. Each technical concept is intended to highlight a core technical consideration making the all-important technical side of swimming more easily understood and applied.

1. Swimming in the Middle

Most swimmers fail to extend fully at the point of entry or push back fully through the finish phase of freestyle. Shortening the stroke on both ends or swimming in the middle makes the stroke easier to swim but far less productive. Ideally the lead arm and finishing arm must achieve a fully extended position before switching. This style of freestyle is ideally suited for swimming distances of two hundred yards/meters or above, where the need for stroke efficiency reigns supreme. In races one hundred yards/meters or less, shortening the stroke to a minor degree is permitted to increase stroke rates.

Note: *Underwater video footage of Michael Phelps reveals one arm totally extended forward of the shoulder and the other arm totally extended backward against the side of the body before the arms switch. An aggressive, six-beat kick is maintained throughout each stroke cycle to facilitate length. Underwater video footage of Australian superstar Ian Thorpe reveals the same stroking pattern.*

2.   Creation Versus Elimination

To achieve ultimate speed, swimmers must create as much propulsion as possible while eliminating as much drag as possible. All
too often the focus is placed on the creation side at the expense of
the elimination side. Without question the creation and elimination sides must work hand in hand for swimmers to realize their
full speed potential.

> **Note:** *The creation side of swimming is more physical*
> *in nature while the elimination side is more mental.*
> *Physical swimmers by nature tend to struggle with the*
> *elimination side.*

3.   Arm Cycle Versus Breathing Cycle

The breathing cycle must fit perfectly within the arm cycle to achieve
ideal timing/flow within a stroke. For example the breathing cycle
in butterfly begins as the arms transition into the catch phase of
the arm cycle and ends prior to the arms returning to the water
at the point of entry. The same arm cycle versus breathing cycle
relationship exists within breaststroke and freestyle.

> **Note:** *A more detailed explanation is outlined in the*
> *Strokes section of this chapter.*

4.   A Drill is a Teacher

Swimming drills play a major role in a holistic approach, often-
times replacing the coach as the teacher of skills. For drills to be
most effective, the holistic coach provides swimmers with a clear
understanding of the purpose of each drill together with step-by-
step instructions. In addition drills are repeated frequently and in
an exacting manner.

> **Note:** *Unfortunately many coaches use drills for warm*
> *up purposes with little or no instruction or follow-up*
> *given. In addition drills are oftentimes performed with*

minimal supervision or correction. As a result swimmers typically go through the motions, missing out on the potential benefits. Another common practice is to place drills on super-fast intervals, making it virtually impossible for swimmers to perform them correctly.

5.   Whole-Body Swimming

Ideally swimmers should rely upon the whole body for speed production including the arms, legs, and core. Unfortunately most tend to rely disproportionately upon the arms when performing butterfly, backstroke, and freestyle due to the fact that greater leg and core involvement places greater physical demands on the body as a whole. While restricting whole-body involvement may be easier in the short term, it dramatically reduces speed potential over the long term.

6.   Swimming on an Allowance

The majority of swimmers have little idea how many strokes they perform over a twenty-five distance. In a holistic approach, swimmers are given an allowance of strokes that must be adhered to when performing specific training sets in practice. For example a twelve-year old swimmer may be given an allowance of seventeen freestyle strokes per twenty-five when performing a set of 10 x 100 FR. While staying within an allowance can be extremely challenging, swimmers adapt quickly. As a result distance per stroke and overall stroke efficiency improve significantly.

Note: *To determine individual allowances a twenty-five stroke count test is conducted in each stroke. The test consists of a series of twenty-fives performed at a predetermined speed. Upon completion an average stroke count per twenty-five is determined. The twenty-five stroke count test is repeated every three to four weeks in order to measure improvements in stroke efficiency.*

7.   Beads on a String

Disjointed strokes (strokes that lack cohesion) are all too common, especially at the age-group level. To address and illustrate this shortcoming, the holistic coach scatters five beads on the pool deck and instructs swimmers to imagine that each bead represents a different part of a stroke. The first bead represents the body position; the second, the kick cycle; the third, the arm cycle; the fourth, the breathing cycle; and the fifth, timing/flow. From here the beads are strung together on a string. The scattered beads are intended to represent a disjointed stroke while the beads on the string are intended to represent a fully connected, elite-level stroke.

> **Note:** *As an alternative kickboards may be used instead of beads. The holistic coach scatters five kickboards randomly on the pool deck. From here the boards are organized in a straight line, one behind the other.*

8.   Swimming on Video

One of the quickest ways to improve start, stroke, or turn technique is to have swimmers imagine they are being filmed for a swimming video. The results can be truly amazing! The concept works particularly well during the warm up and warm-down portions of practice.

> **Note:** *Another concept involves swimmers pretending to be in a fashion show where they get to model their strokes. The lane serves as the runway.*

9.   Water Bottle Kick

Maintaining a shoulder-width distance or slightly wider than shoulder width distance during the propulsive phase of the breast-stroke kick cycle is commonly recommended. While effective for most, I believe knee width is swimmer-specific or individual in nature and swimmers must be allowed to experiment with various kicking widths to discover the ideal size for them. Kosuke Kitajima, the two-time Olympic gold medalist, has a very narrow kick while Amanda Beard, the most decorated female breaststroker in Olympic history, had an extremely wide kick. One proven method of experimentation involves the following four-step progression:

Step 1:   Swimmers place a water bottle between the upper legs and perform a 25 breaststroke kick.

Step 2:   A second 25 breaststroke kick is performed with an imaginary water bottle placed between the upper legs. The width of the kick is similar to step one.

Step 3:   A third 25 breaststroke kick is performed beginning at the imaginary water bottle width and expanding outward from there one kick at a time.

Step 4:   The drill sequence is continued until the ideal knee width is determined.

When performing steps three and four, the knees must spread gradually in order to experience subtle changes in propulsion. Through the process of trial and error, the ideal knee width is determined, delivering maximum propulsion with minimal drag.

Note: *The skinny, fat, in between kick drill (listed under Breaststroke Drills in Chapter 4) is another effective way to determine ideal kicking width.*

10. Fluidity in Body = Fluidity in Water

The term *fluid* has two meanings: 1) a substance with no fixed shape, and 2) the ability to flow easily and gracefully. To maximize speed potential, swimmers must be as fluid as possible, flowing easily and gracefully from stroke to stroke. Therefore yoga or swim-specific stretching must be an essential part of the daily routine.

Note: *Many swimmers resist stretching for a variety of reasons. Some find it boring; others question its importance; still others find it painful or hopeless. Whatever the reason, the need for flexibility (fluidity) cannot be denied. In addition swimmers who lack this all-important necessity generate far less propulsion within each stroke cycle. Flexibility self-tests/exercises are outlined in Chapter 5.*

11. Sinker Arm

Sinking the lead arm in freestyle immediately upon entry is an extremely common stroke error that impacts the total amount of propulsion generated. The error occurs when swimmers rest on the lead arm while breathing to the opposite side, causing it to sink past the desired catch point. The following four-step progression is one proven method of correction:

Step 1: Swimmers perform a 25 freestyle without breathing. The goal is to move from a fully extended arm positioned just beneath the surface to an immediate high elbow catch with a focus on both arms.

Step 2: Step one is repeated only breathing to the right side. The goal is to move from a fully extended arm positioned just beneath the surface to an immediate high elbow catch with a focus on the left arm.

Step 3: Step one is repeated only breathing to the left side. The goal is to move from a fully extended arm positioned just beneath the surface to an immediate high elbow catch with a focus on the right arm.

Step 4: Step one is repeated only with bilateral breathing. The goal is to move from a fully extended arm positioned just beneath the surface to an immediate high elbow catch with a focus on both arms.

Note: *Swimmers may need to repeat step one a number of times to develop a feel for a fully extended arm and immediate high elbow catch.*

12. Breaststroke Versus Rest Stroke

Over the years breaststroke has developed an aggressive edge to it. Therefore swimmers must possess a high degree of technical expertise and physical fitness to flow from stroke to stroke with little or no glide. This aggressive style is much different from another style of breaststroke I refer to as *rest-stroke*, where a glide of varying lengths is placed between strokes. While obviously easier and more restful, it cannot compete with modern-day breaststroke.

Note: *Elite-level swimmers typically perform the 100 breaststroke with little or no glide between strokes but add some degree of glide for a portion of the 200 breaststroke. In either case the body must achieve a fully streamlined position at the end of each stroke cycle.*

Food for Thought

Most coaches and swimmers consider butterfly the most physically challenging stroke of all, with breaststroke a close second. Butterfly has no glide between strokes, yet breaststroke does (in most cases). *If gliding, for the sake of energy conservation, is considered necessary for breaststroke, why is there no glide in butterfly*? In my view, breaststrokers should condition themselves to the point where they achieve a fully streamlined position between strokes but resist the urge to glide. When exposed the body will adapt to most anything. So in time the body will adapt to a lack of glide if it's performed that way in practice.

13. Pretty Fast

In a holistic approach the concept *pretty fast* is used in both practice and competition. *Pretty* defines the desired look of the stroke while *fast* defines the desired speed.

14. 385 and Counting

The amount of technical knowhow required in swimming today is mind-boggling. Swimmers are expected to perfect four strokes, three starts, seven turns, and four finishes. Each stroke consists of at least five parts with a minimum of ten technical points per part. Each start consists of at least four parts with a minimum of five technical points per part. Each turn consists of at least three parts with a minimum of five technical points per part. Each finish consists of one part with a minimum five technical points per part. Added together this represents a total of 385 technical points! An approach that ignores or pays lip service to the technical side of swimming severely handicaps swimmers' potential.

> Note: *The 385 technical points represent just one portion of required knowledge and do not include points pertaining to mental conditioning, racing strategies, training systems/protocol, nutrition, Dry Land training, etc.*

15. An Environment for Learning

To maximize the learning process the ideal environment must be created. For example the Montessori School places a high emphasis on independence, freedom with limits, and respect for a child's natural psychological development. The Suzuki method of learning music is another example where creating the right environment for learning is paramount. Here learning music by ear is emphasized over reading musical notation, and students are expected to retain and review every piece of music ever learned on a regular basis. In a holistic approach to competitive swimming, the coach creates an ideal environment for learning where trying to achieve is just as important as achieving, where skills and drills are taught with clarity in a progressive and repetitive manner, and where recommendations for improvement are presented in a positive and uplifting way.

16. Technical Fitness Requires Physical Fitness

To develop best-form start, stroke, and turn technique, swimmers require a certain degree of strength, flexibility, and endurance. For example strength is needed to execute a high elbow catch in freestyle successfully; flexibility is needed to chest press sufficiently in butterfly; and endurance is needed to windmill the arms at an accelerated rate for the duration of a backstroke race. Without question best-form technique and physical fitness go hand in hand.

17. Focus on the Fastest

Performed correctly, the fastest part of any race is the start (including the underwater travel portion) followed by the turn (including the underwater travel portion). Ideally swimmers should spend a significant amount of time mastering starts and turns, as both have the greatest potential for speed. Typically swimmers are given only a day or two prior to competition, leaving little time for effective skill acquisition. In a holistic approach, starts and turns are rehearsed and refined on a daily basis. Information on the methods used to effectively integrate starts and turns into practice is outlined in Chapter 4.

Note: *It is not uncommon for elite level swimmers to travel sixty meters underwater in both the 100 butterfly and 100 backstroke, as traveling underwater is faster than traveling above water if performed correctly.*

18. Swimming in Control

Elite level swimmers swim in control with their strokes fully maximized. As a result they achieve speeds equal to the amount of energy expended. Unfortunately most swimmers swim out of control, failing to take the time needed to maximize stroke length and speed potential. As a result they achieve speeds far below the energy expended. Research indicates a greater amount of energy is expended by moving quickly from stroke to stroke than by remaining with an existing stroke until its full propulsive potential is realized.

Note: *Elite-level swimmers may actually look slower when swimming fast compared to less accomplished swimmers. This is due to the fact that the arms and legs work with greater amounts of water from start to finish.*

19. Boil Versus Splash

Pulling with the hands out of the water would make absolutely no sense at all, yet kicking with the feet out of the water for a portion of each freestyle kick cycle is common practice. Kicking in this manner reduces foot contact with the water, resulting in less propulsion per kick. Elite-level swimmers maintain a bottom-up kick versus a top-down kick, with the feet kicking up to the surface as opposed to down through the surface. Kicking up to the surface creates a boil while kicking down through the surface creates a splash.

Note: *The only exception may be in sprint events, where kicking with the feet partially out of the water has the* *potential to increase stroke rates.*

20. Stroke Foundation

Each of the four competitive strokes is built upon a foundation. In butterfly and breaststroke, the foundation is reestablished at the end of each stroke cycle while in backstroke and freestyle, the foundation is maintained throughout each stroke cycle. Failure to reestablish or maintain a stroke foundation undoubtedly leads to stroke decay and a decline in speed. In a holistic approach, reestablishing or maintaining the foundation of each stroke is a top priority, especially in the latter part of practice when the onset of fatigue can make it increasingly difficult.

Note: *Foundations for each stroke are outlined in the Stroke section of this chapter.*

21. Uncooked Versus Cooked Spaghetti

An uncooked piece of spaghetti travels through the water more easily than does a cooked piece due to the fact that the uncooked piece has a more solid form. This scientific fact is not only true for spaghetti but for swimmers as well. Achieving a more solid form (via greater core strength and enhanced stroke technique) allows swimmers to pass through the water with greater precision and ease.

22. Wobble Speed

If one were to roll a car tire down the road it would remain upright as long as it traveled above a particular speed. As the speed dropped, the rate of forward movement would decrease, and the amount of side-to-side movement (wobble) would increase. The same thing occurs when a swimmer performs strokes too slowly. In backstroke and freestyle, the body spends more time going side to side than forward. In butterfly and breaststroke, the body spends more time going up and down than forward. Left unchecked these undesired and unproductive movements create a variety of bad habits and severely limit speed potential.

Note: *It is not uncommon for swimmers to waste more than fifty percent of their effort on unwanted movements within a stroke. In addition, rather than correcting these errors, they train harder to compensate for them.*

23. Add Rotation to the Foundation

The foundation in backstroke and freestyle consists of a horizontal or near-horizontal body position. Achieving this position requires a neutral or near-neutral head position, a plank-like upper body, and a tight, symmetrical, continuous kick. Once that's established rotation is added via the hips. As the right arm passes by the right shoulder, the hips rotate the entire foundation (minus the head) to the right and vice versa. Rotation increases stroke length, strengthens the pull, and reduces drag. Within one backstroke stroke cycle, swimmers spend more time rotated to the right or left than flat on their backs. Within one freestyle stroke cycle, swimmers spend more time rotated to the right or left than flat on their stomachs.

Note: *The hips act as the centerpiece for backstroke and freestyle rotation. Therefore the pull and kick must never override the rotational responsibilities of the hips. Overriding results in disjointed strokes and reduced stroking power. In addition the hips must achieve the desired amount of rotation before the pull is initiated to maximize pulling potential.*

24. Muscle Memory

To observe muscle memory in action, place three pens on a table. Pick up the first pen and sign your name, then repeat the process with the second and third pens. Notice how on each occasion your fingers grasped the pen in the same manner, with no conscious thought on your part. This simple experiment illustrates the concept of muscle memory, where muscles become trained to repeat a series of movements automatically. In a holistic approach, creating the ideal muscle memory for each start, stroke, turning, and racing skill is reinforced daily, allowing swimmers to be free and clear of technical thought on race day.

25. B.O.B.

The acronym B.O.B. stands for *best of both* or best stroke length combined with best stroke rate. To maximize speed potential, swimmers must find the perfect balance between a long stroke and a fast rate, as a long stroke with a slow rate or a short stroke with a fast rate will not suffice.

> **Note:** *At the elite level, maintaining near-maximal stroke length at maximal speed is the rule rather than the exception.*

26. Three Types of Breaststrokers

When it comes to breaststroke, swimmers can be categorized into three types: natural, IM, and everybody else. Natural breaststrokers are the fastest of all and make breaststroke look easy. IM breaststrokers are not as fast as natural breaststrokers but can put together a solid breaststroke leg in the IM. Everybody else breaststrokers lack total understanding and feel. To them breaststroke is like speaking a foreign language.

27. The Three Lines

The line running along the bottom of the pool, together with the lane lines on either side of the lane, can be used to teach the ideal non-breathing and breathing head positions in freestyle. During the non-breathing phase, swimmers sight the line running along the bottom of the pool. When breathing to the right, swimmers sight the right lane line. When breathing to the left, swimmers sight the left lane line. This simple concept assists swimmers in achieving a lower and steadier head position while keeping the amount of head turn to a minimum during the breathing cycle.

Note: *When sighting the line running along the bottom of the pool, a slight forward head tilt is permitted.*

28. Red Light, Green Light

Once in motion swimmers must stay in motion to transfer the greatest amount of momentum from stroke to stroke. The two most common stroke errors adversely affecting momentum are 1) pausing the hands at the entry point in butterfly and 2) pausing the hands at the breathing point in breaststroke. A pause within a stroke is similar to a car stopping at a red light. Once stopped additional energy is required to regain the momentum lost. At the elite level, swimmers see only green lights.

29. Links of a Chain

A swimmer's body consists of a series of links, similar to links in a chain, including: the hand-arm link, the shoulder link, the upper back link, the core link, the hip-leg link, and the ankle-foot link. Combined they provide numerous stroke benefits including improved body position, greater stability, and increased stroking power. Unfortunately one weak link can lead to serious stroke decay, placing greater stress on the remaining links and risking potential injury. Swimmers must think beyond their extremities (arms and legs) and understand the entire body plays a role in stroke quality and speed production.

Note: *The above concept was written with simplicity in mind and barely scratches the surface in terms of a full explanation. To gain greater insight, I highly recommend Complete Conditioning for Swimming by David Salo. The term kinetic chain is the official name used to describe this all-important concept.*

30. A Perfect Match

To achieve ideal timing/flow, both sides of a stroke must match. In backstroke and freestyle, the pulling, kicking, and rotational patterns on the right must match the pulling, kicking, and rotational patterns on the left. Butterfly and breaststroke are much easier to match, as both arms pull and both legs kick at the same time. A lopsided stroke can never match a symmetrical one in terms of speed production.

31. Two Body Positions

Butterfly and breaststroke have a non-breathing body position and breathing body position. Swimmers alternate between these two positions every stroke or every other stroke (in the case of butterfly) or every stroke (in the case of breaststroke). For the sake of drag reduction and flow, the difference between the two body positions must be kept to a minimum. Backstroke and freestyle have a head-to-toe body position and a side-to-side body position. For the sake of body alignment, drag reduction, and flow, the head-to-toe body position must be maintained as the body rotates from side to side.

> **Note:** *Many undulating-style breaststrokers choose to rise higher on the breath to lunge over the water during the shoot phase of the arm cycle. It is not uncommon to see their shoulders completely out of the water during the entire shoot. In a holistic approach, the term lift and lunge is used to describe this all-important concept.*

32. Training Hard Versus Training Smart

Most swimmers determine the success of a practice based on how hard they trained. While training hard is important, training smart via sound technical principles is equally important. Swimmers who emphasize only the physical training gain an advantage in one way, but lose significantly in other ways.

> **Note:** *Training hard in the absence of technique can*

give swimmers a false sense of preparedness.

33. The Race Car Analogy

If a racecar driver experienced steering issues and was unable to achieve the desired speed, would the pit crew replace the engine with a larger one or fix the steering? While the answer seems obvious, it is not so obvious to swimmers who typically choose the wrong response. For example rather than fix an offending stroke error, they choose to work harder in an attempt to increase speed. Unfortunately this type of response is totally self-defeating.

> **Note:** *Many swimmers refuse to slow down to fix technical errors for various reasons including an addiction to hard work, a fear of being passed by fellow teammates, a fear of missing an interval, and a fear of being chastised by the coach.*

34. Water Height

Swimmers must strive to achieve their water height at all times. Water height is measured from the fingertips of an extended arm placed overhead to the toe tips. To maximize stroke length and propulsion, swimmers must achieve their water height prior to initiating a stroke.

35. Weight Shifting

To achieve a stronger backstroke and freestyle pull, swimmers must shift their body weight over the entry arm prior to initiating the pull. To illustrate this all-important concept, the holistic coach offers the following two-step progression:

Step 1:   Swimmers perform a 25 backstroke with zero rotation (flat on the back).

Step 2:   Step one is repeated only with the body weight shifted forty-five degrees to either side in unison with the pulling arm.

Note: *As one might expect, swimmers feel much stronger with the body weight shifted. Once complete the two-step progression is repeated with freestyle.*

36. Minimal Kick

A tight, symmetrical, continuous kick is ideal for backstroke and freestyle, but kicking in this manner can be extremely taxing from both technical and physical standpoints. To encourage this type of kicking action, the holistic coach offers the following three-step progression:

Step 1: Swimmers lie face up in the water for backstroke or face down in the water for freestyle with the head placed in a neutral or near-neutral position. The arms are squeezed against the sides of the body with the legs and feet together. From here swimmers attempt to maintain a horizontal body position with a minimal kick (the least effort possible). The kick must be hard enough to maintain a horizontal position without added forward momentum.

Step 2: Step one is repeated only with one arm extended directly behind the shoulder for backstroke or directly in front of the shoulder for freestyle with added kicking intensity. The kick must be sufficiently hard to propel swimmers slowly down the pool.

Step 3: Step two is repeated only swimmers transition from the step two position into full stroke backstroke or freestyle. In the case of freestyle, breathing is initially eliminated or reduced, as improper breathing technique can interrupt the flow of the kick. Through repeated attempts swimmers develop the ability to maintain a tight, symmetrical, continuous backstroke or freestyle kick with minimal effort, greatly enhancing the technical quality of the stroke.

Note: *Once a minimal kick is established, greater kicking intensity is added. The minimal kick concept adds the many benefits of a six-beat kick without a dramatic increase in workload. Its use is highly recommended in extended backstroke sets, endurance-type freestyle events, or distance training.*

37. Perpendicular Paddles

The hands and forearms combine to form paddles by which swimmers propel through the water. To propel efficiently and effectively, the hand/forearm paddle must be perpendicular or near perpendicular to the surface at the point of catch. The more the elbow points upward and the more the fingertips point downward, the greater the propulsion produced.

38. Negative Resistance Versus Positive Resistance

Swimming resistance comes in two forms: negative and positive. Negative resistance slows swimmers down while positive resistance speeds swimmers up. Examples of negative resistance include poor body alignment in backstroke and toes that point downward at the completion of the breaststroke kick. Examples of positive resistance include the correct positioning of the hand/forearm paddle during the catch phase of the freestyle arm cycle and the correct positioning of the foot/leg paddle during the downbeat phase of the butterfly kick cycle. To maximize speed swimmers must decrease the amount of negative resistance while increasing the amount of positive resistance.

39. Stroke Counts

Establishing a predictable stroke count from the flags to the wall at full speed is key to a fast backstroke turn. Although seldom taught, the same performance-improving concept holds true for butterfly, breaststroke, and freestyle turns. Teaching swimmers to identify the ideal number of strokes from the flags to the wall in all four strokes has many benefits, including sustained turning momentum, elimination of short stroking, reduced likelihood of missed turns, and enhanced turning confidence. In a holistic approach, swimmers know and practice their turn counts in all four strokes on a frequent basis.

> **Note:** *Some may wonder how swimmers determine the location of the flags when swimming on the stomach. While unable to see, experienced swimmers can sense the flags. The holistic coach offers experimental opportunities on an ongoing basis to teach this performance-improving concept.*

40. Swimming on a Tightrope

To convey the concept of symmetry and balance, the holistic coach instructs swimmers to imagine performing backstroke or freestyle on an invisible tightrope running from one end of the pool to the other, positioned just beneath the surface. To stay upright a perfectly balanced stroke must be maintained throughout each stroke cycle.

41. Seamless Swimming

Elite-level swimmers have seamless strokes, free of any imbalance or hesitation. Each stroke component fits perfectly within the stroke cycle and each stroke moves smoothly from one to the next with the maximum amount of momentum transferred. While there are always exceptions to the rule (Gallup Freestyle), seamless swimming is the way to go.

42. Pulling Versus Pushing

The term *pull* is commonly used to describe the underwater portion of the butterfly, backstroke, and freestyle arm cycles. But in reality the arms pull the body forward from shortly after the hands enter the water to the rib cage. From here the arms push the body forward until the recovery phase begins. Due to the fact that pushing muscles are inherently stronger than pulling muscles, swimmers must do their utmost to maximize push length.

43. A Small Ball Spins Faster Than a Big Ball

A golf ball spins faster than a basketball due to its smaller circumference. The same scientific rule applies to flip turns. Swimmers who execute a tight ball somersault turn faster than those who don't. In a holistic approach, the term *ball on the wall* is used to convey this all-important concept.

> **Note:** *The term small on the wall is also used.*

44. The Four Lines

The freestyle arm cycle consists of four imaginary lines: 1) shoulder line 2) head line 3) midline, and 4) hip line. The shoulder line is intended to convey the idea of entering the hand in line with the shoulder; the head line is intended to convey the idea of catching the water via a high elbow catch before the elbow passes the top of the head; the midline is intended to convey the idea that the arm never pulls across the center of the body; the hip line is intended to convey the idea of finishing past the hip.

> **Note:** *The backstroke arm cycle consists of three imaginary lines: 1) shoulder line 2) head line, and 3) hip line.*

45. Power Triangle

Swimmers must assume a power-triangle position before pushing off the wall. To envision this position, picture a swimmer sitting upright in a chair with his upper body held in a streamlined position. The pointed fingers represent the tip of the triangle while the shoulder-width foot position represents the base of the triangle. The ninety-degree knee bend achieved by sitting in a chair is considered ideal for a powerful push off.

46. Kicking With the Knees Locked Out

Kicking butterfly, backstroke, and freestyle with the knees locked out and the butt squeezed as tightly as possible is an excellent way to develop kicking uniformity and whole leg involvement while eliminating excessive knee bend or an asymmetrical kick. Once mastered, swimmers gently relax the knees and butt, allowing the knees to play a more active role. As a result the kick is more uniform and propulsive.

47. Breaststroke Timing

Correct timing in breaststroke is critical to flow but can be easily thrown off if too much slow breaststroke is performed in practice. To prevent this from occurring, swimmers must execute the breathe-shoot-kick phase of each stroke cycle as quickly as possible regardless of the overall training speed. An extended glide between strokes may be added to control the total effort expended, but the quickness within the stroke cycle must be preserved.

48. Watered-Down Technique

The term *water down* means to weaken. Swimmers often water down technique in practice to reduce workloads. Examples include reduced kicking rates, shorter stroke lengths, dropped elbows at the point of catch, floating turns, legs that float together in breaststroke kick, increased breathing, and inferior streamlining off the walls. While watered-down technique may make it easier to survive practice, it does little to enhance performance.

49. Arm-Dominant Versus Leg-Dominant

When performing freestyle, the majority of swimmers rely more heavily on the arms, allowing the legs to dangle or follow randomly.

Unfortunately this approach produces an arm-dominant stroke, unlike the leg-dominant stroke performed by many elite-level sprint and middle-distance freestylers. In a holistic approach, freestyle is taught through the legs to connect the stroke from top to bottom and to deliver the eight benefits derived from the kick.

> **Note:** *The eight benefits are listed in the Freestyle section of this chapter.*

50. Full, Fast Finish
The faster the hand/forearm paddle moves through the water, the greater the amount of resistance encountered. While increased resistance on the torso impedes forward progress, increased resistance on the hand/forearm paddle enhances it. To maximize this law of physics, a full, fast finish is emphasized in butterfly, backstroke, and freestyle.

> **Note:** *To further understanding, the holistic coach offers the following three-step progression:*
>
> **Step 1:** Swimmers slowly scull the arms back and forth underwater.
>
> **Step 2:** Step one is repeated only at a faster rate. As one might expect, greater resistance is encountered with faster-moving arms.
>
> **Step 3:** Swimmers perform a series of 25s (butterfly, backstroke, and freestyle), applying the concept to the stroke.

51. Lay It on the Line
This simple concept is used to encourage ideal streamlining and a horizontal body position in breaststroke. Swimmers perform breaststroke on top of an imaginary line running from one end of the pool to the other, just beneath the surface. As the hands shoot forward, ending the recovery phase of the arm cycle, and as the

feet snap together, ending the propulsive phase of the kick cycle, the body is laid entirely on top of the line. Once this is complete, the next stroke cycle is initiated.

> Note: *In addition, setting the line just beneath the surface prevents swimmers from diving down too deeply during the shoot phase of the breaststroke arm cycle.*

52. Lean, Mean Swimming Machines

Elite-level swimmers could easily be described as lean, mean swimming machines. The term *lean* suggests a solid work ethic and sound nutritional habits; the term *mean* suggests an all-powerful mind capable of performing in the most challenging situations; the term *machine* suggests flawless and enduring execution.

53. Ladder Swimming

The swimmer imagines performing freestyle on top of a ladder positioned just beneath the surface. As the hand enters, it proceeds to grab a rung. From here the hand/forearm paddle pulls the body forward until the hand passes underneath the shoulder. From here the hand/forearm paddle pushes the body forward until the hand passes underneath the hip. A high elbow catch and maximum distance per stroke are emphasized throughout. The intention of this performance-improving concept is to promote the idea of pulling and then pushing the body past the arm as opposed to pulling and then pushing the arm past the body.

> Note: *To further enhance this concept, an actual garden hose may be used. In this scenario the hose is stretched and submerged just beneath the surface, from one end of the pool to the other. A coach or volunteer is positioned at both ends of the pool to secure the hose. From here the swimmer performs freestyle over top of the hose, grabbing it as far out in front of the shoulder*

*as possible at the point of entry. From here the hand/
forearm paddle pulls and then pushes the body forward
down the pool. A high elbow catch and maximum distance per stroke is emphasized throughout.*

54. Minutes Versus Weeks

Swimmers can experience improvements in performance via
technical conditioning in a matter of minutes while the same
rate of improvement via physical conditioning may take weeks
to months. Therefore frequent technical adjustments are essential
for ongoing improvement. Examples include finishing fully in
butterfly, driving the arm deeper in backstroke, snapping the feet
together in breaststroke, and kicking continually in freestyle.

> **Note:** *Over the years I have encountered numerous
> swimmers who train upwards of 50,000 yards/meters
> per week or 2.5 million yards/meters per year and
> realize minimal improvements (if any at all) after
> taper. If yardage were solely the answer, these swim-
> mers should experience dramatic improvements year
> to year. Unfortunately this type of training leaves little
> room for ongoing mental and technical conditioning.
> As a result swimmers are ill prepared to swim up to
> their potential when it counts.*

55. A Stroke is Only as Strong as its Weakest Link

Like a chain, a stroke is only as strong as its weakest link. For example
swimmers may possess a tight, symmetrical, continuous freestyle kick
when kicking on a kickboard but not when performing freestyle. The
reason for the change in kick is most likely weak links within the stroke,
including over-entering, over-breathing, over-pulling, over-rotation, or a
combination of the four.

56. Plastic Versus Elastic

When stretched and released, elastic returns to its natural state;

plastic remains unchanged. To achieve the desired goals in swimming, technical changes must become permanent like plastic, requiring constant and correct repetition.

> **Note:** *In a holistic approach, technical expectations remain high throughout the season. Swimmers are expected to perform skills to the best of their ability at all times. Unfortunately many coaches insist on correct technique early in the season but grow lax once the season gets fully underway. The holistic coach remains consistent in technical expectations week to week and month to month.*

57. The Hip-Arm Connection

The hips act as stabilizers in the backstroke and freestyle pull. Prior to commencing a pull with the right arm in either stroke, the hips achieve a forty-five-degree rotation to the right. Once the pull commences, the hips begin rotating to the left in preparation for a pull with the left arm. Rotating back and forth in this manner connects the hips with the pulling arm, creating a greater stabilizing force within each stroke cycle and adding increased stroking power.

58. Grin Versus Smile

In a holistic approach, the concept *grin versus smile* is used to correct a deep dive off the starting block. The holistic coach draws a smile and grin on a whiteboard to familiarize swimmers with both shapes. From here swimmers perform two starts off a block located at the deep end of the pool. On the first a smile-shaped pathway is followed to the surface while on the second a grin-shaped pathway is followed. Once that's complete swimmers are asked to choose the pathway that allowed them to retain the greatest amount of speed to the breakout point. Not surprisingly, the grin-shaped pathway is chosen every time. This concept can also be used to teach the correct turning depth off the walls.

Note: *To further familiarize swimmers with a grin shape versus a smile shape, the holistic coach asks swimmers to grin and then smile before introducing the concept.*

Warning: *All starts must be practiced in deep water only. USA Swimming rules state: "minimum water depth for teaching racing starts in any setting from any height starting block or deck shall be 5 feet or 1.53 meters for a distance of 16 feet 5 inches or 5 meters from the starting wall." In addition starts should be practiced only under a coach's supervision in a lane free of swimmers.*

59. Three Breakout Points

Ideally swimmers should have three distinct breakout points when performing starts and turns. The freestyle breakout point is the shortest, as freestyle is typically faster than body whip for an extended period of time; the breaststroke breakout point is next due to the underwater pullout requirement; the butterfly and backstroke breakout points are the farthest, as body whip can actually be faster than butterfly or backstroke if performed correctly.

Note: *In some swimming circles, body whip is considered the fifth stroke. If one were to rank each of the five strokes in terms of speed, freestyle would rank first, body whip second, butterfly third, backstroke fourth, and breaststroke fifth. In some cases swimmers like Natalie Coughlin actually travel faster performing body whip than freestyle. Most swimmers, on the other hand, would find freestyle faster.*

60. Thread the Needle

In a holistic approach, the *thread the needle* concept is used to teach streamlining. Here swimmers imagine the water as the eye of the needle and their bodies as pieces of thread. In order to pass through the eye, the body must be as thin as thread. To further enhance this concept, swimmers perform the streamline stance drill to familiarize themselves with near-perfect streamlining. A description of the drill can be found in the Practice Glossary in Chapter 6.

61. 180 Versus 180

The arm cycle actions in butterfly, backstroke, and freestyle are cyclical in nature with approximately 180 degrees occurring above the water and approximately 180 degrees occurring below the water. Obviously the above-water portion is non-propulsive while the below-water portion is propulsive to varying degrees. Elite-level swimmers maximize the 180-degree, below-water portion due to an early catch and late finish while most swimmers achieve far less propulsion due to a late catch and early finish.

62. 2 + 3 = 1

In a holistic approach, the concept *2 + 3 = 1* is used to teach breaststroke starts and turns. Here swimmers are challenged to travel the same distance on the second and third phases of the breaststroke pullout when compared to the first. Most swimmers have it reversed, traveling farther on the first phase due to a powerful departure of the block or wall than on the other two combined. The concept provides swimmers with a tangible goal and encourages greater distance traveled underwater.

> **Note:** *The first phase of the breaststroke pullout is known as the streamline; the second, the pull down; the third, the kick up.*

63. Swimming Fitness Versus Turning Fitness

Swimming hard in practice will definitely improve swimming fitness, but turning hard in practice is the only way to improve turning fitness. This is due to the fact that many of the actions involved in turns, including somersaulting actions, knee driving actions, hip swiveling actions, and push off actions are unique to turns. Unfortunately most swimmers miss out on countless opportunities to improve turning fitness by floating into the walls and resting off of the walls in practice.

> **Note:** *In a holistic approach, training sets are often designed to focus on both conditioning needs. For example swimmers perform 12 x 75s with repeats one, four, seven, and ten geared toward developing swimming fitness; repeats two, five, eight, and eleven geared toward developing turning fitness; and repeats three, six, nine, and twelve geared toward developing both forms of fitness.*

64. Fatigue: Public Enemy #1

Fatigue is the biggest enemy of all when it comes to maintaining best-form stroke and turn technique. At the onset of fatigue, strokes shorten, kicking becomes weaker or less frequent, and turns become less powerful. To maintain best-form technique over the course of a race, swimmers must possess fitness that can go the distance. At the elite level, the final fifty of a race looks the same, if not better, than the first.

> **Note:** *In a holistic approach, swimmers are expected to perform one style of butterfly, backstroke, breaststroke, and freestyle throughout the entire practice at various speeds. The notion of having a warm up butterfly, a practice butterfly, and a swim-meet butterfly is totally unacceptable and completely outdated in the demanding world of swimming today. Swimmers must*

train with one style of technique at varying speeds to develop the fitness required to maintain best-form technique at the fastest speed possible throughout the entire race. The only exception to the rule is freestyle, where a 50 style versus a 100 style (and above) is permitted. Obviously the speed of the stroke determines the look of the stroke. In other words butterfly at warm up speed will look different from butterfly at race pace, but the concept in theory remains the same.

65. Test Drive

Imagine if swimmers could take world-class strokes out for test swims, similar to taking a new car out for a test drive. In some ways they would find the strokes easier, as they would consist of the correct components linked flawlessly together, while in other ways they would find the strokes more demanding, requiring much higher degrees of strength, flexibility, and endurance. With that said, swimmers must work diligently at improving swim-specific strength, flexibility, and endurance to develop elite-level technique.

66. Seamless Turns

Right-handed swimmers tend to initiate more backstroke and freestyle turns with the right arm while left-handed swimmers tend to initiate more backstroke and freestyle turns with the left arm (even if the arm chosen is not the best choice). As a result floating turns are commonplace. To rectify this shortcoming, the holistic coach introduces a concept called *seamless turns*, where the forward somersaulting action of a backstroke or freestyle turn must be initiated the moment the turning arm or the last stroking arm enters the water. At this point the chin tucks aggressively into the chest, commencing the somersaulting action. All too often the chin tuck occurs after the arm enters the water, as it pulls back to the side of the body. This delay adds a significant amount of time to the turn and has the potential to place swimmers at risk of disqualification (in the case of backstroke).

To perform seamless turns, the forward somersaulting action must occur the moment the turning arm enters the water whether swimmers are close enough to the wall or not. At first a good number of turns are missed. To rectify this shortcoming, swimmers are instructed to accelerate into the turn (flags to the wall) to bridge any potential gap. Adding more speed to the last five yards/meters delivers the additional momentum needed to perform turns in a seamless manner.

> **Note:** *I have used this concept successfully for many years. At first most swimmers experience difficulty due to the increased physical demands of accelerating into the wall. Those who adopted and adapted dropped massive amounts of time.*

67. Skipping Versus Hopping

The following two-step progression is designed to create a better understanding of butterfly timing/flow:

Step 1:   Swimmers skip down the pool deck, transferring energy from foot to foot.

Step 2:   Step one is repeated only swimmers hop down the pool deck, pausing from foot to foot with no energy transfer.

The holistic coach then draws a comparison to butterfly, explaining how elite-level swimmers skip rather than hop.

> **Note:** *Hopping or pausing between strokes is epidemic amongst swimmers, especially at the age-group level. Infrequent stroke correction and/or extreme workloads are the two main culprits.*

68. Seeing is Believing

Swimmers require a visual understanding of the various start, stroke, and turn techniques to acquire elite-level skills and perform as expected. The holistic coach offers weekly YouTube video sessions providing swimmers with opportunities to view the world's best in action. Suggested videos include Misty Hyman and Michael Phelps for butterfly, Natalie Coughlin and Ryan Lochte for backstroke, Rebecca Soni and Kosuke Kitajima for breaststroke, and Ian Thorpe and Alexander Popov for freestyle. Another worthwhile option involves creating a scrapbook filled with photographs of swimmers performing elite-level starts, strokes, and turns. The scrapbook is kept on the pool deck during practice for easy reference.

> **Note:** *The names listed above are just the tip of the iceberg with dozens of great swimmers to choose from. The holistic coach is free to choose whatever swimmers he or she feels represent the best examples of elite-level technique.*

69. Hand-Led

The hands play a leading role in swimming propulsion. For example both hands face outward and downward, then inward, during the transition from the entry phase to the catch phase in butterfly. From here the hands face backward and inward toward the bellybutton. From here the hands face backward during the transition from the catch phase to the finish phase. From here the hands face outward in preparation for the recovery phase. The same hand-led concept applies to the respective pulling patterns of backstroke, breaststroke, and freestyle.

> **Note:** *The hands play a vital role in swimming, making hand strength critical. Squeezing tennis balls to failure or sculling in a tub of rice can dramatically improve the strength needed to benefit from this concept.*

70. The Lower the Slower

The lower a boat rides in the water the slower it goes, and the same holds true in swimming. To reach peak speeds, a swimmer must maintain an on-the-water body position versus an in-the-water body position. To achieve the desired position, key technical points must be employed.

In butterfly key technical points include pressing the chest down at the point of entry; two powerful kicks per stroke; a high elbow catch coupled with a full, fast finish; a long and low recovery; a minimal breath with the chin remaining in the water; and a constant stroking rhythm.

In backstroke key technical points include a neutral or near-neutral head position; a plank-like upper body joining the head to the lower body; fully extended arms throughout the entry and finish phases of the arm cycle; a powerful, continuous kick; and a constant stroking rhythm.

In breaststroke key technical points include a streamlined body position between strokes; a wider-than-shoulder-width outward sweep; a medium to high elbow inward scull; a super-fast shoot; a forward lunge off the breath; a shoulder width or slightly wider kick coupled with a full, fast finish.

In freestyle key technical points include a neutral or near-neutral head position; a plank-like upper body joining the head to the lower body; fully extended arms throughout the entry and finish phase of the arm cycle; a high elbow catch coupled with a full fast finish; a symmetrical arm recovery; a powerful con-tinuous kick; and a constant stroking rhythm.

71. Power Points

Generating the most power per arm cycle is a key to fast swim-ming. Butterfly, backstroke, and freestyle have two power points, which must be emphasized fully within each arm cycle. The first takes place during the catch phase, the second during the finish phase. Both positions contribute to maximum power output. Unfortunately many swimmers execute the catch phase with a dropped or partially dropped elbow or fail to finish fully reducing the total amount of power generated.

Note: *The inward scull is the only power point within the breaststroke arm cycle.*

72. Three Keys to a Fast Start

There are three keys to a fast front start: 1) the speed of departure off the block, 2) the total distance traveled throughout the entire start, and 3) the depth of entry.

To achieve a fast departure, swimmers must execute the blastoff phase of the start in the blink of an eye. In addition reaction-type drills must be performed frequently in practice.

To achieve the desired distance, the maximum amount of power via the legs, arms, and head must be generated off the block.

To achieve the desired entry depth, the fingers must point to the desired point of entry. Fingers pointed more downward than forward result in a deeper start while fingers pointed more forward than downward result in a shallower start.

Note: *The holistic coach offers various types of reaction-type drills in practice. Two of the most popular include:*

1. At the coach's command swimmers take their marks. From here the coach counts out loud from one to ten or ten to one slowly, quickly, or using a variation of speeds, placing greater emphasis on one particular number. Swimmers are expected to depart the block once that number is called.

2. The drill involves the use of a kickboard and is performed one swimmer at a time. The swimmer takes his or her mark while the holistic coach stands nearby with a kickboard in hand. From here the coach taps the kickboard on the side of the block, then immediately swings the kickboard in the direction of the swimmer's

butt. The tap on the block is intended to represent the starter's signal. A swimmer with a fast reaction time will depart the block before the kickboard reaches its intended target while a swimmer with a slow reaction time will feel the impact of the kickboard. Swimmers quickly learn to depart the block at a faster rate and find the drill a good deal of fun.

73. Catch Points

Catching water effectively is a key to swimming fast. Ideally the right arm catch point should match the left arm catch point and vice versa in butterfly, backstroke, and freestyle. In addition the catch should take place as early in the arm cycle as possible. All too often swimmers catch earlier, with one arm leading to a lop-sided stroke and reduced propulsion.

> **Note:** *Swimmers who catch earlier with one arm typically do so for one of two reasons. Either one arm is stronger or one arm has a better feel for the water.*

74. Swim Slow to Swim Fast

At first glance the phrase *swim slow to swim fast* seems to be a contradiction in terms. How can swimming slow result in swimming fast? But in reality swimmers must have the opportunity to swim slowly in practice from time to time to master the complexities of elite-level technique. This concept holds true in all aspects of life. For example, when learning to drive a car, student drivers practice their driving skills in a church parking lot rather than on the expressway.

> **Note:** *As a point of interest, Alexander Popov, perhaps the greatest male sprinter of all time, was known to perform thousands of meters at slow speeds to groove and perfect his technique.*

75. Three Levels of Strokes

There are three levels of strokes performed in the IM. A gold-level stroke represents the best of the best and contains all of the technical characteristics found at the elite level. The most popular swimming videos depict swimmers performing strokes at this level. A silver-level stroke is one step below. It may not possess all of the technical characteristics or bling of a gold-level stroke but works well enough to keep swimmers competitive through that portion of the IM. A bronze-level stroke is considered average or commonplace and requires a good deal of stroke correction. In my experience the best IM swimmers have four gold-level strokes; really good IM swimmers have three gold-level strokes; and good IM swimmers have two gold-level strokes. Swimmers who possess only one gold-level stroke shine during that portion of the IM but find it extremely difficult to be competitive.

> **Note:** *The ability to perform gold-level strokes is not based upon age. I work with many young swimmers who have achieved the gold level in one or more strokes.*

The seventy-five technical concepts outlined above represent less than half of the total number of concepts used in a holistic approach. Additional concepts are posted on The Swimming Triangle website at www.theswimmingtriangle.com.

STARTS

In a holistic approach, starts are defined as what takes place on the block, off the block, underwater, and during the breakout phase. Starts make up approximately twenty-five percent of total time in all twenty-five-yard/meter races, approximately ten percent of total time in all fifty-yard/meter races; and approximately five percent of total time in 100-yard/meter races. With the exception of breaststroke, the head must break the surface by the fifteen-meter mark. In general the teaching of starts is severely overlooked and a good start is more the exception than the rule. In a holistic approach, race-quality starts are performed frequently throughout the week. Information regarding the format used to integrate starts into practice can be found in Chapter 4.

This section features four forms of front starts and two back starts. The front starts are the weight-forward track start, the slingshot start, the grab start, and the relay start. The back starts are the block start and the gutter start. Each start consists of four phases, including: 1) launch pad, 2) blast off, 3) splash down, and 4) underwater travel/breakout.

In both the weight-forward track start and the slingshot start, the feet split, with one foot placed at the front of the block and the other foot placed at or near the rear of the block. In the grab start, both feet are placed at the front of the block. The track start is the most popular start in the United States. At the 2004 US Olympic trials, 99.8 percent of all swimmers used some version of the track start. On the contrary many international superstars prefer or have reverted back to the grab start. As one can see, one start does not fit all, nor should it.

The weight-forward track start and the slingshot start are considered more stable due to the placement of the feet, thus reducing the risk of a false start. When perfected, the weight-forward track start can result in a faster reaction time off the block with less time spent in the air. The slingshot start, when perfected, can result in increased power production off the block, greater time spent in the air (as compared to the weight-forward track start), and greater entry speed.

The grab start provides a stronger leg drive off the block, as both legs are used at once. It is not uncommon for elite-level swimmers to depart the block at speeds in excess of fifteen miles per hour. When perfected the grab start encourages a higher arch of travel over the water, increasing the amount of time spent in the air. In light of the fact that water is approximately 800 times denser than air, a higher arch may be desirable. A higher arch of travel also increases entry velocity and entry depth, thus improving the speed and distance traveled underwater. Contrary to popular belief, a fast departure off the block is not the single most important factor in determining the best start but rather which start places swimmers in the lead at the breakout point. In a holistic approach, swimmers are given the opportunity to experience all three forms of starts to determine the best fit.

The two most popular forms of backstroke starts include the block start and the gutter start. In the block start, swimmers start from the block while in the gutter start, swimmers start from the gutter or the side of the pool. Some coaches teach only the block start while others allow younger swimmers to start from the gutter before graduating to the block. Starting from the gutter requires less overall strength and in most cases provides greater foot stability, particularly when performing starts from a slippery wall. Both backstroke starts have choices of two starting positions. In one swimmers curl into a crouched or fetal position with the chin tucked toward the chest, providing the opportunity to throw the head back at the point of departure. In the other, the head remains in a neutral position with the back flat (Japanese Start) allowing for a quicker departure from the block.

Relay starts are performed in either a conventional manner or a step up fashion where swimmers step forward into the start from the rear of the block. In either case a well-timed relay start can provide a half-second to a full-second advantage over a signaled start.

Warning: *All starts must be practiced in deep water only. USA Swimming rules state: "minimum water depth for teaching racing starts in any setting from any height starting block or deck shall be 5 feet or 1.53 meters for a distance of 16 feet 5 inches or 5 meters from the starting wall." In addition starts should be practiced only under a coach's supervision in a lane free of other swimmers.*

═══ Food for Thought ═══

Swimming borrowed the track start from the sport of track, and both "take your mark" positions are similar in design. The biggest difference lies in the method used by swimmers to achieve the ideal starting position versus runners. Swimmers stand up first, lowering into position at the starter's command. Runners squat down first, rising into position at the starter's command. I believe swimmers (particularly age groupers) would be better served to follow the method used by runners. In this scenario they would squat down immediately upon mounting the block with hands and feet preset in the track start position, then rise into a weight-forward full-stance position or slingshot position upon the starter's command. Choosing this option provides greater security and stability as swimmers are positioned lower on the block initially and are able to grab the block immediately upon mounting. Another advantage is it automatically guides them into the ideal starting position as the arms and legs extend from a squatted position.

Weight-Forward Track Start

> **Note:** *As a point of interest, Fred Bousquet (FR), former world record holder in the fifty-meter freestyle, uses this form of start.*

1. Launch Pad

To achieve the ideal stance on the block, the hands grasp the front edge of the block on either side of the feet. Grasping the front edge of the block provides greater stability. From here the feet split, with one foot placed at the front of the block and the other foot placed at or near the rear of the block and the body weight centered over the front foot. Typically the strongest leg is placed at the rear of the block for increased push-off power. The toes of the front foot wrap around the front edge of the block for greater stability. The ball of the rear foot is positioned at or near the rear of the block with the heel pointing upward at a forty-five-degree angle. Placing the ball of the foot (rather than the whole foot) on the block increases push-off power at the time of departure, as the ball is the most explosive part of the foot. In a holistic approach, the term *high heel* is used to convey this all-important concept. The degree of knee bend must be sufficient enough for the hands to grab the front edge of the block but no greater, as excessive knee bend places the center of mass farther to the rear of the block, resulting in a slower start. The head is placed in a near-neutral or neutral position with the eyes facing downward or backward. Additionally the ideal stance position much be assumed immediately upon the starter's command with no additional movement permitted. Otherwise swimmers run the risk of disqualification.

> **Note:** *Younger swimmers may choose to grasp the front edge of the block while keeping the entire back foot positioned on the block. Choosing this position helps to avoid slippage, reduces potential movement on the block, and reduces the risk of disqualification.*

2. Blastoff

Upon the starter's signal, the hands quickly release from the front edge of the block to move the center of mass forward. From here the head snaps upward, the arms snap forward and upward toward the ears, and the legs drive off the block in a quick, one-two fashion. Once airborne the hands, arms, head, legs, and feet achieve a streamlined position to minimize the loss of speed at the point of entry. This is particularly critical for the legs, as each leg departs the block at a different time. The flight path on a weight-forward track start is forward and downward.

3. Splashdown

At the point of entry, the pointed feet pass through the same hole as the fingertips. The fingertips open the hole and the toe tips close it. To a great extent, the entry depth is determined by the direction of the fingertip point during flight. The more the fingertips point outward, the greater the back arch upon entry, resulting in a quicker breakout. The ideal entry depth is approximately one meter beneath the surface.

4.   Underwater Travel/Breakout

While the total distance covered underwater is important, the speed of travel underwater is most important. Once the desired combination of underwater travel is perfected, the holistic coach challenges swimmers to break the surface within a certain time-frame depending upon proficiency levels. One-hundred meter start breakout times for elite-level female and elite-level male swimmers are listed at the end of the Start section

> **Note:** *The desired form used during the underwater travel/breakout phase depends upon the stroke performed. The forms are outlined in the Turns section of this chapter.*

Strike the Line

In a holistic approach the following five-step progression is used to encourage the correct course of travel off the block with maximum force:

Step 1:   The swimmer assumes a weight-forward track start "take your mark" position on the pool deck.

Step 2:   From here the holistic coach uses a kickboard to draw a straight imaginary line from the swimmer's lower back (the highest point in the "take your mark" position) to a point two feet in front of the swimmer at the same level. The board remains at this point to serve as a target.

Step 3: From here the holistic coach instructs the swimmer to strike the kickboard forcefully with streamlined arms. The arms follow a semicircular pathway from start to finish. An upward head snap may be added for additional force. Throughout this step the legs and feet remain motionless with only the arms and head snapping forcefully upward.

Step 4: From here steps one and two are repeated on the block only the swimmer strikes the kickboard with one arm and uses the other arm to secure his or her position on the block. In this step the striking action is performed in slow motion to maintain balance on the block.

Step 5: From here the swimmer executes the start on the coach's command.

Note: *I have used this progression for many years with amazing results. Swimmers travel off the block farther and faster and enter the water at the ideal depth, thus eliminating the tendency to dive too deep.*

Pull Buoy Dive Progression

Entering with split legs is a common problem in track starts, as the legs are split upon departure from the block. To rectify the problem, the holistic coach offers the following three-step progression:

Step 1: The swimmer stands at the front of the block with the feet together and a pull buoy placed between the lower legs.

Step 2:   The swimmer dives into the water, attempting to keep the pull buoy in place.

Step 3:   Once perfected the lesson of the drill is applied to the full start.

Slingshot Start

The term *slingshot* is used to define this start due to the fact that the resultant action off the block is similar to the action of a slingshot. The slingshot start can deliver amazing results if performed properly and is ideally suited for swimmers with superior athletic ability. Many elite-level swimmers use this start including South Korean swimmer Park Tae-Hwan, 2008 Olympic gold medalist in the 400 FR. Park also won a gold medal in the same event at the 2011 FINA World Championships in Shanghai. Michael Phelps and Cesar Cielo (BRA), the current world record holder in the fifty-meter freestyle, use a modified version of the slingshot start.

1.   Launch Pad

To achieve the ideal stance on the block, the feet, hands, and head are positioned in the same manner as in the weight-forward track start only the center of mass is shifted to the rear foot, with the weight shift taking place seamlessly at the starter's command.

> **Note:** *Shifting the center of mass to the rear foot places the butt over the center of the block as opposed to the back of the block.*

2.   Blastoff

Upon the starter's signal, the hands pull forcefully against the front edge of the block to move the center of mass forward. This forward-pulling action greatly increases the amount of starting power off the block. As the body passes over the front edge of the block, the head snaps upward, the arms snap backward then forward toward the ears, and the legs drive off the block in a quick, one-two fashion. The head must not snap upward until the body passes over the front edge of the block or the departure off the block will be more upward than outward. Once airborne, the hands, arms, head, legs, and feet achieve a streamlined position to minimize the loss of speed upon entry. This is particularly true for the legs as each leg departs the block at a different time. The flight path on a slingshot start is forward and downward.

3.   Splashdown

At the point of entry, the pointed feet pass through the same hole as the fingertips. The fingertips open the hole and the toe tips close it. To a great extent, the entry depth is determined by the direction of the fingertip point during flight. The more the fingertips point outward, the greater the back arch upon entry and the quicker the breakout. The ideal entry depth is approximately one meter beneath the surface.

4.   Underwater Travel/Breakout

While the total distance covered underwater is important, the speed of travel underwater is most important. Once the desired form of underwater travel is perfected, the holistic coach challenges swimmers to break the surface within a certain timeframe depending upon proficiency levels. One-hundred meter start breakout times for elite-level female and elite-level male swimmers are listed at the end of the Start section.

Note: *The desired form used during the underwater travel/breakout phase depends upon the stroke performed and outlined in the Turns section of this chapter.*

Note: *Many coaches believe the slingshot start is slower than the weight-forward track start due to the fact that the center of mass is shifted backward to the center of* *the block. On the contrary swimmers who have mastered the slingshot start typically travel farther through the air, enter the water with increased velocity, and achieve greater speed underwater. Each start has its advantage but overall I believe the slingshot start is a better start once mastered.*

Grab Start

Note: *As a point of interest, Britta Steffen (GER), current world record holder in the women's fifty and one-hundred-meter freestyle, uses this form of start.*

1.   Launch Pad

To achieve the ideal stance on the block, both feet are placed shoulder width apart at the front of the block with the toes curled over the front edge of the block for greater stability and push-off power. Placing both feet at the front edge of the block delivers more power to the start, as two legs are better than one. The hands grasp the block either between or outside the feet with the arms slightly bent. The head is placed between the arms with the eyes facing downward or backward. Some swimmers prefer to split the hands while others prefer to place one hand on top of the other to increase the likelihood of a streamlined entry. Knee bend is approximately forty degrees. Choosing this degree of knee bend places the center of mass over the front edge of the block. Bending the knees more than forty degrees shifts the center of mass backward. This is an important consideration because the sooner the center of mass passes over the front edge of the block, the sooner the drive off the block begins.

Note: *Upon the starter's command, the ideal stance must be achieved instantaneously.*

Note: *To increase the speed of departure further, the center of mass may be shifted onto the balls of the feet. Although faster, it does place the body in a less stable position. As a result swimmers must remain perfectly still until the starter's signal or risk disqualification.*

2. Blastoff

Upon the starter's signal, the hands push against the front edge of the block to move the center of mass forward. From here the head snaps upward, the arms snap forward toward the ears, and the legs drive off the block together. Once airborne, the hands, arms, head, legs, and feet achieve a streamlined position to minimize the loss of speed upon entry. The flight path on a grab start is forward and upward on the first half and forward and downward on the second half.

3. Splashdown

At the point of entry, the pointed feet pass through the same hole as the fingertips. The fingertips open the hole and the toe tips close it. To a great extent, the entry depth is determined by the direction of the fingertip point during flight. The more the fingertips point outward, the greater the back arch upon entry and the quicker the breakout. The ideal entry depth is approximately one meter beneath the surface.

4. Underwater Travel/Breakout

While the total distance covered underwater is important, the speed of travel underwater is most important. Once the desired form of underwater travel is perfected, the holistic coach challenges swimmers to break the surface within a certain timeframe depending upon proficiency levels. One-hundred meter start breakout times for elite-level female swimmers and elite-level male swimmers are listed at the end of the Start section.

Note: *The desired form used during the underwater*

travel/breakout phase depends upon the stroke per-
formed and outlined in the Turns section of this chapter.

Back Start

1. Launch Pad

The hands grip the bar shoulder width apart while the feet are placed shoulder width apart either side by side or staggered. If staggered, the foot of the strongest leg is typically placed on top. From here the weight of the body is balanced on the balls of the feet positioned high on the wall. USA Swimming rules permit swimmers to place the toes out of the water prior to the start; however the toes cannot wrap over or rise above the edge of the pool. Placing the toes near or slightly above the surface is pre-ferred, as it positions the hips closer to the surface. The head is placed in a neutral position with the eyes facing forward. Upon the starter's command, the arms pull the body into a crouched or fetal position while the hips rise to or above the surface. Raising the hips in this manner increases the likelihood that they will clear the surface during the blastoff phase. The final head position ranges from neutral to a chin-tucked-in position. The arms bend approximately ninety degrees with the elbows pointing downward or outward. The ideal knee bend is determined through trial and error. Some swimmers prefer a ninety-degree bend while others prefer to draw the butt closer to the heels. In a holistic approach, swimmers are free to experiment to determine the best fit.

> **Note:** *Unlike a front start, where swimmers have the advantage of leverage and little strength is required to achieve the ideal starting position, the back start requires a great deal of strength. In many cases younger, size-strength proportionate swimmers perform better backstroke starts than their senior counterparts due to a lack of strength relative to size. Many coaches prefer to teach the backstroke start from the gutter first, as*

strength requirements are far less. In addition mastering the gutter start first has the potential of boosting swimmers' confidence levels, making it easier to master the block start at a later date. The mechanics of the gutter start are similar to the block start.

2. Blastoff

On the starter's signal, the hands push downward on the bar while the hips drive upward. At this point it appears as if swimmers are attempting to sit on the surface. From here the arms and head snap upward and backward as the hips continue to drive upward and the feet push off the wall. The head continues backward until the eyes face the opposite end of the pool. The arms throw over the shoulders into streamline. Throwing the arms over the shoulders is the most direct method of achieving a streamlined position prior to entry. Unfortunately it also generates a greater degree of downward force and may cause a premature entry. To combat this force, sufficient height must be attained during the blastoff phase. In addition throwing the arms directly over the shoulders can make it more difficult to achieve a streamlined position prior to the splashdown phase. As an alternative the arms may be directed around the shoulders, making it easier to position them behind or alongside the head. Unfortunately this method encourages a shallower entry, thus reducing potential distance traveled underwater during the underwater travel/breakout phase.

Note: *Swimmers with great backstroke starts are capable of drawing the entire body out of the water during the blastoff phase. This is by no means an easy feat, as the start begins in the water. To master this position, a relatively high angle of trajectory must be achieved off the block. In addition the back must arch sufficiently to clear the hips, legs, and feet from the water. Swimmers with a tight core will find this action most impossible to achieve. Performing back bridges on*

*a mat (under a coach's supervision) is an excellent way
to prepare for a backstroke start session.*

3. Splashdown

Ideally the entire body should pass through a hole no larger than
the body's circumference. Fingertips enter first and toe tips last.
An upward foot flick is added at the point of entry to prevent the
feet from catching the surface.

4. Underwater Travel/Breakout

While the total distance covered underwater is important, the
speed of travel underwater is most important. Once the desired
form of underwater travel is perfected, the holistic coach challenges swimmers to break the surface within a certain timeframe
depending upon proficiency levels. One-hundred meter start
breakout times for elite-level female swimmers and elite-level
male swimmers are listed at the end of the Start section.

> **Note:** *The desired form used in the underwater travel/
> breakout phases of the backstroke start are similar to
> the techniques outlined in the Turns section of this
> chapter.*

> **Note:** *All too often swimmers enter too steeply and
> struggle to return to the surface in a timely manner.
> To rectify the problem, a simple chin tuck to the chest
> is recommended. Tucking the chin instantly redirects
> swimmers to the surface.*

Simple Yet Effective

Creating the all-important head back/hips up connection is key to
a great backstroke start. One simple yet effective method involves
having swimmers look back as far as possible while pushing
the hips up as far as possible prior to assuming the "take your

mark" position. Ideally the position should be held for at least five seconds. The resultant neck stretch, hip stretch, and back arch promote the necessary feel essential to a great start. The results can be truly amazing!

Hip Lift Start Progression

Clearing the hips from the water is key to a great backstroke start. To develop this essential skill the holistic coach offers the following four-step progression:

Step 1: Swimmers perform a modified backstroke start from the gutter while keeping the head in a neutral position (neither forward nor backward) and the arms at the sides of the body. The goal is to clear the hips from the water.

Step 2: Step one is repeated only with the head snapping backward. Snapping the head in this manner adds more power to the start, thus increasing hip lift. Ideally swimmers should be able to see the opposite end of the pool upside down in midflight.

Step 3: Step two is repeated only with the arms throwing backward. Throwing the arms in this manner adds more power to the start, thus increasing hip lift.

Step 4: Step three is repeated only off the block. Starting off the block adds more power to the start, thus increasing hip lift.

Relay Start

On a relay start, the second-, third-, and fourth-positioned swimmers begin the start before the incoming swimmer touches the wall, although part of the outgoing swimmer's foot must remain in contact with the block until the incoming swimmer's hand touches the wall. Being in motion prior to the takeoff may result in a savings of up to one second. None of the front starts listed above should be used as a relay start except by the lead swimmer. For the sake of brevity, the conventional reverse-swing relay start or windup start is outlined below, although other types of relay starts exist.

> **Note:** *As a point of interest, the reverse-swing relay start is still preferred by most elite-level swimmers.*

1.   Launch Pad

The feet are positioned at the front of the block with the toes wrapped around the edge for greater stability and push-off power. The knees are slightly bent with the arms fully extended forward of the shoulders. From here swimmers position as far forward as possible to move the center of mass over the front edge of the block.

2.   Blastoff

Proper execution and timing of the reverse swing is critical to gain maximum power off the block. Throughout the entire swing, swimmers remain in a forward-leaning position. The swing begins as the incoming swimmer initiates the final recovery into the wall and ends when the hand touches the wall. As the arms enter the final third of the swing, the legs drive off the block. On average it takes half a second for the incoming swimmer to recover the arm over the water—sufficient time for the outgoing swimmer to perform a quick and legal departure. In the case of the breaststroke to butterfly exchange, the outgoing swimmer begins the reverse swing as the incoming swimmer initiates the final breathing cycle into the wall. To avoid disqualification the incoming swimmer must establish a predictable stroking pattern into the wall, avoiding any last-minute stroke adjustments as a change in the stroking pattern may cause the outgoing swimmer to misjudge the departure. Relay starts and relay takeoffs must be practiced often in order for swimmers to develop the skills and confidence necessary to excel.

Note: *In a holistic approach, swimmers are introduced to the step up relay start once the reverse-swing relay start is perfected.*

3.   Splashdown
The techniques used in the splashdown phase of the reverse-swing relay start are similar to the techniques found in the Front Start section of this chapter.

4.   Underwater Travel/Breakout
The techniques used in the underwater travel/breakout phases of the reverse-swing relay start are similar to the techniques used in the Turns section of the chapter.

Note: *In a reverse-swing relay start the arms travel (circle) 360 degrees from beginning to end. Ideally the departure from the block should begin as the arms enter the final third of the swing.*

Start Breakout Times for 100-Meter Events

Obviously start breakout times vary amongst elite-level female swimmers and elite-level male swimmers. In my research I have found that elite-level female swimmers spent (on average) 4.5 seconds underwater in the 100 butterfly, 5.5 seconds underwater in the 100 backstroke, 4.0 seconds underwater in the 100 breast-stroke, and 3.0 seconds underwater in the 100 freestyle. Elite-level male swimmers spent (on average) 5.0 seconds underwater in the 100 butterfly, 6.0 seconds underwater in the 100 backstroke,

5.0 seconds underwater in the 100 breaststroke, and 4.0 seconds underwater in the 100 freestyle.

STROKES

There are four strokes in competitive swimming: 1) butterfly, 2) backstroke, 3) breaststroke, and 4) freestyle. Some coaches include body whip or underwater dolphin kick as the fifth stroke.

Unlike the other strokes, butterfly was introduced in the twentieth century. It was first swum with butterfly arms and breaststroke kick, then switched to butterfly kick in the 1950s. The modern-day backstroke was introduced at the 1912 Olympics in Stockholm, although people had swum on their backs for thousands of years prior to that. The oldest stroke of all is breaststroke, dating back thousands and thousands of years. Since becoming a distinct stroke in the 1950s, it has undergone more changes than any other stroke. Ancient Egyptian wall murals depict people swimming over-arm freestyle some 3,200 years ago; however the Australians are credited with creating the original prototype of the modern-day freestyle called the Australian Crawl.

Butterfly

Of the four strokes, butterfly is the most fishlike and physically challenging. All too often swimmers are introduced to butterfly in an inappropriate manner, forced to swim too many lengths incorrectly with too little rest. As a result they incur numerous bad technical habits and a possible negative view of the stroke, and risk potential injury. To avoid these pitfalls, the holistic coach offers physically demanding sets that provide enough rest so best-form technique may be maintained throughout. Drills are often combined with full-stroke butterfly to encourage best-form technique while improving physical fitness. As swimmers progress, the amount of full-stroke butterfly is increased.

Strength also plays a major role in swimmers' ability to perform butterfly correctly. Size-strength proportionate swimmers find it much easier to perform butterfly compared to swimmers whose size is greater than their strength. It is not uncommon to find size-strength proportionate age-group swimmers able to perform elite-level butterfly technique. In a holistic approach, swimmers participate in an extensive dry land training program designed to narrow the gap between strength and body size.

Common Stroke Errors in Butterfly

To excel in butterfly, swimmers must be free and clear of the most common stroke errors, including:

- No chest press
- Minimal chest press
- Excessive chest press
- Swimming more vertical than horizontal
- An asymmetrical kick
- No kick
- One kick per stroke
- Three kicks per stroke
- An incomplete kick
- Mini-breaststroke kicks versus butterfly kicks
- Inadequate knee bend on either kick
- Flutter kick
- An asymmetrical arm cycle
- Pulling with fingers apart
- An oversized outsweep
- Diving down at the point of entry
- Entering inside shoulder width
- Entering short with elbows bent
- No catch
- Late catch
- Pulling with straight arms

- Pulling outside the body width from start to finish
- Lack of acceleration through the pull
- Finishing short
- An asymmetrical recovery
- Bent-arm recovery
- Palm-down recovery
- Dragging the arms through the recovery
- Holding the breath
- Breathing too late
- Driving the head down as the arms complete the finish
- Lifting the head to breathe
- Breathing with the chin off the surface
- Failure to exhale underwater
- Entering the hands before the head
- Pausing the arms at the point of entry
- Pausing the arms at the finish
- Kicking twice at the point of entry
- A disjointed stroke

As you can see, there are numerous stroke errors associated with the butterfly, each the result of improper teaching or training. Allowing swimmers to perform improper technique is extremely counterproductive and demoralizing and can place them at greater risk of injury. In a holistic approach, swimmers are stopped and corrected at the first sign of improper technique, before bad habits have a chance to form.

> **Note:** *All too often coaches allow swimmers to perform butterfly incorrectly, believing swimmers will eventually or magically find their strokes. I happen to believe this theory is absolute nonsense! Swimmers must be led to the ideal stroke under the watchful eye of a qualified and concerned coach.*

The Butterfly Puzzle

Butterfly consists of five distinct puzzle pieces: 1) body position, 2) arm cycle, 3) kick cycle, 4) breathing cycle, and 5) timing/flow. Swimmers who solve the puzzle enjoy butterfly to a much higher degree and achieve far greater success.

Puzzle Piece 1: Body Position

While there are a series of body positions within one stroke cycle, the single most important one occurs at the point of entry. It is here that swimmers have the best opportunity to achieve a horizontal body position producing the least amount of drag per stroke cycle. To envision this position, picture a swimmer lying face down on the water with the head in a neutral position just beneath the surface, the eyes facing downward, the arms fully extended and forward of the shoulders, the palms pitched slightly outward with the fingertips pointing directly forward, the chest pressed downward with the butt peeking through the surface, the legs together, and the feet pointed. Achieving a horizontal body position at the end of each stroke cycle fulfills many of the foundational requirements essential to best-form butterfly technique. Ideally swimmers should move in and out of this position seamlessly. Unfortunately many choose to rush through the stroke and struggle as a result.

> **Note:** *Pressing the chest downward as the arms enter the water causes the hips to rise. This, in turn, forces the feet deeper, resulting in a greater range of motion and a more propulsive kick.*

Puzzle Piece 2: Kick Cycle

Butterfly is a 2:1 stroke, meaning two kicks per one arm cycle. Performed correctly the kick can contribute up to thirty percent or greater of total propulsion within the stroke. The first kick takes place as the arms enter the water, while the second kick takes place as the arms exit the water. Each kick consists of a downbeat and upbeat. The downbeat begins with a slight flexion of the hips followed by a downward extension of the knees and ankles in a whip-like fashion. The upbeat consists of a rebounding action back to the starting position. In addition to providing significant propulsion, both kicks play essential roles in body positioning and timing. The second kick adds an additional boost to the arms as they exit the water to initiate the recovery phase.

> **Note:** *All too often swimmers rush from stroke to stroke, resulting in shorter downbeat and upbeat phases of the kick and reduced propulsion. In the case of Michael Phelps, it appears his knees bend a quarter of the way on the first kick and greater than that on the second kick.*

Ankle flexibility also plays a major role in the propulsive potential of the kick, as floppy feet generate the greatest amount of propulsion. Ideally the feet should extend seventy degrees or more from vertical. In a holistic approach, improving and maintaining ideal ankle flexibility is a top priority.

Puzzle Piece 3: Arm Cycle

The butterfly arm cycle consists of four phases: 1) entry, 2) catch, 3) finish, and 4) recovery.

To perform the correct entry, the fully extended arms enter the water shoulder width apart or slightly wider. A shoulder-width entry maximizes reach and reduces drag while a wider than shoulder-width entry may result in a quicker catch. The hands enter the water fingers together with the thumb sides facing slightly downward and the palms facing slightly outward.

> **Note:** *A wider than shoulder-width entry allows*

swimmers to initiate the catch sooner. Swimmers who struggle with butterfly may find this method easier to perform.

Immediately upon entering, the hands and forearms transition into the catch phase to engage the water and establish a hold. In a holistic approach, the term *hand/forearm paddles* is used to convey the idea that the hands and forearms work in unison to provide maximum propulsion. For ease of reading, the term *paddles* is used from this point onward. Optimal elbow bend at the point of catch is near ninety degrees with the elbows positioned over the hands. In a holistic approach, the term *L-arms* is used to convey this all-important concept as the arms look like inverted Ls at this point in the arm cycle. At the point of catch, maximum force is applied. The catch phase is executed quickly and completed by or before the shoulders. Catching or maintaining a hold on the water effectively is no easy feat; it requires a great deal of skill and strength. It is not uncommon for swimmers to move through the catch phase with the paddles more parallel to the surface than perpendicular, resulting in reduced propulsion. By the end of the catch phase the paddles face directly backward.

Upon completion of the catch phase, the paddles transition into the finish phase, the second most propulsive phase of the arm cycle due to the forceful acceleration of the paddles that occurs at this point. It should be noted the paddles shrink as they travel through to the finish. At the beginning the hands and forearms face directly backward while at the end only the hands face backward. In a holistic approach, the term *shrinking paddles* is used to convey this all-important concept. As the arms near completion of the finish phase the hands come in close proximity of each other with the thumbs almost touching beneath the belly button. From here the hands push explosively past the hips with the arms achieving a fully extended position.

The recovery phase begins as the fully extended arms exit the water pinkies first, with the palms facing upward. As the arms recover forward, the palms naturally rotate to a palm-back position, and as the arms prepare to enter the water the palms naturally rotate to a near palm-down position. The arms travel forward long and low to the surface. Achieving this position ensures maximal extension, assists in maintaining a horizontal body position, and reduces the amount of physical effort required.

Puzzle Piece 4: Breathing Cycle

Ideally the breathing cycle should be performed in a manner that allows swimmers to maintain a near-horizontal body position without the loss of flow. Within each breathing cycle the body moves from a non-breathing body position to a breathing body position. At the height of the breath, the chin and shoulders rest on the surface with the eyes facing forward or slightly downward. The transition from the non-breathing body position to the breathing body position is the result of the catch phase. As the paddles catch or engage the water, the shoulders and head naturally rise, providing space for the breath. In a holistic approach, the term *elevator arms* is used to convey this all-important concept. The height of the breath is determined by the quality of the catch. Swimmers who possess a strong catch easily create the clearance necessary to breathe without the need to add additional head lift, while swimmers who possess a weak catch are compelled to lift the head, resulting in dropped elbows, excessive hip drop, and increased drag. Adding a slight forward push of the chin during the up-breath phase of the breathing cycle is also promoted. In a holistic approach, the term *PEZ head* is used to convey this all-important concept, as the movement of the head is similar to a PEZ candy dispenser. Additional information regarding PEZ head breathing can be found in Chapter 4 under Butterfly Drills.

Note: *Pushing the chin slightly forward as the shoulders and head rise is not universally taught although many* *elite-level swimmers breathe in this manner. In the case of Michael Phelps, above- and below-water video footage reveal his face facing downward during the chest press and completely forward during the breath. The only way to achieve this position is through a slight forward push of the chin.*

Breathing is continued through the finish and the first half of the recovery phase. As the arms recover past the shoulders, the process of returning the head to the water begins. The head must be fully returned prior to the hands' entering the water. At this point swimmers appear headless. In a holistic approach, the term *head first, hands second* is used to convey this all-important concept.

The most common breathing pattern in butterfly is one nonbreathing stroke followed by a breathing stroke. The advantage of this pattern is that the body remains in a horizontal position for a longer period of time between breaths, thus reducing drag. In addition it encourages a fuller finish and enhanced propulsion. The disadvantage of this pattern is that swimmers may experience premature oxygen debt. In recent years breathing every stroke has become increasingly popular due to the fact that Michael Phelps breathes in this manner.

Puzzle Piece 5: Timing/Flow

To achieve the ideal timing/flow within the stroke of butterfly, the arm, kick, and breathing cycles must work together in harmony. In addition swimmers must move seamlessly from stroke to stroke, resisting the urge to pause at any given point within the stroke cycle. Pausing at the point of entry or exit is particularly common among younger or less experienced swimmers. While a slowing down of the arms at the point of entry is natural, the arms must never fully stop. Stopping results in a cessation of forward momentum. In addition it can cause the hands to float together prior to the initiation of the catch phase, which can have a detrimental effect upon propulsion.

Cycle rates, which measure the number of strokes performed in one minute, may be used to promote ideal butterfly timing/flow. In the 100 butterfly, elite-level female swimmers achieve cycle rates of fifty-two and higher, as do their male counterparts. In a holistic approach, swimmers are challenged to hit these rates over ever-increasing distances with best-form technique. To measure cycle rates accurately, a stopwatch with a cycle rate function is recommended.

Stroke length also impacts timing/flow as swimmers who enter and exit the water with the arms fully extended create the time and space necessary to execute each puzzle piece as intended. A fully finished stroke looks and performs much differently from an unfinished one.

Note: *The Finis Tempo Trainer is an excellent tool and can be used to encourage ideal timing/flow in butterfly. For further information, go to www.finisinc.com.*

Backstroke

Backstroke is unique in that it is the only stroke performed on the back. Swimming on the back places greater demands on the lower back, abdominals, hamstrings, and quadriceps. In addition the high, arching recovery style of the arms exerts greater downward force upon the body compared to the recovery styles used in butterfly and freestyle. Therefore swimmers must rely upon the legs more heavily to maintain the ideal backstroke body position.

Common Stroke Errors in Backstroke

To excel in backstroke, swimmers must be free and clear of the most common backstroke errors, including:

- Side-to-side head movement
- Bobbing the head
- Excessive upward head tilt
- Sinking hips
- Squirming
- Bouncing
- Under-rotation
- Over-rotation
- Uneven rotation
- Disjointed rotation (body does not rotate as a whole)
- Asymmetrical kicking pattern
- Sputter kick (non-continuous)
- Breaststroke feet (kicking with one or both feet turned out)
- Split kick (legs that spread beyond body width)
- Excessive knee bend
- Knees that break the surface
- Dominant entry arm
- Bent-arm entry
- Shallow entry (not driving arm down deep enough)
- Pausing at the point of entry
- Over-entry (crossover)
- Under-entry
- Asymmetrical entry
- Entering with the back of the hand (slapping the water)
- Pulling with fingers apart
- Asymmetrical pull
- Dominant pulling arm
- No catch
- Late catch
- Catching air through the pull
- Straight-arm pull
- Pushing more down than back
- Lack of acceleration through the finish

- Incomplete finish
- Pausing at the point of finish
- Asymmetrical recovery
- Bent-arm recovery
- Recovering around the shoulder instead of over the shoulder
- Holding the breath
- Inconsistent breathing pattern
- Irregular arm-cycle timing
- Starting one arm before the other
- A disjointed stroke

As you can see, there are numerous stroke errors associated with the backstroke, each the result of improper teaching or training. Allowing swimmers to perform improper technique is extremely counterproductive and demoralizing, and can place them at greater risk of injury. In a holistic approach, swimmers are stopped and corrected at the first sign of improper technique, before bad habits have a chance to form.

> **Note:** *All too often coaches allow swimmers to perform backstroke incorrectly, believing swimmers will eventually or magically find their strokes. I happen to believe this theory is absolute nonsense! Swimmers must be led to the ideal stroke under the watchful eye of a qualified and concerned coach.*

The Backstroke Puzzle

Backstroke consists of five distinct puzzle pieces: 1) body position, 2) arm cycle, 3) kick cycle, 4) breathing cycle, and 5) timing/flow. Swimmers who solve the puzzle enjoy backstroke to a much higher degree and experience far greater success.

Puzzle Piece 1: Body Position

Similar to the other three strokes, body position forms the foundation of backstroke. The backstroke body position actually consists of two body positions rolled into one: head to toe and side to side. Swimmers who achieve the ideal head-to-toe body position ride higher in the water, enjoy a greater degree of stability, and swim straighter while swimmers who achieve the ideal side-to-side body position experience less drag, increased stroke length, and generate greater amounts of propulsion. Achieving the ideal head-to-toe body position requires a steady, neutral, or near-neutral head position, a plank-like upper body, and a tight, symmetrical, continuous kick. The head acts like a balancing tool, drawing the hips, legs, and feet toward the surface; the plank-like upper body acts like a bridge connecting the head with the lower body; and the kick acts like an elevator, raising the body upward toward the surface.

Achieving the ideal side-to-side body position requires forty-five-degree rotation to both sides in unison with the recovery arms. As the right arm recovers past the right shoulder, the entire body (minus the head) rotates to the right via the hips, and as the left arm recovers past the left shoulder, the entire body (minus the head) rotates to the left via the hips. In most cases rotation should not exceed forty-five degrees. In a holistic approach, rotation is restricted to less than forty-five degrees until the kinetic chain is firmly established. Adding the full amount of rotation prematurely can have an adverse effect on both body positions and kick.

Note: *Further information regarding the kinetic chain can be found under Technical Concepts in this chapter.*

To encourage proper rotation, the holistic coach introduces a concept called *connect the dots*, where swimmers imagine having brightly colored dots painted on their shoulders, hips, and ankles. As the body rotates from side to side, all three dots must remain in line and connected. Keeping the dots in line maintains a connection from the tip of the shoulder to the ankle. As mentioned previously, maintaining the recommended amount of rotation reduces drag, lengthens the stroke, and strengthens the pull. In fact rotation can add four to six inches to stroke length, translating to one or two fewer strokes per fifty. While some coaches teach rotation through the shoulders, rotation through the hips works best and guarantees full body rotation. This is due to the fact that the hips are located in the center of the body, having full access to the strength of the core. In addition an approach that emphasizes hip rotation versus shoulder rotation supports the all-important hip-hand connection.

> **Note:** *Further information regarding the hip-hand connection can be found under Technical Concepts in this chapter.*

Sink or Swim

Maintaining a horizontal body position in backstroke is more challenging than in freestyle as it places a greater demand on the kick. To prove the point, the holistic coach offers the following two-step progression:

> **Step 1:** Swimmers push off the wall on top of the water in a face-up position with the arms at the sides of the body while attempting to maintain a horizontal position for as long as possible without the use of the arms or legs.
>
> **Step 2:** Step one is repeated only in a facedown position.

In most cases swimmers find it easier to maintain a horizontal position on the stomach as opposed to the back. Results may vary depending upon a percentage of body fat; a higher percentage makes it easier for swimmers to float in either position.

Puzzle Piece 2: Kick Cycle

Backstroke is a 6:1 stroke, meaning six kicks per one arm cycle or two strokes. Swimmers capable of maintaining six kicks per cycle have the greatest potential to excel. Aside from helping to establish and maintain the ideal body position, a six-beat kick provides maximum propulsion, promotes balance and stability, enhances flow, assists in rotation, encourages greater stroke length, and spreads out the work between the arms and the legs. No other kicking pattern delivers as many benefits to the stroke. While the demands of a six-beat kick are greater, so are the rewards.

> **Note:** *In a holistic approach, swimmers are introduced to kicking in this manner through a concept called minimal kick, as outlined in the Technical Concepts section of this chapter.*

Each backstroke kick consists of an upbeat and downbeat action with the upbeat being the most propulsive. The upbeat begins with a slight flexion of the hip followed by an upward extension of the knee and ankle in a whip-like fashion. At the height of the upbeat, the toes come to the surface but not through the surface. The downbeat consists of a straight-leg rebounding action back to the starting position.

The ideal backstroke kick is tight, symmetrical, and continuous. To convey this idea, the holistic coach introduces a concept called *kick in the box*, where swimmers imagine kicking inside an imaginary box with the sides of the box representing the sides of the body, the top of the box representing the chest, and the bottom of the box representing the back. Kicking in this manner is a prerequisite to high-performance backstroke.

Ankle flexibility also plays a major role in the propulsive potential of the kick as floppy feet generate the greatest amount of propulsion. Ideally the feet should extend seventy degrees or more from vertical. In a holistic approach, improving and maintaining ankle flexibility is a top priority.

> **Note:** *One of the greatest detractors of backstroke kick is over-rotation. Swimmers who do this break the kinetic chain connecting the body from hand to foot. Once broken, a number of technical errors typically occur, including excessive knee bend, severe splitting of the legs, and disjointed rotation. In a holistic approach, swimmers earn the right to rotate based on the strength of the kinetic chain.*

Puzzle Piece 3: Arm Cycle

The backstroke arm cycle consists of four phases: 1) entry, 2) catch, 3) finish, and 4) recovery.

To perform the correct entry, the fully extended arm enters the water directly behind the shoulder, pinkie first and below body depth.

Once the entry phase is complete the hand and forearm move quickly into the catch phase to establish a hold on the water. In a holistic approach, the term *hand/forearm paddle* is used to convey the idea that the hand and forearm work in unison to provide maximum propulsion. For ease of read, the term *paddle* is used from this point onward. Optimal elbow bend at the point of catch is near ninety degrees from forearm to upper arm. In a holistic approach, the term *L-arm* is used to convey this all-important concept, as the arm looks like an L on its side at this point in the arm cycle. At the point of catch, maximum force is applied. The catch phase is executed quickly and completed before the shoulder. By the end of the catch, the paddle faces directly backward. Catching or maintaining a hold on the water is no easy feat; it requires a great deal of skill and strength.

Upon completion of the catch phase, the paddle transitions into the finish—the second-most propulsive phase of the arm cycle due to the forceful acceleration that occurs at this point. The paddle shrinks as it travels through to the finish. At the beginning both the hand and forearm face directly backward, while at the end only the hand faces backward. In a holistic approach, the term *shrinking paddle* is used to convey this all-important concept.

Once the finish phase is complete, the fully extended arm exits the water thumb first in unison with the body rotation to begin the recovery phase. From here the arm travels upward and forward, directly over the top of the shoulder. As the arm passes over the shoulder it switches from a thumb-led recovery to a pinkie-led recovery in preparation for a pinkie-first entry.

Note: *Not all swimmers follow the same pulling pattern in backstroke. Some execute a shallow pull, described as a shallow S pattern with lesser amounts of downward and upward movement, while others execute a deeper pull, described as a deep S pattern with greater amounts of downward and upward movement. In general the shallower the pull, the faster the stroke rate, and the deeper the pull, the slower the stroke rate.*

Puzzle Piece 4: Breathing Cycle

Typically, little is mentioned about breathing in backstroke due to the fact that the face remains out of the water at all times. Timing the inhalation and exhalation of the breath with each stroke is the most popular method, with the inhalation taken as the arm enters and the exhalation taken as the arm exits. While simple and effective, swimmers must be permitted to experiment with various breathing patterns to determine the best fit. In addition the air exchange must remain constant at all times. From time to time, the holistic coach will highlight the importance of a regular air exchange, particularly at the age group level, as swimmers often forget to maintain a predictable pattern.

Puzzle Piece 5: Timing/Flow

To achieve the ideal timing/flow within the stroke, the arm cycle, kick cycle, and body rotation must work together in harmony. Ideally swimmers should move seamlessly from stroke to stroke, resisting the urge to pause at any given point.

There are two different timing methods used in backstroke: windmill and overlap. In windmill timing one arm begins the recovery phase of the arm cycle as the other arm begins the pull/push phase. In overlap timing one arm begins the recovery phase of the arm cycle slightly before the other arm begins the pull/push phase. This method of timing is not the common practice but can significantly increase cycle rates.

> **Note:** *In my experience swimmers either get overlap timing immediately or struggle. For those who struggle, windmill timing is the way to go.*

Cycle rates, which measure the number of strokes performed in one minute, may also be used to promote ideal backstroke timing/flow. In the 100 backstroke, elite-level female swimmers achieve cycle rates of fifty and higher, while their male counterparts cycle at rates of forty-eight and higher. In a holistic approach, swimmers are challenged to hit these rates over ever-increasing distances with best-form technique. To measure cycle rates accurately, a stopwatch with a cycle rate function is recommended.

Stroke length also impacts timing/flow, as swimmers who enter and exit the water with arms fully extended create the time and space necessary to execute each puzzle piece as intended. A fully finished stroke looks and performs much differently from an unfinished one.

> **Note:** *The Finis Tempo Trainer is an excellent tool and can be used to encourage ideal timing/flow in backstroke. For further information, go to www.finisinc.com.*

Breaststroke

Breaststroke is the second most physical stroke if swum in an aggressive manner versus a restful one. Reasons include the length of time required to swim a breaststroke race versus other strokes performed over the same distance, the recovery style of the arms used in breaststroke versus the recovery style used in other strokes, and the recovery style of the legs used in breaststroke versus the recovery style used in other strokes.

In the case of time required, the world record for the men's 200 breaststroke in 2009 was 2:07.31 compared to 1:51.1 in the 200 butterfly, 1:51.92 in the 200 backstroke, and 1:42.0 in the 200 freestyle. As you can clearly see, breaststrokers must endure for longer.

In the case of the breaststroke arm recovery, the arms travel forward through or partially through the water, resulting in greater resistance compared to the arm-recovery styles used in butterfly, backstroke, and freestyle. In the case of the breaststroke leg recovery, the knees execute a greater bend throughout the recovery phase, resulting in greater resistance compared to the leg recovery styles used in butterfly, backstroke, and freestyle.

> **Note:** *The legs also extend beyond body width throughout the propulsive phase of the kick cycle, adding even greater resistance.*

Breaststroke is performed in two unique styles: conventional and undulating. In conventional style the body remains relatively flat throughout, while in undulating style the body moves in a sinuous, wavelike fashion. Both styles have been used to capture Olympic gold. Other unique breaststroke features include an underwater versus a partial overwater recovery style; a nonmoving head versus a moving head; the amount of glide between strokes; a pulling arm action versus a sculling arm action; a narrow versus wide kick; and hips that remain in the water throughout the kick cycle versus hips that rise above the surface at the completion of the kick cycle. In a holistic approach, conventional style is taught first and recommended for most. The undulating style is taught to those swimmers who exhibit a natural disposition.

Common Stroke Errors in Breaststroke

To excel in breaststroke, swimmers must be free and clear of the most common stroke errors, including:

- Incomplete streamline
- A less-than-horizontal body position at the end of each stroke cycle
- Knee-led recovery
- Wider than shoulder-width leg recovery
- Setting the knees prior to the kickback, then spreading them wider during the kickback
- Partial recovery of the heels
- No outward rotation of the ankles
- Limited outward rotation of the ankles
- Lack of acceleration through the kick
- An incomplete finish of the kick
- Toes that point downward at the completion of the finish
- Scissor kick
- Kicking too far beyond shoulder width
- Pulling with fingers apart
- Extra-wide pull
- Narrow pull
- Pulling past the shoulders
- An oversized outward sweep
- Dropped elbows
- Catching earlier with one arm
- Tilted shoulders
- Lack of acceleration through the pull
- Pausing the hands beneath the chin before shooting forward

- Jumping the hands out of the water during the shoot
- Shooting downward rather than forward
- Breathing too early
- Breathing too late
- Lifting the head to breathe
- A tilted head
- Excessive head movement
- Pausing between the pull and kick
- Delayed heel recovery
- Failure to streamline between strokes (unless desired)
- Too much glide between strokes
- Starting the pull before finishing the kick (unless desired)
- Beginning and ending each stroke cycle under the chin

As you can see, there are numerous stroke errors associated with breaststroke, each the result of improper teaching or training. Allowing swimmers to perform improper technique is extremely counterproductive and demoralizing, and can place them at greater risk of injury. In a holistic approach, swimmers are stopped and corrected at the first sign of improper technique, before bad habits have a chance to form.

> **Note:** *All too often coaches allow swimmers to perform breaststroke incorrectly, believing swimmers will eventually or magically find their strokes. I happen to believe this theory is absolute nonsense! Swimmers must be led to the ideal stroke under the watchful eye of a qualified and concerned coach.*

The Breaststroke Puzzle

Breaststroke consists of five distinct puzzle pieces: 1) body position, 2) arm cycle, 3) kick cycle, 4) breathing cycle, and 5) timing/flow. Swimmers who solve the puzzle enjoy breaststroke to a much higher degree and achieve far greater success.

Puzzle Piece 1: Body Position

Breaststroke consists of a non-breathing body position and a breathing body position with the non-breathing body position forming the foundation of the stroke. To achieve a non-breathing body position, a concept called *seven squeezes* is used, where swimmers squeeze seven different parts of the body together in sequence at the end of each stroke cycle. The seven parts are thumbs, arms, head, shoulders, butt, feet, and legs. At the completion of the final squeeze, the body achieves a horizontal position. From here the next stroke cycle begins unless a glide between strokes is desired. As the arms transition from the sweep phase to the scull phase of the breaststroke arm cycle, the body naturally rises, transitioning into the breathing body position. In a holistic approach, the term *elevator arms* is used to convey this all-important concept as the arms help to elevate the body for the breath. Throughout the breathing cycle the chin remains tilted toward the chest, and at the height of the breath the chin hovers over the hands with the eyes facing forward or downward to one degree or another. From here the arms transition into the shoot phase of the arm cycle. As the hands shoot directly forward at or just below the surface, the body returns to the non-breathing body position.

> **Note:** *At the elite level, some breaststrokers keep the head still throughout the breathing cycle while others add a slight upward head movement during the up-breath phase and a slight downward head movement during the down-breath phase. In a holistic approach, the technique of keeping the chin tilted toward the chest is taught first with individual adjustments made where needed.*

Puzzle Piece 2: Kick Cycle

Breaststroke is a 1:1 stroke, meaning one kick cycle per one arm cycle. Regardless of the event distance, the same number of kicks and pulls are performed. As a result the kick plays a larger role in breaststroke than any other stroke. With such a heavy reliance on the kick, the legs must be in superior condition.

> **Note:** *One of my favorite test sets involves swimmers performing an all-out 100 breaststroke pull with a pull buoy. Dolphin kicks and/or underwater pullouts (at the turns) are not permitted. Upon completion an all-out 100 breaststroke kick with a kickboard is performed. From here the 100 pull time is compared to the 100 kick time. Natural breaststrokers typically have much faster kick times than pull times. For most, the kick time and pull time should match or be near equal.*

The breaststroke kick consists of a recovery phase and a propulsive phase. To eliminate any deceleration between strokes, the recovery phase must begin at the conclusion of the propulsive phase unless a glide between strokes is desired. The recovery is initiated by drawing the heels toward the butt while keeping the knees within hip width. In a holistic approach, the term *narrow knee recovery* is used to convey this all-important concept. It is important to note the recovery is heel-led versus knee-led. Leading with the heels decreases drag while leading with the knees increases drag. As the heels rise and the knees near a fully flexed position, the knees spread from hip width to shoulder width and the feet rotate fully outward. At this point the feet and legs resemble the letter W, with the feet positioned outside of the knees. To maximize propulsion and minimize drag, the feet rotate beyond shoulder width while the knees remain at or near shoulder width. From here the feet drive back and down in a quick out, around, and together action. Initially the inside edges of the feet push back against the water, followed by the soles of the feet. The propulsive drive of the legs continues until the feet snap together at the finish.

Note: *Some elite-level swimmers spread the knees beyond shoulder width before initiating the propulsive phase of the kick. In a holistic approach, starting at shoulder width is taught first with individual adjustments made where needed. Swimmers should be cautioned about spreading the knees too wide. While a wider kick may feel more propulsive it also produces more drag and may have a detrimental effect on the overall timing of the stroke.*

Flexibility is All-Important

The degree of propulsion generated in breaststroke kick is hugely dependent upon flexibility. Swimmers must have the ability to rotate the lower legs away from the center of the body as the knees bend (knee external rotation); rotate the ankles outward toward the baby toes (ankle inversion); and pull the legs apart to the desired width (outer thigh abduction). Swimmers who have the ability to manipulate the legs and feet in this manner succeed in breaststroke while swimmers who are unable to do so struggle. In a holistic approach, addressing the flexibility demands of the breaststroke kick is a primary focus of Dry Land training.

Conventional Kick Versus Snap Butt Kick

There are two types of breaststroke kick. In one the hips remain underwater throughout the entire kick cycle while in the other the hips draw upward through the surface as the feet snap together at the finish. Drawing the hips upward is a better option as it increases muscle involvement and lengthens the duration of the propulsive phase of the kick cycle. In a holistic approach, the term *snap butt* is used to convey this all-important concept. Some swimmers will find this technique easier to perform than others. Those who struggle should stick with the conventional style of kicking. To demonstrate the potential benefit of a snap butt kick, the holistic coach offers a set of alternating 25s. On the odd 25s swimmers perform conventional kicks, while on the even 25s snap butt kicks are performed. Typically fewer kicks are performed using the snap butt version.

Puzzle Piece 3: Arm Cycle

In a holistic approach, the term *three-S pull* is used to describe the breaststroke arm cycle. The first S stands for sweep; the second scull; and the third shoot. In general the entire three-S pull is performed in front of the shoulders, although some elite-level swimmers pull past the shoulders. For most pulling past the shoulders causes a pausing of the hands prior to the forward shoot and a sliding backward of the elbows. It can also have a detrimental effect on the overall timing/flow of the stroke.

> **Note:** *Russian Roman Sludnov, the first male to break the magic one-minute barrier in the 100 breaststroke (LCM), pulls well past his shoulders. He currently trains at the National Training Center in Clermont, Florida, where I frequently have the opportunity to watch him in action.*

The arms begin the three-S pull by sweeping directly outward, just beneath the surface, to a wider than shoulder-width position with the arms straight and the palms pitched slightly outward. Typically, stronger swimmers sweep wider than weaker ones. Once the sweep phase is complete, the arms transition into the scull phase. This is the point within the arm cycle where the hand and forearms establish a strong hold on the water. In a holistic approach, the term *hand/forearm paddle* is used to convey this all-important concept as the hands and forearms work in unison to provide maximum propulsion. For ease of read, the term *paddles* is used from this point onward. In a holistic approach, the term *L-arms* is used to convey this all-important concept as the arms look like inverted Ls at this point in the pull, with the elbows positioned over the hands.

The paddles accelerate throughout this phase as maximum force is applied. Applying maximum force is no easy feat; it requires a great deal of skill and strength. It is not uncommon for swimmers to move through the scull phase with the paddles more parallel to the surface than perpendicular, resulting in reduced propulsion. From here the paddles slice upward at an increased rate of speed into the shoot phase. The hands shoot forward slightly above the waterline, slightly below the waterline, or on the waterline with the elbows remaining in the water throughout. At the completion of the shoot phase, swimmers return to a streamlined position.

> **Note:** *Some may question the wisdom of emphasizing a wide, outward sweep, thinking there's little propulsion to be had. However, the wider the arms travel outward (to a degree), the greater the distance the hand/forearm paddles travel inward during the scull phase. Extending the length of the scull phase dramatically increases the amount of propulsion generated. Breaststroke legend Ed Moses (among others) had an extremely wide outward sweep.*

Three-S Pull—A Piece of Cake

To teach the three-S pull, the holistic coach pretends to lay his streamlined arms across the top of an imaginary cake with the foremost edge of the cake pressed against the chest. From here the arms sweep outward across the top of the cake with the palms pitched slightly outward until reaching the outside edges of the cake, slightly wider than shoulder width. From here the elbows position over the hands, sending the hands and forearms down into the cake. From here the thumb-side edge of the hands and forearms slice up through the cake, back to the top. From here the hands shoot across the top of the cake and back to the starting position. The sculling action is similar to the one used by world champion and six-time NCAA champion Rebecca Soni.

Puzzle Piece 4: Breathing Cycle

While the breaststroke breathing sequence was outlined in the previous section, there is one other important point that must be noted. If the scull phase is performed correctly, the head and shoulders will rise naturally for the breath. In a holistic approach, the term *natural breathing spot* is used to convey this all-important concept. Therefore swimmers should avoid moving the head independently of the upper body. Swimming with a tennis ball tucked beneath the chin may be used to control head movement and create the ideal upper-body angle.

> **Note:** *The shoulders play an important role in the undulating style of breaststroke. At the peak of the breath, the shoulders achieve near ear-level height via a lift or shrug before lunging forward in unison with the hands. The shoulders remain squeezed together and above the surface until the final portion of the shoot phase, at which point they return to the water. In order for the shoulders to remain above the surface, the hands must move forward at an accelerated rate.*

> **Note:** *In a holistic approach, the term lift and lunge is used to convey this all-important concept. Swimmers who fail to lift the shoulders upward to the required height during the breathing cycle and fail to shoot the hands forward at the required speed during the shoot phase will be unable to create a lunging effect. In addition failure to lift the shoulders increases frontal drag.*

Puzzle Piece 5: Timing/Flow

To achieve ideal timing within the stroke, the arm, kick, and breathing cycles must work together in harmony. Breaststroke has three unique timing/flow styles. The first is commonly referred

to as *glide timing*, where a glide of one second is held between each stroke. Adding a glide controls the rate of physical exertion and provides swimmers with more time to achieve a streamlined position between strokes. The second is commonly referred to as *continuous timing*, where swimmers move from stroke to stroke the instant a streamlined body position is achieved. While more aggressive in nature, it respects the need for stroke efficiency. The third is commonly referred to as *overlap timing*, where the arms and legs pull and kick continuously in an overlapping fashion. Swimming in this manner makes it impossible to achieve a fully streamlined position between strokes. Although extremely inefficient, it can be extremely effective over shorter distances, when energy conservation is a lesser concern.

⚊⚊ Food for Thought ⚊⚊

As mentioned previously, butterfly is the most physically challenging stroke. Breaststroke, on the other hand, is the second-most challenging stroke. Therefore, teaching swimmers to glide in breaststroke seems counterintuitive, as no glide is taught in butterfly. In a holistic approach, swimmers are first introduced to glide timing and transition to continuous timing once the stroke is technically sound.

Cycle rates, which measure the number of strokes performed in one minute, can also be used to promote ideal breaststroke timing/flow. In the 100 breaststroke, elite-level female swimmers achieve cycle rates of forty-eight and higher while their male counterparts achieve cycle rates of fifty-two and higher. In a holistic approach, swimmers are challenged to hit these rates over ever-increasing distances with best-form technique. To measure cycle rates accurately, a stopwatch with a cycle rate function is recommended.

Stroke length also impacts breaststroke timing/flow as swimmers who finish each stroke with arms and legs fully extended create the time and space necessary to execute each puzzle piece as intended. A fully finished stroke looks and performs differently from an unfinished one.

> **Note:** *The Finis Tempo Trainer is an excellent tool and can be used to encourage ideal timing/flow in breaststroke. For further information, go to www.finisinc.com.*

Freestyle

Freestyle is unique in that it is the only stroke with side breathing. While some swimmers choose to breathe to the side in butterfly, side breathing is not an inherent part of butterfly as it is in freestyle. Although breathing to the side may seem like a simple skill, it has the potential to cause a host of problems including over-rotation, over-entering, over-pulling, over-breathing, and a broken kick. Ideally the breathing cycle should work harmoniously within each stroke cycle.

> **Note:** *Breathing is a non-propulsive action as compared to pulling or kicking. At no time can a non-propulsive part of a stroke interfere with a propulsive part. All too often swimmers delay the breath slightly to get more air. As a result propulsion is impacted in a negative way. Ideally all stroke parts should work together harmoniously.*

Common Stroke Errors in Freestyle

To excel in freestyle, swimmers must be free and clear of the most common freestyle errors, including:

- Side-to-side head movement (not related to breathing)

- Bobbing the head
- Excessive upward head tilt
- Burying the head
- Non-horizontal body position
- Squirming
- Bouncing
- Under-rotation
- Over-rotation
- Uneven rotation
- Disjointed rotation (body does not rotate as a whole)
- Sputter kick (non-continuous)
- Breaststroke feet (kicking with one or both feet turned out)
- Split kick (legs that spread beyond body width)
- Kicking air
- Lack of extension on entry
- Dominant entry arm
- Pausing at the point of entry
- Over-entry (crossover)
- Under-entry
- Asymmetrical entry
- Thumb-down entry (ninety degrees)
- Pulling with fingers apart
- Over-pulling (pulling across midline)
- Asymmetrical pull
- Dominant pulling arm
- No catch
- Late catch
- Straight-arm pull
- Lack of extension on finish
- Lack of acceleration through the finish
- Pausing at the point of finish
- Asymmetrical recovery
- Over-breathing
- Asymmetrical breathing

- Dropping the lead arm during the breath
- Breathing backward (as opposed to directly sideways)
- Early breathing
- Late breathing
- Failure to exhale underwater
- Pausing during the breath
- Irregular timing of the stroke as a whole
- A disjointed stroke

As you can see, there are numerous stroke errors associated with freestyle, each the result of improper teaching or training. Allowing swimmers to perform improper technique is extremely counterproductive and demoralizing, and can place them at greater risk of injury. In a holistic approach, swimmers are stopped and corrected at the first sign of improper technique, before bad habits have a chance to form.

> **Note:** *All too often coaches allow swimmers to perform freestyle incorrectly, believing swimmers will eventually or magically find their strokes. I happen to believe this theory is absolute nonsense! Swimmers must be led to the ideal stroke under the watchful eye of a qualified and concerned coach.*

The Freestyle Puzzle

Freestyle consists of five distinct puzzle pieces: 1) body position, 2) arm cycle, 3) kick cycle, 4) breathing cycle, and 5) timing/flow. Swimmers who solve the puzzle enjoy freestyle to a much higher degree and achieve far greater success.

Puzzle Piece 1: Body Position

Similar to the three other strokes, body position forms the foundation of freestyle. The freestyle body position actually consists of two body positions rolled into one: head to toe and side to side. Swimmers who achieve the ideal head-to-toe body position ride higher in the water, enjoy a greater degree of stability, and swim straighter while swimmers who achieve the ideal side-to-side body position experience less drag and increased stroke length and generate greater amounts of propulsion. Achieving the ideal head-to-toe body position requires a steady, neutral, or near-neutral head position, a plank-like upper body, and a tight, symmetrical, continuous kick. The head acts like a balancing tool, drawing the hips, legs, and feet toward the surface; the plank-like upper body acts like a bridge, connecting the head with the lower body; and the kick acts like an elevator, raising the body upward toward the surface. Achieving the ideal side-to-side body position requires a forty-five-degree rotation to both sides in unison with the recovery arms. As the right arm recovers past the right shoulder, the entire body (minus the head) rotates to the right via the hips, and as the left arm recovers past the left shoulder, the entire body (minus the head) rotates to the left via the hips. In most cases rotation should not exceed forty-five degrees. In a holistic approach, rotation is restricted to less than forty-five degrees until the kinetic chain is firmly established. Adding the full amount of rotation prematurely can have an adverse effect on both body positions and the kick.

> **Note:** *Further information regarding the kinetic chain can be found under Technical Concepts in this chapter.*

To encourage proper rotation, the holistic coach introduces a concept called *connect the dots,* where swimmers imagine having brightly colored dots painted on their shoulders, hips, and ankles. As the body rotates from side to side, all three dots must remain in line and connected. Keeping the dots in line maintains a connection from the tip of the shoulder to the ankle. As mentioned previously, maintaining the recommended amount of rotation reduces drag, lengthens the stroke, and strengthens the pull. In fact rotation can add four to six inches to stroke length, translating to one or two fewer strokes per 50.

While some coaches teach rotation through the shoulders, rotation through the hips works best and guarantees full body rotation. This is due to the fact that the hips are located in the center of the body and have full access to the strength of the core. In addition an approach that emphasizes hip rotation versus shoulder rotation supports the all-important hip-hand connection.

Note: *Further information regarding the hip-hand connection can be found in the Technical Concepts section in this chapter.*

Note: *While a neutral head makes it easier to maintain a horizontal body position, the majority of swimmers prefer to tilt the head forward to one degree or another to see down the pool. To orientate swimmers on an acceptable degree of head tilt, the holistic coach introduces a concept called nose number in a five-step progression, with each step consisting of one 25. On the first 25, swimmers pretend to dial the nose to zero; on the second 25, swimmers pretend to dial the nose to one. The process is continued until they're dialing the nose to five on the last 25. Dialing the nose to zero places the head in a neutral position with the eyes facing directly downward while dialing the nose to five places the head out of the water with the eyes facing directly forward, similar to water polo freestyle. Upon completion, swimmers are asked to choose the nose number that felt best yet allowed them to maintain a horizontal or near-horizontal body position. Typically a one to three nose number is chosen.*

Puzzle Piece 2: Kick Cycle

Freestyle is a 6:1 stroke, meaning six kicks per one arm cycle or two strokes. Swimmers capable of maintaining six kicks per cycle have the greatest potential to excel. Aside from helping to establish and maintain the ideal body position, a six-beat kick provides maximum propulsion, promotes balance and stability, enhances flow, assists in rotation, encourages greater stroke length, and spreads out the work between the arms and the legs. No other kicking pattern delivers as many benefits to the stroke. While the demands of a six-beat kick are far greater, so are the rewards.

Note: *In a holistic approach, swimmers are introduced to kicking in this manner through a concept called minimal kick, as outlined in the Technical Concepts section of this chapter.*

Each freestyle kick consists of a downbeat and an upbeat action with the downbeat being the most propulsive. The downbeat begins with a slight flexion of the hip followed by a downward extension of the knee and ankle in a whip-like fashion. The upbeat consists of a straight-leg rebounding action back to the starting position. The ideal freestyle kick is tight, symmetrical, and continuous. To convey this idea, the holistic coach introduces a concept called *kick in the box,* where swimmers imagine kicking inside an imaginary box with the sides of the box representing the sides of the body, the top of the box representing the chest, and the bottom of the box representing the back. Kicking in this manner is a prerequisite for high-performance freestyle.

Ankle flexibility also plays a major role in the propulsive potential of the kick, as floppy feet generate the greatest amount of propulsion. Ideally the feet should extend seventy degrees or more from vertical. In a holistic approach, improving and maintaining ankle flexibility is a top priority.

Note: *One of the greatest detractors of freestyle kick is over-rotation. Swimmers who over-rotate break the kinetic chain connecting the body from hand to foot. Once it's broken a number of technical errors may* *occur including excessive knee bend, severe splitting of the legs, and disjointed rotation. In a holistic approach, swimmers earn the right to rotate based on the strength of the kinetic chain.*

Puzzle Piece 3: Arm Cycle

The freestyle arm cycle consists of four phases: 1) entry, 2) catch, 3) finish, and 4) recovery.

To perform the correct entry, the fully extended arm enters the water forward of the shoulder, fingertips first. Some swimmers prefer to enter fingertips first with the palm rotated slightly outward while others prefer fingertips first, palm side down. Entering with the palm side rotated completely outward is not recommended as it has the potential to cause unwanted stress on the shoulder. If a high-elbow recovery is used, the hand enters the water forward of the shoulder, sliding to full extension before initiating the pull. If a low-elbow recovery or straight-arm recovery is used, the hand enters the water with no additional extension required.

Immediately upon entering, the hand and forearm transition into the catch phase to engage the water and establish a hold. In a holistic approach, the term *hand/forearm paddle* is used to convey the idea that the hand and forearm work in unison to provide maximum propulsion. For ease of read, the term *paddle* is used from this point onward. Optimal elbow bend at the point of catch is near ninety degrees with the elbow positioned over the hand. In a holistic approach, the term *L-arm* is used to convey this all-important concept as the arm looks like an inverted L at this point in the arm cycle. At the point of catch, maximum force is applied. The catch is executed quickly and completed by or before the shoulder. Catching (or establishing a hold on the water) is no easy feat; it requires a great deal of skill and strength. It is not uncommon for swimmers to move through the catch with the paddle more parallel to the surface than perpendicular, resulting in minimal propulsion. By the end of the catch phase the paddles face directly backward.

Upon completion of the catch phase, the paddle transitions into the finish phase, the second-most propulsive phase of the arm cycle due to the forceful acceleration of the paddle that occurs at this point. It should be noted the paddle shrinks as it travels through to the finish. At the beginning the hand and forearm face directly backward while at the end only the hand faces backward. In a holistic approach, the term *shrinking paddle* is used to convey this all-important concept.

> **Note:** *Not all swimmers follow the same pulling pattern in freestyle. Some virtually pull straight back from entry to finish with little outside or inside sculling action while others follow an elongated, narrow S pattern.*

Once the finish phase is complete, the fully extended arm begins the recovery phase in one of three styles: 1) high elbow, 2) low elbow, or 3) straight arm. For the sake of brevity, a description of straight-arm recovery style is not included. Many coaches discourage the use of this style; however, its popularity is growing especially in sprint events. In a holistic approach, swimmers who demonstrate a natural inclination to recover in this manner are encouraged to do so via a concept known as *rainbow arms*.

> **Note:** *At the 2000 Olympic Games, Dutch swimmer Inge de Bruijn set a world record in the 50 freestyle using a straight-arm freestyle recovery.*

High-elbow recovery refers to the classic style of recovery performed by many elite-level swimmers. As the arm nears the end of the finish phase, the shoulder, upper arm, and elbow rise upward, led by the elbow. The upper arm, elbow, and hand continue to rise until the hand nears the side of the body (palm facing inward) and the fingertips clear the surface. From here the hand travels forward, past the shoulder, along a linear pathway to the point of entry. As the hand passes the shoulder, the body rotates toward the entering arm and the hand enters the water forward of the head, in line with the shoulder. The hand continues to reach forward until the arm is fully extended. A high-elbow recovery is the most direct and least evasive of all three recovery styles. A low-elbow recovery begins much the same as the high-elbow recovery only the elbow rise is less pronounced and the hand remains farther off the side of the body. Once the hand exits the water, the slightly bent arm swings forward, via the shoulder, along a semicircular pathway to the point of entry. As the hand passes the shoulder, the body rotates toward the entering arm and the hand enters the water forward of the head, in line with the shoulder. From here the hand joins the forearm in initiating the catch. There is no extension of the arm required at the point of entry as the arm is already extended. Due to the semicircular nature of the low-elbow recovery, the arm produces a greater amount of negative force, which has the potential to destabilize the stroke, causing swimmers to squirm and bounce. Therefore swimmers must possess a strong core and maintain a tight, symmetrical, continuous kick to combat its effects.

Puzzle Piece 4: Breathing Cycle

When asked to demonstrate best-form freestyle technique, most swimmers will eliminate or limit their breathing to reduce the number of potential stroke errors. As mentioned previously, improper breathing technique can cause a host of stroke errors. In order to breath correctly and maintain the ideal body position, the head must be positioned appropriately prior to the breath, and the side of the head must remain as parallel to the surface as possible during the breath. In a holistic approach, the term *parallel breathing* is used to convey this all-important concept, where swimmers position the side of the head parallel or near parallel to the surface throughout the inhalation period of the breathing cycle. For body alignment purposes, the eyes must face directly outward as opposed to facing backward or forward during the inhalation period. In addition the breath should be taken in the smallest space possible and be difficult to see from the pool deck. In a holistic approach, the term *invisible breathing* is used to convey this all-important concept.

The timing of the breath within the arm cycle is also critical. When breathing to the right, the face turns out as the right arm pulls past the right shoulder, and the face turns in as the right arm recovers past the right shoulder. The same process is repeated on the left. The breathing cycle must work harmoniously within each stroke cycle.

Breathing bilaterally, or every third stroke, is a common practice with many advantages, including greater balance as swimmers breath alternately to both sides; matched muscle development as the breathing action alternates to both sides; and opportunities to view competitors on either side. Disadvantages include a reduced supply of oxygen (when compared to single-sided breathing) and a lopsided stroke for swimmers who breathe more efficiently to one side.

As an alternative, single-sided breathing is recommended. Many of the world's greatest freestylers, including Ian Thorpe of Australia, have perfected the art of single-sided breathing. In addition breathing patterns must be adjusted based on the event distance. For example in the 50 freestyle, elite-level swimmers may choose not to breathe at all, while in the 200 freestyle a bilateral or single-sided pattern is recommended.

> **Note:** *The Finis front-mounted snorkel is an excellent tool for teaching proper breathing mechanics. Swimming with a snorkel encourages symmetry throughout the entire stroke cycle, thus creating greater balance and flow. Upon removal of the snorkel, swimmers feel compelled to breathe in a manner that maintains the acquired symmetry, balance, and flow.*

Puzzle Piece 5: Timing/Flow

To achieve the ideal timing/flow within the stroke, the arm, kick, and breathing cycles, together with body rotation, must work in harmony. Ideally swimmers should move seamlessly from stroke to stroke, resisting the urge to pause at any given point.

There are three different timing methods used in freestyle: 1) hip-driven, 2) shoulder-driven, and 3) a combination of both with each creating a unique style of timing/flow. For the sake of brevity the combination style, better known as gallup freestyle, is not described in this chapter.

In hip-driven freestyle the hips dominate by leading the arm into and out of the entry and finish phases of each stroke cycle. Emphasizing the hips in this manner increases stroke length and stroking power while reducing drag through increased rotation. A tight, symmetrical, continuous kick must be maintained throughout. Hip-driven freestyle is used by the majority of elite-level swimmers in races 200-yards/meters and above. In the case of hip-driven, one arm is held forward of the shoulder until the other arm begins to recover past the opposite shoulder, at which point the arms switch positions. It is essential that the extended arm remains just beneath the surface until the switch is made. Cycle rates are lower in hip-driven freestyle due to the fact that hip rotation must be coordinated with the arm cycle. In other words the arm cannot begin to pull until the hip is rotated forty-five degrees to the pulling arm side. A lower stroke rate increases distance per stroke and encourages a more drag-free position.

In shoulder-driven freestyle, the shoulders dominate by leading the arm into and out of the entry and finish phases of each stroke cycle. Emphasizing the shoulders in this manner increases cycle rates and is ideally suited for racing distances of 100-yards/meters or below. Rotation is less as the hips play a lesser role. In shoulder-driven freestyle the arms remain opposite each other at all times, similar to paddling a kayak. As one arm enters, the other arm exits. Although more physically demanding and less efficient when compared to hip-driven freestyle, shoulder-driven freestyle can be extremely effective over shorter racing distances. When performing shoulder-driven, kicking rates must match pulling rates or at least seem that way. To understand the intensity of kicking required, I suggest viewing the world's greatest sprint free-stylers in action, including Britta Seffen (GER), Lisbeth Trickett (AUS), Cesar Cielo (BRA), Eamon Sullivan (AUS), and Nathan Adrian (USA). Videos are available for viewing on YouTube.

Cycle rates, which measure the number of strokes performed in one minute, may also be used to promote ideal freestyle timing/flow. In the 100 freestyle, elite-level female swimmers achieve cycle rates of fifty-four and higher while their male counterparts cycle at rates of fifty and higher. In a holistic approach, swimmers are challenged to hit these rates over ever-increasing distances with best-form technique. To measure cycle rates accurately, a stopwatch with a cycle rate function is recommended.

Note: *In a holistic approach, the freestyle flow drill is used to integrate the arms and legs. To begin swimmers perform a 25 freestyle with the fastest kick possible combined with the slowest arms possible. This usually takes a few attempts before being mastered. From here swimmers perform a series of 25s, adding slightly faster arms per 25 while maintaining the fastest kick possible. Eventually the arm speed catches up to the kick speed and ideal timing/flow is achieved.*

Stroke length also impacts freestyle timing/flow, as swimmers who enter and exit the water with arms fully extended create the time and space necessary to execute each puzzle piece as intended. A fully finished stroke looks and performs differently from an unfinished one.

Note: *The Finis Tempo Trainer is an excellent tool and can be used to encourage ideal timing/flow in freestyle. For further information, go to www.finisinc.com.*

TURNS

There are seven basic turns in competitive swimming: butterfly, backstroke, breaststroke, freestyle, butterfly to backstroke, backstroke to breaststroke, and breaststroke to freestyle. In addition there are four variations of the backstroke to breaststroke turn: open, backward somersault, swivel, and crossover, though I have heard other names used to describe the three IM turns. In a holistic approach, turns are divided into three phases: 1) before the wall, 2) at the wall, and 3) after the wall. Each of these phases can take years to master.

Food for Thought

Turns are all-important and can make or break a race. Unfortunately the turns executed by most swimmers in practice are well below the quality needed to excel in competition. In many cases practice turns serve only as rest stops between lengths. To ensure race-quality turns in competition, swimmers must have frequent opportunities to perform race-quality turns in practice. Performing hundreds of subpar turns practice after practice has no correlation to the type of turns executed by elite-level swimmers in competition. The adage *garbage in, garbage out* rings true here.

> **Note:** *Swimmers typically receive constructive feedback from the coach upon completing a race. Of all criticisms given, poor turns usually top the list. While the need to develop race-quality turns is unquestioned, few coaches provide swimmers with meaningful opportunities to improve turning skills upon returning to practice after competition. It is not unusual to hear a coach state, "We don't need to spend additional practice time working on turns. We do hundreds every week." But common circle turns can never compete with the type of turns required in competition. In a holistic approach, race-quality*

turns are performed frequently throughout the week. Information regarding the format and structure used to integrate turns into practice can be found in Chapter 4.

Each turn outlined below consists of a series of components executed seamlessly in rapid succession. To increase turning speed, each component must be executed within the smallest space possible. In a holistic approach, the term *small on the wall* is used to convey this all-important concept.

Streamlining is a common and essential component in all turns. The streamline stance drill is an excellent way to improve swimmers' streamline ability. To perform the drill, swimmers stand on deck in a streamlined position with the arms squeezed against the back of the head or ears and the fingertips pointed toward the sky. The hands are placed one behind the other with the thumb of the backward hand wrapped around the palm of the forward hand. In a holistic approach, the term *hand sandwich* is used to convey this all-important concept. The head is placed in a neutral position with the eyes facing directly forward. The legs and feet are squeezed tightly together. To complete the stance, swimmers rise up on their tiptoes, squeezing the body as tightly as possible while holding a streamlined position for as long as possible. In a holistic approach, the term *narrow as an arrow* is used to convey the desired objective of the drill.

While streamlining has always been an essential skill, its importance has risen due to the advent of the body whip or underwater dolphin kick. When it's performed correctly, swimmers can travel as fast or faster underwater compared to above. Throughout the body whipping process, the arms remain motionless. While it's difficult to imagine, elite-level swimmers execute two or more body whips per second!

Note: *Determining the right size body whip, as well as the speed of execution, is critical. An oversized body whip performed at a slow speed, or an undersized body* *whip performed at a fast speed, will not suffice. To determine the right size and speed, the holistic coach offers the following three-step progression:*

Step 1: Swimmers push off the wall underwater in a streamlined position, performing a series of large body whips as quickly as possible.

Step 2: Step one is repeated only a series of small body whips are performed as quickly as possible.

Step 3: Step two is repeated only a series of medium body whips are performed as quickly as possible.

Upon conclusion, swimmers are asked to choose the size that felt the fastest. Typically the medium-size body whip is chosen. From here swimmers practice a concept called *kick counting* to determine the ideal number of kicks performed underwater. Typically, novice-level swimmers choose three to five kicks off the wall, junior-level swimmers five to seven, and senior-level swimmers seven to nine.

Current USA Swimming rules permit swimmers to travel fifteen meters off the turns in all butterfly, backstroke, and freestyle races provided the head breaks the surface by the fifteen-meter mark. Rather than focus on distance, the amount of time spent underwater can also be used to enhance turns. In my research I have found elite-level female swimmers spent (on average) 3.5 seconds underwater in the 100 butterfly, 5.0 seconds underwater in the 100 backstroke, 4.0 seconds underwater in the 100 breaststroke, and 2.5 seconds underwater in the 100 freestyle. Elite-level male swimmers spent (on average) 5.0 seconds underwater in the 100 butterfly, 6.0 seconds underwater in the 100 backstroke, 5.0 seconds underwater in the 100 breaststroke, and 3.5 seconds underwater in the 100 freestyle.

Note: *Accomplished senior-level swimmers typically*

perform thousands of strokes per practice, compared to hundreds of turns. Therefore it is not surprising to find that they place a higher value on swimming than turning. But nothing could be further from the truth. The need to develop elite-level turns is just as important as the need to develop elite-level strokes. In a holistic approach, quality strokes and turns go hand in hand.

Fail to Plan, Plan to Fail

In the world of competitive swimming, executing great turns and finishes in competition is a top priority, but sadly the majority of swimmers miss more turns and finishes than they hit. The reasons are many, but perhaps the biggest lies in the fact that swimmers either fail to plan for an upcoming wall or plan too late, thus leaving little room for error. In light of this unfortunate truth, during practice, swimmers should begin planning for an upcoming turn or finish immediately off the start or the previous turn. In other words planning for the wall should begin approximately twenty yards/meters before the wall rather than the typical five yards/meters. Planning well in advance of the wall by standardizing the number of strokes per 25 or stroke counting at race pace dramatically increases the chance of executing the level of turn or finish desired. For some coaches this may seem like too much work from a preparation point of view, but within a holistic approach, rehearsing race-quality turns and finishes is a top priority.

> **Note:** *The concept of stroke counting for an entire 25 can deliver exceptional results. I have used this concept for years with swimmers hitting turn after turn. Periodic retesting should occur to ensure stroke count consistency.*

Butterfly Turn

1.   Before the Wall

The wall must be timed perfectly in order to maintain maximum momentum through the turn. Therefore planning well in advance the wall is key. Swimmers must also resist the urge to dive beneath the surface prior to touching the wall, as this results in a serious loss of speed. In a holistic approach, the term *wall, not water* is used to convey the idea that the hands must find the wall at the completion of the final stroke. In addition the skills required to execute this portion of the butterfly turn are very similar to those required to execute a well-timed butterfly finish. Information regarding the butterfly finish can be found later in this chapter.

2.   At the Wall

The hands touch the wall simultaneously at the water level. At this point the body assumes a horizontal position with the arms fully extended and the head tucked between the arms. Achieving this position maximizes reach while minimizing drag.

At the point of contact, the elbows flex slightly or remain straight depending on the type of touch preferred. From here the hands depart the wall in a quick one-two fashion. The first hand is removed by way of a strong, backward elbow drive toward the ribs while the second hand is removed in a quick karate chop action before the feet plant on the wall. The second hand travels behind the head, joining the awaiting hand in streamline. Ideally, advanced junior- and senior-level swimmers should spend one second (or less) between the time the hands touch the wall and the feet touch the wall. Swimmers should also strive to maintain the one-second standard on every turn within a race. To develop the level of conditioning needed, attacking the walls in practice must be a constant theme.

Note: *Butterfly hand-touch to foot-touch speeds for elite-level swimmers can be as fast as 0.70 seconds.*

As the hands depart the wall in a quick one-two fashion, an optional backward head snap is added. Snapping the head in this manner redirects the body toward the other end of the pool. Although not universally taught, it can result in amazingly fast turns. If the right hand departs the wall first, the hips swivel to the right and vice versa. As the hips swivel, the feet swing to the wall in a pendulum-like fashion and a breath is taken. In a holistic approach, the term *small on the wall* is used to convey the importance of remaining compact throughout this phase of the turn. To achieve the desired power, alignment, and trajectory off the wall, the feet plant shoulder width apart and parallel to the surface.

3. After the Wall

Upon planting the balls of the feet on the wall, the feet drive off the wall instantaneously. At this point the body assumes a streamlined position, first on the side, then rotating to the chest. According to current USA Swimming rules, "the shoulders must be kept at or past vertical toward the breast when the swimmer leaves the wall." In a holistic approach, the concept *grin versus smile* is used to teach the correct push off angle, as outlined in the Technical Concepts section of this chapter.

The number of body whips performed of the wall is dependent upon swimmers' skill and fitness levels. Kicking underwater may continue up to fifteen meters provided the speed achieved underwater is greater than the potential speed achieved above water.

From here the arms pull the body to the surface. The timing of the pull is critical, as surfacing too early or too late results in a serious loss of speed. The pull begins with the body fully underwater and ends with the body on top of the water. Swimmers must sense the surface as opposed to sighting the surface. Tilting the head forward to sight the surface is not recommend, as it increases drag and decreases speed. Swimmers should also resist the temptation to breathe on the first stroke off the turn. In addition the underwater portion of the turn must be timed perfectly to blend seamlessly into the swimming portion. In a holistic approach, the term *seamless transition* is used to convey this all-important concept.

Backstroke Turn

> **Note:** *There are two kinds of backstroke turns. In one the turning arm throws over the opposite shoulder. In the other the turning arm remains on its original side with the body rotating over it. For the sake of brevity, the turn in which the turning arm throws over the opposite shoulder is featured.*

1. Before the Wall

The correct turn count (one stroke less than the finish count) must be performed accurately and at full speed to avoid a loss of momentum into the wall and throughout the turn. From here the turning arm throws diagonally over the opposite shoulder to initiate the turn. For added speed and momentum, the turning arm remains straight and close to the surface, as a straight arm generates greater throwing force and lengthens the turning arm's reach to the wall. As the arm throws, the body rotates from back to front.

> **Note:** *In a holistic approach, the concept stroke counts is used to teach the correct approach to the wall, and to remove any doubt, indecision, or fear of the wall, as outlined in the Technical Concepts section of this chapter.*

2. At the Wall

At this point in the turn, the turning arm is positioned forward of the shoulder with the non-turning arm positioned against the side of the body. It should be noted the moment the turning arm enters the water the chin tucks aggressively into the chest to initiate a forward somersault. In a holistic approach, the term *ball on the wall* is used to convey the need to remain compact throughout the somersaulting action. A small dolphin kick is added at this point to accelerate turning speed. In a holistic approach, the concept *seamless turns* is used to teach the correct execution of the turn, as outlined in the Technical Concepts section of this chapter. Ideally, advanced junior- and senior-level swimmers should spend one second or less between the time the final stroke is initiated and the feet push off the wall. Swimmers should also strive to maintain the one-second standard on every turn within a race. To develop the level of conditioning needed, attacking the walls in practice must be a constant theme.

> **Note:** *Elite-level swimmers achieve speeds of 0.75 seconds or faster between initiating the final stroke into the wall and the push off.*

Upon completion of the forward somersault, the feet plant on the wall shoulder width apart and perpendicular to the surface, with the body in a face-up position and the knees bent ninety degrees. In a holistic approach, the concept *power triangle* is used to teach the correct push-off position, as outlined in the Technical Concepts section of this chapter.

3. After the Wall

Upon planting the balls of the feet on the wall, the feet drive off the wall instantaneously. At this point the body assumes a streamlined position on the back. In a holistic approach, the concept *grin versus smile* is used to teach the correct push-off angle, as outlined in the Technical Concepts section of this chapter.

The number of body whips performed off the wall is dependent upon swimmers' skill and fitness levels. Kicking underwater may continue up to fifteen meters provided the speed achieved under the water is greater than the potential speed achieved above water.

Prior to the breakout point, the legs transition from body whip to backstroke kick as the arm pulls the body to the surface. The timing of the pull or breakout arm is critical, as surfacing too early or too late results in a serious loss of speed. The pull begins with the body fully underwater and ends with the body on top of the water. At the completion of the pull, the shoulder tip of the pulling arm breaks the surface first. This allows the body to shed water off the chest, resulting in a quicker breakout with less energy expended. The underwater portion of the turn must be timed perfectly to blend seamlessly into the swimming portion. In a holistic approach, the term *seamless transition* is used to convey this all-important concept.

> **Note:** *If the body is rotated toward the right at the point of push-off, the right arm pulls to the surface and vice versa. In addition, if the body is rotated toward the right, the right arm is placed beneath the left arm during the streamline phase and vice versa, with the thumb of the right hand wrapped around the palm of the left hand.*

Breaststroke Turn
1.   Before the Wall
The wall must be timed perfectly in order to maintain maximum momentum through the turn. Therefore planning well in advance of the wall is key. Swimmers must resist the urge to dive beneath the surface prior to touching the wall or glide into the wall, as both errors result in a serious loss of speed. In a holistic approach, the term *wall, not water* is used to convey the idea that the hands must find the wall at the completion of the final stroke. In addition, the skills required to execute this portion of the breaststroke turn are very similar to those required to execute a well-timed breaststroke finish. Information regarding the breaststroke finish can be found later in this chapter.

2.   At the Wall

The hands touch the wall simultaneously at water level or above. Current USA Swimming rules permit the elbows to be out of the water on the final stroke to the wall. If timed correctly, the hands should touch as the kick finishes. At this point the body assumes a horizontal position with the arms fully extended and the head tucked between the arms. Achieving this position maximizes reach while minimizing drag.

At the point of contact, the elbows flex slightly or remain straight depending on the type of touch preferred. From here the hands depart the wall in a quick one-two fashion. The first hand is removed by way of a strong, backward elbow drive toward the ribs while the second hand is removed in a quick karate chop action before the feet plant on the wall. The second hand travels behind the head, joining the awaiting hand in streamline. Ideally, advanced junior- and senior-level swimmers should spend one second or less between the time their hands touch the wall and their feet push off the wall. Swimmers should also strive to maintain the one-second standard on every turn within a race. To develop the level of conditioning needed, attacking the walls in practice must be a constant theme.

> **Note:** *Breaststroke hand-touch to foot-touch speeds for elite-level swimmers can be as fast as 0.70 seconds.*

As the hands depart the wall in a quick one-two fashion, a backward head snap is added. Snapping the head in this manner redirects the body toward the other end of the pool. Although not universally taught, it can result in amazingly fast turns. If the right hand departs the wall first, the hips swivel to the right and vice versa. As the hips swivel, the feet swing to the wall in a pendulum-like fashion and a breath is taken. In a holistic approach, the term *small on the wall* is used to convey the importance of remaining compact throughout this phase of the turn. To achieve the desired power, alignment, and trajectory off the wall, the feet plant shoulder width apart and parallel to the surface.

3.   After the Wall

Upon planting the balls of the feet on the wall, the feet drive off the wall instantaneously. At this point the body assumes a streamlined position first on the side, then rotating to the chest. According to current USA Swimming rules, "the shoulders must be kept at or past vertical toward the breast when the swimmer leaves the wall." In a holistic approach, the concept *grin versus smile* is used to teach the correct push-off angle, as outlined in the Technical Concepts section of this chapter.

From here a three-phase underwater pullout is performed, consisting of a streamline, pull down, and kick up. In a holistic approach, the concept *streamline stance* is used to achieve the desired streamline position of the wall. A description can be found in Chapter 6 under the Practice Glossary. Swimmers hold the streamline position for a count of one before transitioning to the pull-down phase.

The pull down resembles an exaggerated butterfly pull combined with a dolphin kick. Current USA Swimming rules permit one dolphin kick to be performed during the pull-down phase or at the completion of the pull-down phase, and the dolphin kick must be followed by a breaststroke kick. At the conclusion of the pull down, the arms squeeze against the sides of the body with the palms pressed firmly against the thighs. Pressing the palms against the thighs as opposed to the sides of the body helps to round the shoulders; thus reducing drag. The head is held in a neutral position with the eyes facing downward. Swimmers hold the pull-down position for a count of one before transitioning to the kick-up phase.

From here the arms recover underneath the body in preparation for the kick-up phase. To reduce drag the arms draw forward, thumbs first, with the palms and elbows remaining close to the sides of the body. As the arms recover, the feet draw toward the butt heels first, and as the arms pass underneath the chin the propulsive phase of the kick begins.

At the completion of the kick-up phase, the head breaks the surface and the first above-water stroke is initiated. The first above-water stroke can actually be initiated while still below the surface provided the head breaks the surface before the hands turn inward at the end of the outward sweep. Swimmers must sense the surface as opposed to sighting the surface. Tilting the head forward to sight the surface is not recommended as it increases drag and decreases speed.

While maximum distance per phase is the ultimate goal, a point of deceleration between phases must never occur. The underwater portion of the turn must be timed perfectly to blend seamlessly into the swimming portion. In a holistic approach, the term *seamless transition* is used to convey this all-important concept.

> **Note:** *In a holistic approach, the concept 2 + 3 = 1 is used to enhance the three-phase underwater pull out, as outlined in the Technical Concepts section of this chapter.*

Freestyle Turn

> **Note:** *There are two types of freestyle flip turns. In one a forward somersault is combined with a twist, placing the feet on the wall parallel or near parallel to the surface and shoulder width apart. From here the feet drive off the wall as the body assumes a streamline position first on the side, then rotating toward the chest. In the other a simple forward somersault is performed, placing the feet on the wall perpendicular or near perpendicular to the surface and shoulder width apart. From here the feet drive off the wall as the body assumes a streamline*

position first on the back, then rotating toward the chest. For the sake of brevity, the first turn is outlined below, although both turns are taught in a holistic approach. In my experience neither turn is faster overall. It really comes down to what turn works best for the swimmer.

1. Before the Wall

The wall must be timed perfectly to maintain momentum through the turn. Therefore planning well in advance of the wall is key. The T on the bottom of the pool may be used to assist swimmers in determining when to initiate the turn. As an alternative swimmers may choose to tilt the head slightly forward to sight the oncoming wall. While a forward head tilt increases drag, it also increases the chance of a well-timed turn.

Note: *In a holistic approach, the concept stroke counts is used to teach the correct approach to the wall, as outlined in the Technical Concepts section of this chapter.*

Note: *Submerging is another concept taught within a holistic approach, where the entire upper body tilts beneath the surface as the turning arm pulls fully to the side. Tilting in this manner begins the somersaulting process sooner, resulting in a faster turn.*

2. At the Wall

At this point in the turn, the turning arm is positioned forward of the shoulder with the non-turning arm positioned against the side of the body. It should be noted the moment the turning arm enters the water, the chin tucks aggressively into the chest to initiate a forward somersault. In a holistic approach, the term *ball on the wall* is used to convey the need to remain compact throughout the somersaulting action. A small dolphin kick is added at this point to accelerate turning speed. In a holistic approach, the concept *seamless turns* is used to teach the correct execution of the turn, as outlined in the Technical Concepts section of this chapter.

Ideally, advanced junior- and senior-level swimmers should spend one second or less between the time the final stroke is initiated and the feet push off the wall. Swimmers should also strive to maintain the one-second standard on every turn within a race. To develop the level of conditioning needed, attacking the walls in practice must be a constant theme.

> **Note:** *Elite-level swimmers achieve speeds of 0.75 seconds or faster between initiating the final stroke into the wall and the push off.*

As the body continues through the somersault the hips twist sideways, the feet plant on the wall shoulder width apart and parallel or near parallel to the surface with the knees bent ninety degrees. In a holistic approach, the concept *power triangle* is used to teach the correct push-off position, as outlined in the Technical Concepts section of this chapter.

3. After the Wall

Upon planting the balls of the feet on the wall, the feet drive off the wall instantaneously. At this point the body assumes a streamline position first on the side, then rotating toward the chest. In a holistic approach, the concept *grin versus smile* is used to teach the correct push-off angle, as outlined in the Technical Concepts section of this chapter. The number of body whips performed off the wall is dependent upon swimmers' skill and fitness levels. Kicking underwater may continue up to fifteen meters provided the speed achieved is greater than the potential speed achieved above water. In most cases swimmers travel far less than fifteen meters underwater when performing freestyle turns primarily due to the fact that freestyle is typically faster than body whip and the aerobic demands of middle distance/distance freestyle events.

Prior to the breakout point, the legs transition from body whip to freestyle kick as the arm pulls the body to the surface. The timing of the pull or breakout arm is critical, as surfacing too early or too late results in a serious loss of speed. The pull begins with the body fully underwater and ends with the body on top of the water. Swimmers must sense the surface as opposed to sighting the surface. Tilting the head forward to sight the surface is not recommended, as it increases drag and decreases speed.

At the completion of the pull, the shoulder tip of the pulling arm breaks the surface first. This allows the body to shed water off the back, resulting in a quicker breakout with less energy expended. The underwater portion of the turn must be timed perfectly to blend seamlessly into the swimming portion. In a holistic approach, the term *seamless transition* is used to convey this all-important concept. In races of one hundred yards/meters or less, swimmers should refrain from breathing on the first stroke cycle off the wall to maintain turn speed into the swim.

> **Note:** *If the body is rotated toward the right at the point of push off, the right arm pulls to the surface and vice versa. In addition, if the body is rotated toward the right, the right arm is placed beneath the left arm during the streamline phase and vice versa, with the thumb of the right hand wrapped around the palm of the left hand.*

IM/Transition Turns

Butterfly to Backstroke Turn

1.   Before the Wall
See Butterfly Turn/Before the Wall.

2.   At the Wall
The hand touch to foot plant resembles a butterfly turn, as

outlined in the Butterfly Turn. The only difference is in the way the feet plant on the wall, as the feet plant shoulder width apart at a forty-five-degree angle. Positioning the feet in this manner reduces drag off the wall, positions the body for a more powerful pull to the surface, and ensures the body is positioned correctly, avoiding the risk of disqualification.

3.   After the Wall
See Backstroke Turn/After the Wall.

Backstroke to Breaststroke Turn
For the sake of brevity, only the open turn and backward somersault turn are outlined below.

Open Turn
1.   Before the Wall
The correct backstroke turn count must be performed accurately and at full speed to avoid a loss of momentum through the turn. On the final stroke to the wall, the entire body (including the head) rotates toward the turning arm as it reaches for the wall. To avoid disqualification the body must not rotate beyond the vertical plane.

2.   At the Wall
At the point of contact, the hand releases from the wall in a quick karate chop action. From here the hand travels behind the head to join the awaiting hand in streamline. From here the feet swing to the wall in a pendulum-like fashion and a breath is taken. In a holistic approach, the term *small on the wall* is used to convey the importance of remaining compact throughout this phase of the turn. Upon releasing the second hand from the wall, the body drops beneath the surface in preparation for the push off. To achieve the ideal power, alignment, and trajectory off the wall,

the feet plant shoulder width apart and parallel to the surface. In a holistic approach, the concept *power triangle* is used to teach the correct push-off position, as outlined in the Technical Concepts section of this chapter.

3. After the Wall
See Breaststroke Turn/After the Wall.

Backward Somersault Turn

1. Before the Wall
When approaching the wall, the backstroke finish count is used.

> **Note:** *In a holistic approach, the backward somersault with kickboard drill is used. Here swimmers lie in a face-up position with the palm of each hand placed on top of a kickboard and the arms fully extended. The kickboards are placed alongside the legs. From here swimmers aggressively draw the knees into the chest to initiate a backward somersault. The type of somersault performed is similar to the one required in a backward somersault turn. The drill is an excellent way to introduce swimmers to the turn. From here swimmers kick into the wall with the turning arm extended directly behind the shoulder and execute a backward somersault turn at the wall. From here swimmers repeat the process only swimming.*

2. At the Wall
Upon touching the wall, the palm plants firmly with the fingertips pointing downward and the turning arm fully extended. From here the knees flex and drive toward the chin to initiate a backward somersault. In a holistic approach, the term *ball on the wall* is used to convey this all-important concept. As the knees drive, the planted palm slides up on the wall, adding additional

momentum to the backward somersault. Upon completion, the feet land on the wall shoulder width apart and perpendicular to the surface, with the body in a facedown position, the knees bent ninety degrees, and the arms in a streamline position. In a holistic approach, the concept *power triangle* is used to teach the correct push-off position as outlined in the Technical Concepts section of this chapter.

3.   After the Wall
See Breaststroke Turn/After the Wall.

> **Note:** *The backward somersault turn is best suited for the 100 IM and 200 IM. In a holistic approach, all four back-to-breast turns are taught relative to swimmers' ability and inclination.*

Breaststroke to Freestyle Turn
1.   Before the Wall
See Breaststroke Turn/Before the Wall.

2.   At the Wall
See Breaststroke Turn/At the Wall.

3.   After the Wall
Upon planting the balls of the feet on the wall, the feet drive off the wall instantaneously. At this point the body assumes a stream-line position first on the side, then rotating toward the chest. According to current USA Swimming rules, "the body must be kept at or past vertical toward the breast when the swimmer leaves the wall." In a holistic approach, the concept *grin versus smile* is used to teach the correct push-off angle, as outlined in the Technical Concepts section of this chapter.

The number of body whips performed off the wall is depen-dent upon swimmers' skill and fitness levels. Kicking underwater may continue up to fifteen meters provided the speed achieved is greater than the potential speed achieved above water. In most cases swimmers travel far less than fifteen meters underwater when pushing off the wall into the freestyle leg of the IM, primarily due to the fact that freestyle is typically faster than body whip.

Prior to the breakout point, the legs transition from body whip to freestyle kick as the arm pulls the body to the surface. The timing of the pull or breakout is critical, as surfacing too early or too late results in a serious loss of speed. The pull begins with the body fully underwater and ends with the body on top of the water. Swimmers must sense the surface as opposed to sighting the surface. Tilting the head forward to sight the surface is not recommended as it increases drag and decreases speed.

At the completion of the pull, the shoulder tip of the pulling arm breaks the surface first. This allows the body to shed water off the back, resulting in a quicker breakout with less energy expended. The underwater portion of the turn must be timed perfectly to blend seamlessly into the swimming portion. In a holistic approach, the term *seamless transition* is used to convey this all-important concept.

> **Note:** *If the body is rotated toward the right at the point of push off, the right arm pulls to the surface and vice versa. In addition, if the body is rotated toward the right, the right arm is placed beneath the left arm and vice versa, with the thumb of the right hand wrapped around the palm of the left.*

FINISHES

The only length of a race a swimmer must win is the last. Therefore the need for a well-executed finish is paramount. Unfortunately the majority of swimmers rehearse hundreds of subpar finishes practice to practice, and those who seldom have the opportunity to perform race-winning finishes in practice should not be expected to perform them in competition. While most coaches understand the important role finishes play, few create the conditions in practice to allow them to occur. In a holistic approach, swimmers are required to move off to a designated side of the lane upon touching the wall. That way every swimmer in the lane has an equal opportunity to perform the correct finish. In addition race-winning finish progressions are rehearsed often.

> **Note:** *In a holistic approach, finishes are emphasized off the final turn to the wall as opposed to the flags to the wall. Emphasizing the finish from this point provides swimmers with additional time and space needed to ensure a race-winning finish. To take full advantage of this concept, swimmers must standardize and automate the total number of strokes taken over the last twenty-five yards/meters. The concept is highly recommended for advanced junior- and senior-level swimmers.*

Butterfly Finish

Maintaining maximum momentum into the wall is key to a well-executed butterfly finish. Swimmers must resist the urge to dive beneath the surface prior to touching or glide into the wall. Finishing in either manner adds time, giving the competition an advantage at the wall. In a holistic approach, the term *wall, not water* is used to convey the idea that the hands must touch the wall simultaneously upon completion of the final stroke.

At this point in the finish, the body achieves a horizontal position with the arms fully extended and the head tucked between the arms, resulting in maximal reach and minimal drag. If the distance from the wall is more than one stroke but less than two, one or two butterfly kicks are performed upon completion of the final stroke (considered legal by USA Swimming rules). If the finishing distance is less than one stroke, the elbows bend on the final recovery to shorten the distance traveled by the hands.

Ideally the final two to three strokes should be performed without breathing. In a holistic approach, the concept *stroke counts* is used to teach the correct approach to the wall in butterfly, as outlined in the Technical Concepts section of this chapter.

Backstroke Finish

The correct finish count must be performed accurately and at full speed to avoid a loss of momentum into the wall. In order for this to occur, swimmers must know and trust their finish count. To acquire trust, race-winning finishes must be performed regularly in practice. In the event swimmers find themselves positioned too far away from the wall on the final stroke, one of three options is employed: 1) driving the head back as the finishing arm reaches for the wall, 2) driving the head back in combination with one or two dolphin kicks (considered legal by USA Swimming rules), or 3) rotating the body completely sideways toward the finishing arm to extend the overall length and reach of the body. In a holistic approach, the concept *stroke counts* is used to teach the correct approach to the wall in backstroke, as outlined in the Technical Concepts section of this chapter.

> **Note:** *Should swimmers find themselves too close to the wall on the final stroke, flexing the elbow and jabbing the hand directly to the wall is recommended. Flexing the elbow reduces the distance traveled by the hand.*

Breaststroke Finish

Maintaining maximum momentum into the wall is key to a well-executed breaststroke finish. Swimmers must resist the urge to dive beneath the surface prior to touching or glide into the wall. Finishing in either manner adds time, giving the competition an advantage at the wall. In a holistic approach, the term *wall, not water* is used to convey the idea that the hands must touch the wall simultaneously at the water level or above immediately upon completion of the final stroke. Current USA Swimming rules permit the elbows to be out of the water on the final stroke to the wall.

At this point in the finish, the body achieves a horizontal position with the arms fully extended and the head tucked between the arms, resulting in maximal reach and minimal drag. Executing a mini-stroke is recommended should swimmers find they have insufficient space to perform a full stroke into the wall. The purpose of a mini-stroke is to quicken the finish and satisfy USA Swimming rules requiring swimmers to execute a complete stroke cycle into the wall. At times a short glide may be the best option while a mini-stroke may work best on other occasions.

In a holistic approach, swimmers are given the opportunity to rehearse various finishing scenarios in practice. In a holistic approach, the concept *stroke counts* is used to teach the correct approach to the wall in breaststroke, as outlined in the Technical Concepts section of this chapter.

Freestyle Finish

Three common recommendations for a fast freestyle finish are: 1) sighting the wall in advance of the finish, 2) increasing the rate of stroke into the wall, and 3) eliminating the breath from the flags to the wall or sooner. One other beneficial technique involves rotating the body away from the finishing arm as the hand reaches for the wall. Rotating the body can increase reach by as much as four to six inches.

The hand should touch the wall fingertips first, as opposed to palm first. Although tough on the fingers, losing a close race by a fraction of a second is even tougher. While gliding into the wall is never an option, swimmers must resist the temptation of performing another stroke if space is limited. In addition the finishing arm should drive directly forward toward the wall as opposed downward through the surface. In a holistic approach, the concept *stroke counts* is used to teach the correct approach to the wall, as outlined in the Technical Concepts section of this chapter.

FINISH DRILLS

The following four drills (one per stroke) are ideal for improving swimmers' understanding of the ideal finishing position:

Butterfly: Swimmers lie facedown in a floating position with pull buoys between the legs, arms fully extended and positioned shoulder width apart with the fingertips of both hands in contact with the wall.

Backstroke: Swimmers lie face up in a floating position with pull buoys between the legs, one arm fully extended and positioned directly behind the shoulder with the fingertips of the contact hand touching the wall, and the other arm squeezed against the side of the body.

Breaststroke: Swimmers lie facedown in a floating position with pull buoys between the legs; the arms are fully extended and positioned shoulder width apart, and the fingertips of both hands are in contact with the wall.

Freestyle: Swimmers lie balanced completely on the side with a pull buoy between the legs and the arm closest to the surface squeezed against the side of the body, with the lower arm fully extended forward of the shoulder, the fingertips of the contact hand touching the wall, and the bottom ear squeezed tightly against the lower arm.

> **Note:** *Once a clear understanding of each finish is acquired, swimmers perform a series of 25s with the goal of achieving a near-perfect finish on each attempt. To demonstrate competency they must be able to perform three in a row.*

Fearless Finish Drill

Many swimmers are reluctant to attack the wall on a backstroke or freestyle finish because they fear bodily injury, and as a result they decelerate into the finish. To encourage a fearless finish, the holistic coach offers the following three-step progression:

Step 1: Swimmers perform a 25 backstroke or 25 freestyle at race pace and execute a fearless finish at the flags (5 yards/meters) from the wall.

Step 2: Swimmers repeat step one only finish halfway between the flags and the wall.

Step 3: Swimmers repeat step one only finish at the wall. The goal of this step is for swimmers to finish in the same manner as they did in steps one and two.

CHAPTER 4

The Physical Curriculum

INTRODUCTION

The physical curriculum constitutes the third side of the swimming triangle. The material presented here is blended with the content of the mental and technical curriculums to create a holistic effect. Optimal physical conditioning is a prerequisite to achieving the ultimate swimming goal and the primary purpose of the physical curriculum. It also provides the forum whereby mental and technical skills are rehearsed, refined, and automated.

The physical curriculum consists of a wet side and a dry side. The wet side is commonly referred to as *practice* while the dry side is commonly referred to as *Dry Land training*. Although the wet side comprises the majority of practice time, the dry side plays an equally important role in the development of swim-specific strength, power, and flexibility, as well as injury prevention.

Note: *The degree of physical conditioning also affects the degree of mental and technical conditioning. From a mental standpoint, physically fit swimmers feel better prepared, thus raising confidence levels. From a technical standpoint, physically fit swimmers achieve a higher degree of technical competence due to superior strength and flexibility.*

══ **Food for Thought** ══

A holistic approach has its place in the competitive swimming world, although some may feel it does not go far enough in addressing physical requirements. As the former coach of an Olympic swimmer, I am keenly aware of the training required to excel at the elite level. However I do not believe high yardage training is the only way to develop swimmers at the elite level. Even though this type of training has a proven track record and is by far the most popular, a quality-over-quantity approach has also been proven to work and has many similarities to the one proposed in this book.

PRACTICE VERSUS TRAINING

The term *practice* is often used to describe what swimmers do in the pool on a daily basis. The term *training* is also used. In reality both terms can mean the same thing or two different things. I define practice as performing the essential mental, technical, and physical skills necessary to excel in competition, as opposed to training, which I define as undertaking a series of exercises or sets to reach a higher level of physical fitness. The term *practice* is the word of choice in a holistic approach.

THE PURPOSE OF PRACTICE

In a holistic approach, preparing for competition is the number one purpose of practice. Therefore the need to maintain best-form stroke and turn technique over ever-increasing distances at faster and faster speeds is absolutely essential. While this approach may have little appeal to coaches who believe high-volume training is the key to swimming success, regardless of the quality of stroke, turn, or speed, it will appeal to those looking for an alternative approach that stresses quality over quantity and is more race-specific.

While the majority of coaches emphasize the development of an aerobic base, anaerobic development must also play a key role, as every race relies on both. When one considers the fact that most racing occurs over distances of 200 yards/meters or less—and that the overwhelming majority of swimmers compete in distances of 200 yards/meters or less—it is unclear why high-volume training, with slower average training speeds per 25 and inferior technique, is so revered. In my opinion swimming with best-form stroke and turn technique over ever-increasing distances at faster and faster speeds will do far more to prepare swimmers for the rigors of competition.

> **Note:** *A holistic approach does not preclude swimmers from performing high yardage practices. The only restriction is that yardage must be performed with best-form stroke and turn technique at the desired speed.*

Most coaches who stress high-volume training at the age-group level do so believing that a well-established aerobic base is paramount to long-term swimming success. While the need for endurance is unquestioned, swimmers must also develop specific racing skills and race-specific fitness through quality repetition to compete successfully at the elite age-group level and beyond.

> **Note:** *Experiencing ongoing success is vital in sustaining swimmers' interest and motivation levels year to year. A well-established aerobic base means nothing if swimmers quit prematurely due to a lack of interest or lack of success.*

QUANTITY VERSUS QUALITY

Many of the swimmers who participate in my swim camps train for eleven months of the year, attend seven practices or more a week, and perform on average 6,000 yards/meters per practice, for a grand total of 1,848,000 yards/meters a year! One would think that with all that training they would find it easy to perform seamless butterfly, hold their ideal cycle rates for the 100 back-stroke, not die (figuratively speaking, of course) on the third fifty of 200 breaststroke, or maintain a continutous kick in 400 free-style. But nothing could be further from the truth. Therefore the quantity of yardage alone is not the answer. In order to perform the essential skills necessary to excel in competition, the quality of training must be as important as the quantity of training. While many coaches say that they insist on best-form stroke and turn technique during practice I have little evidence to support it. Each year I work with more than a thousand swimmers (of all levels) from every corner of the world and the quality of their technique is average at best.

> **Note:** *"We are what we repeatedly do. Excellence then, is not an act, but a habit"*   *--Aristotle*

RED, WHITE, AND BLUE

Imagine all muscles within the body are made up of three equal parts: one red, one white, and one blue. Red muscles are used for fast-speed swimming both in competition and training; white muscles are used for medium-speed swimming; and blue muscles are used for slow-speed swimming. If one were to track the colors of the muscles trained most often by the majority of swimmers, what would they be? I would venture to say blue and white due to the sheer amount of yardage performed daily in practice. While the need to build a solid aerobic base is unquestioned swim-mers who spend an overabundance of time training blue and white muscles are ill-prepared for most racing distances with the possible exception of distance freestyle events. I see evidence of this in my camps and clinics on a regular basis where swimmers have unlimited endurance to swim slow to medium but limited endurance to swim fast.

> Note: *"I believe speed has to be taught very young. It doesn't mean swimmers have to compete in speed events at a young age, but you have to open them up to speed and speed development very, very early in their swimming careers."* --Bill Sweetenham

PRACTICE BREAKDOWN

While the underlying purpose of practice in a holistic approach is consistent at all levels, novice-level practices differ greatly from junior- and senior-level practices. A typical novice-level practice consists of a warm up set, a technique and/or drill set, a kick set, and one or more challenge sets. A typical junior- or senior-level practice consists of a warm up set, a test set (if applicable), one or more challenge sets, a technique and/or drill set, a kick and/or pull set, and a warm-down set. Sets are mixed and matched to create the ultimate conditioning experience. The length and total number of sets offered is determined by swimmers' competency levels and the practice time available.

> **Note:** *A novice-level swimmer is defined as one having two or fewer years of competitive swimming experience regardless of age; a junior-level swimmer is defined as thirteen or younger with three years or more of competitive swimming experience; and a senior-level swimmer is defined as fourteen or older with multiple years of competitive swimming experience.*

THE NEED FOR FOCUS

While seldom mentioned in discussions or articles pertaining to competitive swimming, the ability to focus plays a critical role in day-to-day practice quality. Research indicates typical teenage swimmers are unable to sustain attention effectively on one thing for more than twenty to twenty-five minutes before a need to refocus is required. The attention span is even less for younger swimmers.

Sustainable attention is vital to learning and maintaining training intensity. Attention can be prolonged provided swimmers show an interest in the task at hand or feel capable and competent. Fatigue, hunger, emotional stress, and distracting conditions also have detrimental effects on attention spans. The holistic coach does his utmost to create a training environment free of distraction. In addition he offers engaging practice sets and provides periodic refocusing opportunities within the practice.

TRAINING CONCEPTS

The following three training concepts are designed to meet the physical conditioning objectives of a holistic approach. Rather than design sets around the various aerobic and anaerobic energy systems via conventional interval training, sets are designed around swimmers' abilities to maintain best-form stroke and turn technique over ever-increasing distances at faster and faster speeds. As a result holistic training is more race-specific, promoting the concept of training to race over training to train.

> **Note:** *Provided the tenets of a holistic approach are fully respected and utilized, conventional interval-training methods may be substituted for the three training concepts outlined in this chapter.*

SIX-SPEED TRAINING

This concept of training is simple to implement, extremely effective, and individual in nature and can be implemented at the novice, junior, and senior levels. Rather than using intervals to determine effort levels, the six-speed training concept allows swimmers to determine effort levels based on how their bodies and strokes feel. Six-speed training fulfills one of the primary objectives of a holistic approach wherein swimmers assume greater responsibility for their swimming.

Note: *The holistic coach also plays a decisive role in helping swimmers determine their best training speed.*

The first step in implementing six-speed training involves an introduction to the six training speeds. Here swimmers perform a series of repeats beginning at speed 1 and ending at speed 6.

SPEED CLASSIFICATIONS

- Speed 1 rates a 1-2 effort out of 10 and is considered low intensity.
- Speed 2 rates a 3-4 effort out of 10 and is considered low to medium intensity.
- Speed 3 rates a 5-6 effort out of 10 and is considered medium intensity.
- Speed 4 rates a 7-8 effort out of 10 and is considered medium to high intensity.
- Speed 5 rates a 9 effort out of 10 and is considered high intensity.
- Speed 6 rates a 10 effort out of 10 and is considered race pace.

Once swimmers become familiar with the feel of each training speed, the technical and physical conditioning process begins. Swimmers who demonstrate the ability to complete a set with best-form stroke and turn technique at speed 1 are free to advance to speed 2. This process is repeated until best-form stroke and turn technique at speed 6 is achieved. This can take years to accomplish.

Swimmers unable to demonstrate best-form stroke and turn technique at a desired speed must remain at that speed until they are able to do so. At first glance this may seem counterproductive. However, swimmers who are technically and physically fit trump swimmers who are physically fit every time.

> **Note:** *Restricting practice speed based on technical proficiency also serves as an excellent motivational tool, as most swimmers dislike having their speeds restricted.*

Repeat distances of any length may be used provided best-form stroke and turn technique at the desired speed is maintained. There is absolutely no sense in offering a set of 100s if technique and speed deteriorate after the first 50. In this case a set of 50s would be more appropriate.

Initially the rest between repeats is longer to ensure set compliance. As technical and physical adaptations take place, the amount of rest is reduced. Intervals, or a guaranteed amount of rest between repeats, may also be used. In the case of intervals, the rest must be sufficient to allow swimmers the opportunity to meet the technical objectives and speed requirements of the set. There is absolutely no sense in offering repeats on a short rest interval if best-form stroke and turn technique at the desired speed is unsustainable.

TOUCH TIME TRAINING

This form of training provides junior- and senior-level swimmers with individual touch times or goal times for each repeat, enhancing the training experience from a specificity and motivational point of view. Test sets used to determine individual touch times are as follows:

> **Note:** *Throughout the book the symbol (") represents seconds and the symbol (') represents minute.*

50 test set: 4 x 25 > 10" @ 25
100 test set: 8 x 25 > 10" @ 25
200 test set: 12 x 25 > 10" @ 25
300 test set: 16 x 25 > 10" @ 25

Note: *All test sets are performed over a twenty-five-yard/meter distance. There is nothing magical about this distance other than the fact that swimmers have a much better chance of maintaining best-form stroke and turn technique at the desired speed. The maximum test set distance is 300 yards/meters, as experience has shown most swimmers find it extremely difficult to meet test objectives beyond this distance. Longer test sets may be added should the need arise.*

Swimmers must strive to maintain the same speed or pace over the entire test set or the results will be less than favorable. Obviously a 100 test set is performed at a faster speed than a 300 test set.

Typically test sets are repeated several times before swimmers gain a full understanding of how to perform them correctly. Upon completion swimmers estimate the average time held per 25. If a 50 test set was performed, the holistic coach multiplies the average time held per 25 by two to determine the 50 touch time with an additional second added to account for the omitted turn. If a 100 test set was performed, the holistic coach multiplies the average time held per 25 by four to determine the 100 touch time with an additional three seconds added to account for the three omitted turns. If a 200 test set was performed, the holistic coach multiplies the average time held per 25 by eight to determine the 200 touch time with an additional seven seconds added to account for the seven omitted turns. If a 300 test set was performed, the holistic coach multiplies the average time held per 25 by twelve to determine the 300 touch time with an additional eleven seconds added to account for the eleven omitted turns.

In a holistic approach, test sets are offered on a weekly basis early in the season and every two to three weeks after that. Most swimmers reach a saturation point by the final third of the short-course and long-course season, at which point improvements in test results are minimal. Once the short-course season ends, the process is repeated for the long-course season, and accurate records must be maintained throughout both. Tracking test results provides the holistic coach with invaluable information and serves as an excellent motivational tool for swimmers. In addition swimmers receive updated copies of individual touch times once a test set is complete.

> **Note:** *The successful execution of test sets is largely dependent on swimmers' willingness to act responsibly and put forth their best efforts. For some coaches this may be a deal breaker; they may believe that given a choice most swimmers will choose the path of least resistance and slack off. While this may be true in some cases, the majority of swimmers are highly responsible, care deeply about swimming, and enjoy a good challenge. In my view the potential action of a few should not disqualify this method of training.*

AN EXAMPLE OF A 200 TEST SET

Step 1: The swimmer performs 12 x 25s with 10 seconds of rest between 25s, holding an average time of 16.0 seconds per 25.

Step 2: The holistic coach multiplies the average time by eight to determine the 200 touch time. An additional seven seconds are added to account for the seven omitted turns, resulting in a touch time of 2:15.0.

Step 3: The swimmer performs a set of 200s with the goal of holding 2:15.0 per 200. The rest interval must be sufficient to provide a realistic chance of achieving the touch time while maintaining best-form stroke and turn technique. It is always best to start with a generous rest interval and reduce from there. By allowing more rest initially, the successful completion of the set is far more likely. In addition the swimmer gains greater confidence in his or her ability to perform the set correctly and successfully.

Note: *The following pace chart was created to assist the holistic coach in determining touch times for swimmers.*

Touch times may be used for virtually any training distance plus drill, kick, and pull sets.

Note: *Swimmers are grouped into lanes according to touch times prior to commencing a set.*

TOUCH TIME SAMPLE SETS

Sample 1

On Monday, Wednesday, and Friday of the same week, a set of 10 x 100 FR is offered. On Monday swimmers are placed on an interval or guaranteed amount of rest between repeats providing approximately thirty seconds of rest between 100s. Swimmers are challenged to maintain best-form stroke and turn technique while achieving their respective touch times. On Wednesday the same set is offered only swimmers are placed on an interval or guaranteed amount of rest between repeats, providing approximately twenty seconds of rest between 100s. Swimmers are challenged to maintain best-form stroke and turn technique while achieving their respective touch times.

On Friday the same set is offered only swimmers are placed

The Swimming Triangle Pace Chart

yards/meters

	25	50	75	100	125	150	175	200	300	400
0:10	0:10	0:20	0:30	0:40	0:50	1:00	1:10	1:20	2:00	2:40
0:11	0:11	0:22	0:33	0:44	0:55	1:06	1:17	1:28	2:12	2:56
0:12	0:12	0:24	0:36	0:48	1:00	1:12	1:24	1:36	2:24	3:12
0:13	0:13	0:26	0:39	0:52	1:05	1:18	1:31	1:44	2:36	3:28
0:14	0:14	0:28	0:42	0:56	1:10	1:24	1:38	1:52	2:48	3:44
0:15	0:15	0:30	0:45	1:00	1:15	1:30	1:45	2:00	3:00	4:00
0:16	0:16	0:32	0:48	1:04	1:20	1:36	1:52	2:08	3:12	4:16
0:17	0:17	0:34	0:51	1:08	1:25	1:42	1:59	2:16	3:24	4:32
0:18	0:18	0:36	0:54	1:12	1:30	1:48	2:06	2:24	3:36	4:48
0:19	0:19	0:38	0:57	1:16	1:35	1:54	2:13	2:32	3:48	5:04
0:20	0:20	0:40	1:00	1:20	1:40	2:00	2:20	2:40	4:00	5:20
0:21	0:21	0:42	1:03	1:24	1:45	2:06	2:27	2:48	4:12	5:36
0:22	0:22	0:44	1:06	1:28	1:50	2:12	2:34	2:56	4:24	5:52
0:23	0:23	0:46	1:09	1:32	1:55	2:18	2:41	3:04	4:36	6:08
0:24	0:24	0:48	1:12	1:36	2:00	2:24	2:48	3:12	4:48	6:24
0:25	0:25	0:50	1:15	1:40	2:05	2:30	2:55	3:20	5:00	6:40
0:26	0:26	0:52	1:18	1:44	2:10	2:36	3:02	3:28	5:12	6:56
0:27	0:27	0:54	1:21	1:48	2:15	2:42	3:09	3:36	5:24	7:12
0:28	0:28	0:56	1:24	1:52	2:20	2:48	3:16	3:44	5:36	7:28
0:29	0:29	0:58	1:27	1:56	2:25	2:54	3:23	3:52	5:48	7:44
0:30	0:30	1:00	1:30	2:00	2:30	3:00	3:30	4:00	6:00	8:00
0:31	0:31	1:02	1:33	2:04	2:35	3:06	3:37	4:08	6:12	8:16
0:32	0:32	1:04	1:36	2:08	2:40	3:12	3:44	4:16	6:24	8:32
0:33	0:33	1:06	1:39	2:12	2:45	3:18	3:51	4:24	6:36	8:48
0:34	0:34	1:08	1:42	2:16	2:50	3:24	3:58	4:32	6:48	9:04
0:35	0:35	1:10	1:45	2:20	2:55	3:30	4:05	4:40	7:00	9:20
0:36	0:36	1:12	1:48	2:24	3:00	3:36	4:12	4:48	7:12	9:36
0:37	0:37	1:14	1:51	2:28	3:05	3:42	4:19	4:56	7:24	9:52
0:38	0:38	1:16	1:54	2:32	3:10	3:48	4:26	5:04	7:36	10:08
0:39	0:39	1:18	1:57	2:36	3:15	3:54	4:33	5:12	7:48	10:24
0:40	0:40	1:20	2:00	2:40	3:20	4:00	4:40	5:20	8:00	10:40

time in minutes & seconds

on an interval or guaranteed amount of rest between repeats that provides approximately ten seconds of rest between 100s. Swimmers are challenged to maintain best-form stroke and turn technique at all times while achieving their respective touch times.

> **Note:** *Swimmers who experience a serious decline in technique, speed, or both are permitted to skip a portion of a repeat before rejoining the set. Those who find the set less than challenging are provided with additional challenges such as traveling extended distances underwater, no breathing off the walls, and/or extended breathing patterns.*

Sample 2

Swimmers perform a set of 4(4 x 50 FL) on an interval or a guaranteed amount of rest between repeats. An additional thirty to sixty seconds of rest is provided between sets. The amount of rest between repeats must be sufficient to provide them with a realistic chance of maintaining best-form stroke and turn technique while achieving their respective touch times. There is no sense in reducing the rest or increasing the speed until swimmers are able to maintain best-form stroke and turn technique at their respective touch time. Once the current set objectives are achieved the amount of rest between repeats and rest between sets is reduced.

> **Note:** *Swimmers who experience a serious decline in technique, speed, or both are permitted to skip a 50 before rejoining the set. Those who find the set less than challenging are provided with additional challenges such as traveling extended distances underwater, no breathing off the walls, and/or extended breathing patterns.*

Sample 3

Swimmers perform a set of 5 x 200 BK or 5 x 100 BR on an interval or guaranteed amount of rest between repeats. The amount of rest between repeats must be sufficient to provide them with a realistic chance of maintaining best-form stroke and turn technique while achieving their respective touch times. There is no sense in reducing the rest or increasing the speed until swimmers are able to maintain best-form stroke and turn technique at their respective touch time. Once the current set objectives are achieved the amount of rest between repeats and rest between sets is reduced.

> **Note:** *Swimmers who experience a serious decline in technique or speed are permitted to skip a portion of a repeat. Those who find the set less than challenging are provided with additional challenges such as traveling extended distances underwater in backstroke or additional underwater pullouts in breaststroke.*

At the risk of sounding repetitious many coaches would consider the sample sets listed above as easy but I would venture to say many of their swimmers (ages 12 and above) would find it challenging to maintain best-form stroke and turn technique at any speed and extremely challenging at speed 4 or higher.

LOCOMOTIVE TESTING

Instead of performing test sets as outlined above, novice-level swimmers perform a locomotive consisting of 12 x 25s with ten seconds rest between each 25. The first two 25s are performed at speed 1, the next two at speed 2, the next two at speed 3, the next two at speed 4, the next two at speed 5, and the final two at speed 6.

Note: *A fifteen-second rest interval is used in butterfly test sets.*

Once this is complete, swimmers are assigned training speeds based on their ability to maintain best-form stroke technique at the desired speed throughout the locomotive. For example a swimmer who maintained best-form stroke technique at speed 3 but struggled at speed 4 would be required to begin training at speed 3.

Note: *Swimmers are not permitted to exceed the assigned training speed until the next test set or unless granted permission by the holistic coach. Swimmers found doing so are issued speeding tickets and instructed to slow down. The locomotive may also be used for drill or kick sets. On average, novice-level swimmers are retested every other week.*

PRACTICE SETS

In a holistic approach, practices are divided into the following sets: warm up, technique, drill, kick, pull, challenge, refocus, and warm-down. With the exception of warm up and warm-down, sets may be ordered as the holistic coach sees fit. In addition test sets as outlined previously are added to the mix. The number and variety of sets used within a practice is at the coach's discretion.

Warm Up Sets

Swimmers are in constant need of start, turn, and finish work. In a holistic approach, these all-important racing skills are the daily focus of warm up. Some coaches may find this method of warm up rather unorthodox, but given the dynamic nature of starts, turns, and finishes it can be extremely effective and beneficial. It also ensures starts, turns, and finishes are not overlooked, as is so often the case.

All warm up sets begin with a review of key technical focus points. Typically a novice-level warm up lasts between five and ten minutes, while warm ups for junior and senior levels last between ten and twenty minutes. The number of focus points emphasized is dependent upon swimmers' proficiency levels and attention spans, and the practice time available.

Novice-, Junior-, and Senior-Level Sample Warm Up Set Using the Relay Start

1. The holistic coach introduces the key technical focus points of the reverse swing relay start.
2. Swimmers perform two relay jumps off the block. The step has two objectives: 1) to coordinate the arm swing with the leg drive, and 2) to maximize the distance traveled off the block. A relay jump involves the same reverse arm swinging action and head snap used in a relay start only swimmers jump into the water feet first.
3. Swimmers perform two relay starts off the block. The step has two objectives: 1) to coordinate the arm swing with the leg drive and 2) to rehearse key technical focus points of the start.
4. Swimmers perform two full relay exchanges in addition to three fast strokes. This step has two objectives: 1) to coordinate the outgoing swimmer's departure off the block with the incoming swimmer's arrival to the wall and 2) to simulate actual swim meet conditions.

Note: *At this point swimmers are warmed up and ready for the next practice set.*

Warning: *All starts must be practiced in deep water only. USA Swimming rules state: "minimum water depth for teaching racing starts in any setting from any height starting block or deck shall be 5 feet or 1.53 meters for a distance of 16 feet 5 inches or 5 meters from the starting wall." In addition starts should be practiced only under a coach's supervision in a lane free of other swimmers.*

Technique Sets

Technique sets play a starring role and are used to introduce new skills or enhance existing ones at any point within a practice. A typical novice-level technique set lasts between five and ten minutes, while typical junior- and senior-level technique sets last between five and fifteen minutes. Technique sets may be offered at any point within practice once warm up is complete and may be repeated more than once. The number of focus points emphasized is dependent upon swimmers' proficiency levels and attention spans, and the time available. Initially, technical sets are performed at speed 1 for novice-level swimmers and speed 1 or speed 2 for junior- and senior-level swimmers.

> **Note:** *Definitions of various drills and practice terminology can be found in the Drill Set section of this chapter or the Practice Glossary in Chapter 6.*

Sample Technique Sets for Backstroke
Novice-Level
1. 8 x 25 BK K > Plank Kick Drill > Butt Squeeze > 10" @ 25
2. 12 x 25 BK K > 1-Arm Plank Kick Drill > 3-5 Knee Bend > Constant Boil > 10" @ 25
3. 16 x 25 BK K/S > Odd 25s > 1-Arm Plank Kick Drill > Constant Boil > Even 25s > Swim > Cup Head >

Constant Boil > 10" @ 25

Junior-Level

1. 10 x 50 BK K/S > Odd 25s > Streamline Kick on Back Drill > Constant Boil > Even 25s > Swim > Cup Head > 10" @ 50
2. 6 x 75 BK D/S > 1st 50 > 3" Switch 1-Arm Plank Drill > 11 & 1 O'clock Entry > 3rd 25 > Swim > 1-4 Arm Cycle > Roll In/Roll Out > 10" @ 75
3. 5 x 100 BK K/D > 1st 50 > 12 O'clock Kick Drill > Constant Boil > 2nd 50 > 1-Arm BK Drill > Cup Head > Roll In/Roll Out > 10" @ 100

Senior-Level

1. 400 BK K/S > Odd 50s > Plank Kick Drill > Even 50s > Swim > Cup Head > Windmill Arms
2. 2 x 300 BK K/D/S > 1st 100 > Streamline Kick on Back Drill > 2nd 100 > Tea Cup Drill > 3rd 100 > Swim > Roll In/Roll Out > 30" @ 300
3. 10 x 75 BK K/S > 1st 25 > Streamline Kick on Back Drill > 2nd 25 > Double Arm 12 O'clock Kick Drill > 3rd 25 Swim > Constant Boil > 10" @ 75

Note: *Intervals or a guaranteed amount of rest between repeats may be used in all technique sets. In the case of intervals, the rest must be sufficient to allow swimmers the opportunity to meet the technical requirements of the set. There is absolutely no sense in offering repeats on a short rest interval if best-form stroke technique at the desired speed is unsustainable. As in all other types of practice sets, the total distance covered is dependent upon the swimmers' abilities to maintain best-form stroke technique at the desired speed. Adjustments may be made should swimmers experience a serious decline* *in technique and/or desired speed.*

Drill Sets

Without question the quality of swimmers' drills reflects the quality of swimmers' skills. In a holistic approach, drills play a major role in every practice and are used to teach, enhance, and condition various skill components and swimming fitness. In the beginning technical conditioning is the major focus, but as swimmers progress technical and physical conditioning become equally important.

Initially drills are performed at speed 1 or speed 2. Once these are mastered, swimmers are encouraged to execute the drills at faster and faster speeds while maintaining best-form technique. Repeat distances range from 25 to 300 yards/meters. A typical novice-level drill set lasts between five and ten minutes while typical junior- and senior-level drill sets last between five and twenty minutes. Drill sets may be offered at any point within practice (once warm up is complete) and repeated more than once. As in all other types of practice sets, the total distance covered and the amount of rest provided (between intervals/repeats) is dependent upon the swimmers' ability to maintain best-form technique at the desired speed.

Note: *There are literally hundreds of swimming drills. For brevity's sake the number has been limited to twenty-five per stroke. Coaches are encouraged to add personal favorites to the mix. are posted on The Swimming Triangle website at www.the swimmingtriangle.com.*

Butterfly Drills
1.   Chest Press on Wall Drill

Note: *The chest press position forms the foundation of* *butterfly in a holistic approach.*

Purpose: To teach the chest press action in butterfly.
Instructions: The drill is performed with a kickboard. Swimmers lie in a facedown floating position. The feet are placed in the gutter with the legs together and the knees locked out. From here the arms extend fully with the palms placed shoulder width apart on the bottom of the kickboard. Fingertips point directly toward the other end of the pool. From here the chest slowly presses downward, causing the hips to rise above the surface. The head moves in unison with the chest press. Three or more chest press actions are performed before a breath is taken.

Note: *The drill is similar to the downward dog pose in yoga.*

2.   Floating Chest Press Drill
Purpose: To enhance the chest press action in butterfly.
Instructions: The drill is performed with a pull buoy. Swimmers lie in a facedown floating position with size-proportionate pull buoys placed between their upper legs. From here the arms extend fully just beneath the surface with the palms placed shoulder width apart. Fingertips point directly toward the other end of the pool. From here the chest slowly presses downward, causing the hips to rise above the surface. The head moves in unison with the chest press. Three or more chest press actions are performed before a breath is taken.

Note: *The fully extended arms must remain just beneath the surface throughout the chest press action.*

3.   Chest Press With Kickboard Drill
Purpose: To enhance the chest press action in butterfly.
Instructions: The drill is performed with a kickboard. Swimmers push off the wall in a facedown position with the arms

fully extended shoulder width apart and the palms placed at the bottom of the kickboard. Fingertips point directly toward the other end of the pool with the legs together and the toes pointed. From here the chest presses downward, causing the hips to rise above the surface. The head moves in unison with the chest press. Three or more chest press actions are performed before a breath is taken. There is no kicking in this drill, although the legs are permitted to move up and down in unison with the chest.

> **Note:** *At first swimmers may find it difficult to move at any appreciable speed.*

4.   Chest Press With Three-Second Pause Drill

Purpose: To coordinate the chest press action with the butterfly arm cycle.

Instructions: Swimmers perform arms-only butterfly, breathing every stroke. A three-second pause is held between each stroke cycle, allowing additional time for the chest press action to occur.

> **Note:** *This is a non-kicking drill.*

5.   Chest Press With No Pause Drill

Purpose: To coordinate the chest press action with the butterfly arm cycle.

Instructions: Similar to drill four only the three-second pause is eliminated.

6.   Chest Press With Kick Drill

Purpose: To coordinate the chest press action with the butterfly kick cycle and butterfly arm cycle.

Instructions: Similar to drill five only two kicks per stroke are added. The first kick takes place as the arms enter the water; the second kick takes place as the arms exit the water.

Note: *Another name for this drill is full stroke butterfly.*

7.   Dolphin Drill

Purpose: To introduce the concept of undulation.

Note: *Undulation is defined as a wavelike motion.*

Instructions: Swimmers perform butterfly kick on the surface or below, with the arms squeezed tightly against the sides of the body, while attempting to imitate a dolphin. Each downward kick is combined with a chest press, encouraging a whole body kick. Breathing is to the front, similar to butterfly. Three or more kicks are performed before a breath is taken.

Note: *Keeping the body as relaxed as possible throughout each dolphin kick is key to maximizing propulsion.*

8.   Whole-Body Kick With Kickboard Drill

Purpose: To teach the first kick in butterfly.
Instructions: The drill is performed with a kickboard. Swimmers perform face-in butterfly kick with the arms fully extended shoulder width apart and the palms placed at the bottom of the kickboard. Each downward kick is combined with a chest press. Breathing is to the front, similar to butterfly. This drill is best performed with a Finis snorkel.

Note: *The first kick-in butterfly combines a chest press with a kick. In a holistic approach, the term whole-body kick is used to convey this all-important concept.*

9.   Half-Body Kick With Kickboard Drill

Purpose: To teach the second kick in butterfly.

Instructions: The drill is performed with a kickboard. Swimmers perform face-out butterfly kick with the arms fully extended shoulder width apart and the hands placed at the top of the kickboard.

> **Note:** *The second kick in butterfly comes from the hips down. In a holistic approach, the term half-body kick is used to convey this all-important concept.*

10. Whole-Body/Half-Body Kick With Kickboard Drill

Purpose: To enhance and condition the butterfly kick cycle.

Instructions: The drill is performed with a kickboard. Swimmers perform face-in butterfly kick for the first half of each 25 and face-out butterfly kick for the second half. On the first half, the arms are extended fully with the palms shoulder width apart and placed at the bottom of the kickboard. On the second half, the arms are extended fully with the hands shoulder width apart grasping the top of the kickboard.

> **Note:** *A whole-body kick is performed on the first half of each 25; a half-body kick is performed on the second half. Combining both kicks in this manner highlights the difference between the two.*

11. Boom Butt Kick Drill

Purpose: To condition the butterfly kick cycle.

Instructions: The drill is performed with a kickboard. Swimmers perform face-out butterfly kick with the arms fully extended shoulder width apart and the hands placed at the bottom of the kickboard. The drill consists of two challenges: 1) to create a loud *boom* sound with the feet during the downbeat phase of the kick cycle and 2) to force the butt out of the water at the completion of the downbeat phase of the kick cycle. Forcing the butt out encourages a hip-down kick versus a less propulsive knee-down kick.

> **Note:** *In a holistic approach, the term boom butt is used to convey this all-important concept.*

12. Streamline Kick on Back Drill

Purpose: To enhance and condition the butterfly kick cycle.

Instructions: Swimmers perform butterfly kick on the back with the arms held in streamline. The feet must boil the surface at the completion of each upbeat phase of the kick cycle. To achieve the ideal streamline position, the arms extend fully, the hands are placed one on top of the other with the fingers together and pointed, and the thumb of the bottom hand wraps around the palm of the top hand. The head is held in a neutral position.

13. Two-Way Kick Drill

Purpose: To enhance and condition the butterfly kick cycle.

Instructions: Swimmers perform butterfly kick on the side with one arm extended forward of the shoulder. The palm of the extended arm faces downward with the other arm squeezed tightly against the side of the body. The face remains in the water with the bottom ear pressed against the extended arm. The top shoulder, hip, and foot must be positioned directly above the bottom shoulder, hip, and foot. A horizontal body position must be maintained throughout. Breathing is to the side (similar to freestyle) and kept to a minimum. Throughout each kick cycle, the feet must travel the same distance forward as backward, emphasizing maximal effort in both directions.

> **Note:** *In a holistic approach, the term two-way kick is used to convey this all-important concept.*

14. PEZ Head Breathing Drill

Note: *The breathing action in butterfly is similar to the head action of a PEZ candy dispenser. To learn more visit www.pez.com.*

Purpose: To enhance the butterfly breathing cycle.
Instructions: The drill is performed with a foam noodle. Swimmers lie in a facedown floating position with a noodle placed beneath the feet. The hands grasp the wall shoulder width apart with the arms fully extended. From here the chin gently pushes forward until the mouth clears the water. The chin must remain in the water throughout each breathing cycle while the noodle remains at the surface. From here the face slowly returns to the starting position. In a holistic approach, the term *PEZ head breathing* is used to convey this all-important concept.

Note: *Tilting the chin slightly forward as the head rises for the breath is not universally taught. However, many elite-level swimmers breathe in this manner. In the case of Michael Phelps, above- and below-water video footage show his face facing directly downward during the chest press action and completely forward during the breath. In my view the only way to achieve a face-forward position (from a face-downward position) is through a slight forward tilting of the chin.*

15. Beat the Coach Drill
Purpose: To enhance the butterfly breathing cycle.
Instructions: The drill is performed one swimmer at a time. The coach stands at the end of the lane, directly behind the swimmer. The swimmer executes a short push-off followed by five full strokes of butterfly with only one breath taken within the five strokes. The breath is taken at the swimmer's discretion. Upon completion the coach attempts to identify the breathing stroke. If

he's correct, he wins; if he's incorrect, the swimmer wins. The drill teaches swimmers to minimize the size of the breath.

Note: *The swimmer is cautioned against using unfair tactics such as choosing not to breathe at all or breathing in an unorthodox manner.*

16. Wall-Tracing Drill
Purpose: To enhance the butterfly arm cycle.
Instructions: Swimmers stand in front of a large sheet of white paper attached to a wall, felt-tipped markers in each hand. From here the arms extend fully overhead with the marker tips placed shoulder width apart on the paper. From here swimmers attempt to trace the correct butterfly pull pattern as the coach stands nearby to offer corrective feedback. Once mastered, the process is repeated only with the eyes closed, using different colored markers. Upon completion, the eyes-closed version is compared to the eyes-open version. Ideally both should match.

17. Water-Tracing Drill
Purpose: To enhance the butterfly arm cycle.
Instructions: Swimmers push off the wall in a facedown position with the arms fully extended shoulder width apart. From here a series of butterfly arm cycles are performed in slow motion together with a slow motion freestyle kick. Initially the drill is performed without breathing; breathing is added once the drill is mastered. The recovery arms skim forward across the surface as opposed to traveling through the air. At the point of exit the hands achieve a palm-up position, while at the point of entry the hands achieve a palm-down position. Best performed with a Finis snorkel

18. Recovery Drill
Purpose: To enhance and condition the recovery phase of the

butterfly arm cycle.

Instructions: Swimmers lie facedown on a mat with the arms fully extended and slightly off the sides of the body. The hands are held in a palm-up position. From here the recovery phase of the butterfly arm cycle is performed in slow motion. As the arms travel toward the shoulders the palms naturally rotate backward, and as the arms near the end of the recovery the palms naturally rotate downward. The arms hold for one second at the entry point before returning to the starting position and must not touch the ground at any point throughout the repetition. The total number of repetitions performed depends upon the swimmers' fitness levels and the quality of execution.

> **Note:** *The drill can be quite strenuous and must be carefully monitored. Weighted wristbands may be used for swimmers needing an additional challenge.*

19. Floating Catch Drill

Purpose: To enhance the catch phase of the butterfly arm cycle.

Instructions: The drill is performed with a pull buoy and foam noodle. Swimmers lie in a facedown floating position with size-proportionate pull buoys placed between their upper legs, while grasping noodles with both hands. The hands are placed shoulder width apart with the arms fully extended. From here the elbows slowly flex, replicating the catch phase of the butterfly arm cycle. Ideally a ninety-degree angle should form at the completion of the catch, with the upper arms parallel to the surface and the forearms and hands perpendicular to the surface. In a holistic approach, the term *perpendicular paddles* is used to convey this all-important concept. The catch position is held for three seconds. From here swimmers slowly return to the starting position and repeat. The drill is best performed with a Finis snorkel.

20. Exaggerated Finish Drill

Purpose: To enhance the finish phase of the butterfly arm cycle.

Instructions: The drill is performed with a pull buoy. Swimmers lie in a facedown floating position with size-proportionate pull buoys placed between their upper legs. The arms are fully extended and shoulder width apart with the fingertips facing the other end of the pool. From here the underwater portion of the butterfly arm cycle is performed. At the conclusion of the finish, the fully extended arms explode through the surface and into the air, producing an exaggerated finish. From here swimmers slowly return to the starting position and repeat. The drill is best performed with a Finis snorkel.

> **Note:** *The fully extended arms should achieve a height of at least one foot above the surface at the completion of the finish.*

21. Double Finish Drill

Purpose: To coordinate the finish phase of the butterfly arm cycle with the finish phase of the butterfly kick cycle.

Instructions: Swimmers lie in a facedown floating position. The arms are positioned just beneath the shoulders in a ninety-degree flexed position to simulate the catch phase of the butterfly arm cycle. The knees are flexed halfway (or near halfway) to simulate the midway point of the second kick. From here the arms and legs explosively extend to a fully finished position. Both finishes must be coordinated to occur at the same time. From here swimmers slowly return to the starting position. The arms recover under the water as opposed to over the water. Three or more repetitions are performed before a breath is taken. The drill is best performed with a Finis snorkel.

> **Note:** *The inspiration for this drill came from watching underwater footage of Michael Phelps on YouTube. I was amazed to see the coordinated and explosive finish*

of his arms and legs and the resultant surge.

22. 1-A FL With Front Breathing Drill

Purpose: To integrate the various components of butterfly.

Instructions: Swimmers perform one-arm butterfly with the right arm while squeezing the left arm against the side of the body. Breathing is to the front, similar to butterfly, and performed every stroke. Swimmers must remain flat on the chest at all times. Once complete, the drill is repeated with the left arm.

> **Note:** *The drill may also be performed while breathing to the front or side, with the other arm fully extended forward of the shoulder. If breathing to the side, the shoulders must remain horizontal to the surface at all times.*

23. Pull With FR Kick Drill

Purpose: To enhance butterfly timing/flow.

Instructions: Swimmers perform the butterfly arm cycle with a super-fast freestyle kick. The purpose of the drill is to encourage a continuous butterfly arm cycle. In a holistic approach, the term *seamless swimming* is used to convey this all-important concept. The drill is initially performed without breathing; breathing is added once ideal timing/flow is achieved.

> **Note:** *The most common pause points in butterfly occur as the hands enter the water and as the hands exit the water.*

24. MDPS Drill

> **Note:** *MDPS is defined as maximum distance per stroke.*

Purpose: To improve butterfly stroke efficiency.

Instructions: Swimmers perform a 25 butterfly with best-form technique at the fastest speed possible while counting strokes. The drill is repeated until the lowest possible stroke count is achieved. For consistency's sake the first stroke is initiated as the head passes beneath the backstroke flags. A diving brick or hockey puck is used to mark the five-yard/meter mark at the bottom of the pool. Beginning the stroke count at this point creates a consistent twenty-yard/meter course for measurement purposes. For accuracy's sake the fastest speed possible is maintained over each repeat. Upon completion, the total number of strokes performed is divided into twenty yards/meters to determine swimmers' MDPS scores.

> **Note:** *To calculate the MDPS score the total number of strokes is divided into twenty yards/meters. For example if a swimmer performed twelve strokes in twenty yards/meters, the MDPS score would be 1.66 yards/meters per stroke.*

25. Stroke-Rate Drill

> **Note:** *Stroke rate is defined as the number of stroke cycles performed in one minute. In the 100 butterfly, elite-level female and male swimmers execute fifty-two or more stroke cycles per minute.*

Purpose: To enhance butterfly timing/flow.

Instructions: Swimmers perform a series of 25s butterfly with best-form technique at the fastest speed possible. Stroke rates are measured using a stopwatch with a stroke-rate function and compared to those of elite-level swimmers. Having a tangible number to strive for can dramatically increase a swimmer's stroke rate. Once an elite-level stroke rate is achieved, swimmers are challenged to maintain it over ever-increasing distances.

Note: *A Finis Tempo Trainer may also be used to increase stroke rate.*

Backstroke Drills

1. Plank on Wall Drill

Note: *The plank position, including the head position, torso, and kick, form the foundation of backstroke in a holistic approach.*

Purpose: To teach backstroke plank position.

Instructions: Swimmers lie in a face-up floating position with the feet in the gutter, the head set in a neutral position, and the eyes facing directly upward. The upper body is fixed in a plank-like position with the arms squeezed against the sides of the body, the legs together, and the toes pointed.

Note: *To understand the plank position further, picture swimmers lying at attention in the water.*

2. Plank Kick With Rotation Drill

Purpose: To introduce rotation to the backstroke plank position.

Instructions: Swimmers perform backstroke kick in the same plank position achieved on the wall only the entire body (minus the head) rotates forty-five degrees to both sides. Rotation must be smooth, symmetrical, and continuous. In a holistic approach, the term *connect the dots* is used to convey this all-important concept, where swimmers imagine having brightly colored dots painted on the shoulders, hips, and ankles. The dots must remain in line and connected as the body rotates from side to side.

3. Cup-Head Drill

Purpose: To enhance backstroke plank position.

Instructions: The drill is performed with a plastic cup, similar to drill two only swimmers perform backstroke kick with a half-filled cup of water on the forehead. Once this is mastered, swimmers perform full-stroke backstroke with a half-filled cup of water on the forehead. Kicking and swimming with a cup on the forehead usually takes a few attempts before being mastered.

4.   1-A Plank-Kick Drill

Purpose: To integrate the various components of backstroke.

Instructions: Swimmers perform backstroke kick in the same plank position achieved on the wall only with one arm extended behind the shoulder. The drill introduces five all-important backstroke concepts. The first is cup head, where swimmers imagine traveling down the pool with a half-filled cup of water on the forehead. The second is plank body, where swimmers attempt to make the upper body feel like a wooden plank. The third is kick in the box, where swimmers maintain a tight, symmetrical, continuous kick inside an imaginary box. The width of the box is equal to the width of the body and the depth of the box is equal to the depth of the body. The fourth is shoulder-width entry, where the extended arm is positioned directly behind and in line with the shoulder, similar to the backstroke entry position. The fifth is pinkie-first entry, where the hand of the entry arm maintains a pinkie-down/thumb-up position.

5.   Butt Squeeze Kick Drill

Purpose: To enhance and condition the backstroke kick cycle.

Instructions: Swimmers perform backstroke kick with the butt squeezed as tightly as possible in plank position. Squeezing the butt firmly prevents the knees from bending, encouraging uniformity and whole-leg involvement. In a holistic approach, the term *butt squeeze kick* is used to convey this all-important concept.

Note: *Swimming backstroke with the butt squeezed is also performed from time to time, encouraging uniformity and whole-leg involvement. The butt is relaxed once both are achieved.*

6. Butt Squeeze/No Butt Squeeze Kick Drill

Purpose: To enhance the backstroke kick cycle.

Instructions: Similar to drill five only swimmers squeeze the butt on the first half of each 25 and relax it on the second half. The drill derives the best of drill five while adding greater propulsion through increased knee bend. The amount of knee bend added must not exceed the swimmer's body width and depth. In a holistic approach, the term *kick in the box* is used to convey this all-important concept.

7. Streamline Kick Drill

Purpose: To enhance and condition the backstroke kick cycle.

Instructions: Swimmers perform backstroke kick with the arms held in streamline while maintaining a tight, symmetrical, continuous kick. The feet must boil the surface at the completion of each upbeat phase of the kick cycle. To achieve the ideal streamline position, the arms extend fully, the hands are placed one on top of the other with the fingers together and pointed, and the thumb of the bottom hand wraps around the palm of the top hand.

8. Side Kick Drill

Purpose: To enhance and condition the backstroke kick cycle.

Instructions: Swimmers perform backstroke kick on the side with one arm fully extended forward of the shoulder. The palm of the extended arm faces downward with the other arm squeezed against the side of the body. The face remains in the water with the bottom ear pressed against the extended arm. The top shoulder, hip, and foot must be positioned directly above the bottom shoulder, hip, and foot. A horizontal body position together with a tight, symmetrical, continuous kick must be maintained throughout. Breathing is to the side, similar to freestyle, and kept to a minimum.

9.   Twelve O'Clock Drill

Purpose: To enhance and condition the backstroke kick cycle.

Instructions: Swimmers perform backstroke kick holding the right arm out of the water directly above the right shoulder (at twelve o'clock) to mimic the midway point of the arm recovery. The left arm is squeezed against the side of the body. For an additional challenge the right shoulder is raised out of the water. From here the drill is repeated holding the left arm out of the water.

10.   Vertical Kick Drill

Purpose: To enhance and condition the backstroke kick cycle.

Instructions: Swimmers begin by treading water, transitioning to vertical backstroke kick with the hands above the surface. Proper posture must be maintained at all times, with the head held in a neutral position and the hips in line with the shoulders. Ideally the shoulders should remain out of the water for the duration of the drill, with a knee bend no greater than three to five out of ten.

> **Note:** *Swimmers may imagine having dials attached to the outsides of the knees. A locked out position equals zero on the dial while a fully flexed position equals ten. A knee bend between three and five is considered ideal, producing maximum propulsion and minimal drag.*

11.   Mirror Drill

Purpose: To enhance the backstroke arm cycle.

Instructions: Swimmers stand tall and perform the backstroke arm cycle in front of a mirror, beginning slowly at first before building to the fastest speed possible. The drill may be performed with or without body rotation. The head remains in a neutral position with the arms opposite each other throughout. The holistic coach stands nearby to offer corrective feedback.

Note: *Swimmers able to perform the correct backstroke arm cycle on land have a much better chance of performing it correctly in the water.*

12. 1-A BK Drill

Purpose: To integrate the various components of backstroke.

Instructions: Similar to drill two only with the addition of one-arm backstroke. Swimmers rotate the entire body via the hips toward the right arm as it enters the water and away from the right arm as it exits the water. Ideally the entire body (minus the head) should rotate forty-five degrees in both directions. The left arm remains squeezed against the side of the body. A tight, symmetrical, continuous kick must be maintained at all times. From here the drill is repeated using the left arm.

Note: *The drill allows swimmers to focus on the body position, kick cycle, and arm cycle at once.*

13. Double-Arm BK Drill

Purpose: To promote a symmetrical backstroke arm cycle.

Instructions: Swimmers perform backstroke pull simultaneously with both arms, comparing the right to the left. Ideally the entry point, catch point, and finish point should match on both sides. The drill is performed with backstroke kick.

14. 1-10 Drill

Purpose: To enhance the entry phase of the backstroke arm cycle.

Instructions: Swimmers perform a total of ten strokes of backstroke, beginning with the right arm. Strokes one and two enter inside the shoulders; strokes three and four enter in line with the shoulders; strokes five and six enter slightly outside the shoulders; strokes seven and eight enter slightly wider than strokes five and six; and strokes nine and ten enter slightly wider than strokes seven and eight. Each set of entry numbers must match. In other words, strokes one and two must be the same distance inside the shoulders, strokes three and four must be directly behind and in line with the shoulders, and so on. Once this is complete, the holistic coach informs swimmers as to what pair of numbers resulted in a shoulder-width entry considered the ideal entry position in backstroke. Typically swimmers are surprised to learn that the numbers they chose differ from those chosen by the coach.

15. Head Back Drill

Purpose: To enhance the entry phase of the backstroke arm cycle.
Instructions: Swimmers perform backstroke with the head tilted backward and submerged beneath the surface. Placing the head in this position provides an unequalled opportunity to observe the hand and arm entry into the water. Adjustments are made should either hand enter other than pinkie first or inside or outside shoulder width.

16. Face Sideways Drill

Purpose: To enhance the catch phase of the backstroke arm cycle.
Instructions: Swimmers perform one-arm backstroke with the right arm rotating the entire body (including the head) toward the right side as the arm enters the water and away from the right side as the arm exits the water. The entire body rotates ninety degrees to the entry-arm side. At the point of entry, the face is totally submerged so the pulling arm can be observed from the point of entry to the point of finish. The pulling action is performed in slow motion to provide ample time for observation. At the point of finish, the body rotates onto the back and a breath is taken. The drill is repeated on the opposite side.

Note: *The pull must not be initiated until the entire body is rotated ninety degrees with the face turned to the side and fully submerged.*

17. Recovery Drill

Purpose: To enhance the recovery phase of the backstroke arm cycle.

Instructions: Swimmers stand tall with the right side of the body turned sideways to the wall. The feet are placed no more than three inches away from the wall with the arms at the sides of the body. From here the right palm is placed against the wall with the fingers together and the right elbow locked out. From here the right palm slides up the wall, mimicking the recovery phase of the backstroke arm cycle. The arm stops upon arriving above the right shoulder. From here the palm slides back to the starting position. The drill is repeated five times with the right arm followed by five times with the left.

Note: *Even though the recovery arm exits the water palm facing inward, teaching the drill in the manner described above works best. The holistic coach may choose to instruct swimmers to rotate the palm from an inward position to an outward position as the arm recovers up the wall.*

18. 1-A BK With Eyes Closed Drill

Purpose: To promote backstroke symmetry.

Instructions: Swimmers perform ten strokes of one-arm backstroke with the eyes closed. If swum straight the drill is repeated using the opposite arm. If swum crooked technical adjustments are made and the drill repeated. Aluminum foil is used to cover the insides of the goggles for those swimmers who have a tendency to peek.

Note: *The causes for swimming crooked vary, including throwing the head to one or both sides, over-rotation to one or both sides, over-entry to one or both sides, over-pulling with one or both arms, a straight arm pull, or a weak/uneven kick.*

Warning: *The drill must be performed with only one swimmer at a time (under strict coaching direction and supervision) in a lane bordered on both sides by lane lines. To prevent serious injury, the drill must never be performed in the lane closest to the wall. In addition the number of one-arm strokes performed must be limited to ten or fewer depending on the size and proficiency level of the swimmer. Limiting the number of strokes is intended to ensure swimmers complete the drill safely and well before reaching the other end of the pool. As an extra precaution, the coach individualizes the number of strokes before implementation. For example novice-level swimmers may be assigned ten strokes based on size and proficiency level while senior-level swimmers may be assigned seven. As an additional safety pre-caution, a second coach or swimmer is positioned in the water at the other end of the pool to prevent the swimmer from hitting the wall due to a miscalculation or a misunderstanding.*

19.   1-A BK With Pull Buoy Drill

Purpose: To enhance and condition backstroke rotation.
Instructions: The drill is performed with a pull buoy. Swimmers perform one-arm backstroke with the right arm and a size-proportionate pull buoy tucked inside the left armpit. From here the body rotates downward via the hips as the right arm enters the water and upward via the hips as the right arm exits the water. Rotation must be equal in both directions. This is no easy feat as

the pull buoy resists being submerged, requiring a greater effort from the core and kick. From here the drill is repeated with the left arm.

Note: *The head must remain motionless, maintaining a neutral position at all times.*

20. Teacup Drill

Purpose: To enhance and condition backstroke rotation.
Instructions: Swimmers perform one-arm backstroke with the right arm while placing the left hand on the left hip. The left arm is bent with the left elbow pointing directly out to the side, resembling the handle of a teacup. From here the handle rotates upward via the hips as the right arm enters the water and downward via the hips as the right arm exits the water. Ideally the handle should rotate forty-five degrees in both directions. This is no easy feat; it requires a greater effort from the core and kick. From here the drill is repeated using the left arm.

21. MDPS Drill

Note: *MDPS is defined as maximum distance per stroke.*

Purpose: To improve backstroke stroke efficiency.
Instructions: Swimmers perform a 25 backstroke with best-form technique at the fastest speed possible while counting strokes. The drill is repeated until the lowest possible stroke count is achieved. For consistency's sake the first stroke is initiated as the head passes beneath the backstroke flags. Beginning the stroke count at this point creates a consistent twenty-yard/meter course for measurement purposes. For accuracy's sake the fastest speed possible is maintained over each repeat. Upon completion the total number of strokes performed is divided into twenty yards/meters to determine swimmer's MDPS score.

Note: *To calculate the MDPS score, the total number of strokes is divided into twenty yards/meters. For example if swimmers performed sixteen strokes in twenty yards/meters, the MDPS score would be 1.25 yards/meters per stroke.*

22. Windmill Drill

Purpose: To enhance backstroke timing/flow.

Instructions: Swimmers stand at attention with the feet slightly wider than shoulder width. The right arm extends above the shoulder as if entering the water. The left arm is placed at the side of the body as if exiting the water. From here a series of backstroke arm cycles are performed, slowly at first and building to the fastest speed possible. The arms remain straight throughout. The arms must remain opposite each other at all times. As the right arm travels down the body, the left arm travels up the body. The head remains in a neutral position throughout.

23. Windmill Transition Drill

Purpose: To enhance backstroke timing/flow.

Instructions: Swimmers perform ten fast backstroke windmills on deck near the edge of the pool. From here a 25 backstroke is performed with the goal of maintaining the same windmill speed achieved on deck. The head remains in a neutral position throughout.

24. Stroke Rate Drill

Purpose: To enhance backstroke timing/flow.

Note: *Stroke rate is defined as the number of stroke cycles performed in one minute. In the 100 BK an elite-level female swimmer performs fifty or more stroke cycles per minute while an elite-level male swimmer* *performs forty-eight or more stroke cycles per minute.*

Instructions: Swimmers perform a series of 25s backstroke with best-form technique at the fastest speed possible. Stroke rates are measured using a stopwatch with a stroke-rate function and compared to those of elite-level swimmers. Having a tangible number to strive for can dramatically increase stroke rate. Once an elite-level stroke rate is achieved, swimmers are challenged to maintain it over ever-increasing distances.

> **Note:** *A Finis Tempo Trainer may also be used to increase stroke rate.*

25. Over Kick Drill
Purpose: To enhance backstroke flow.
Instructions: Swimmers perform a 25 backstroke with a super-fast kick and super-slow arms. This usually requires a few attempts before being mastered. From here the process is repeated beginning with a super-fast kick and super slow arms transitioning to a super-fast kick with super-fast arms.

Breaststroke Drills
1. 7-Squeeze Drill

> **Note:** *The 7-squeeze position forms the foundation of breaststroke in a holistic approach.*

Purpose: To teach breaststroke body position.
Instructions: The drill is performed with a kickboard. Swimmers lie facedown in a floating position with the arms fully extended, the palms placed at the bottom of the kickboard, and the feet in the gutter. From here swimmers achieve a streamlined and

horizontal body position by squeezing seven different parts of the body together in sequential order beginning with the thumbs, arms, head, shoulders, butt, legs, and feet. Back arch must be kept to a minimum throughout the drill.

> **Note:** *In breaststroke streamline, one thumb squeezes against the other versus placing one hand on top of the other.*

2. 7-Squeeze With Three, Two, One-Second Glide Drill

Purpose: To enhance breaststroke body position.

Instructions: Swimmers perform a 75 breaststroke. On the first 25, a 7-squeeze body position is held for a three-second glide, followed by a two-second glide on the second 25 and a one-second glide on the third 25.

3. 7-Squeeze With Zero-Second Glide Drill

Purpose: To enhance breaststroke body position.

Instructions: Similar to drill two only swimmers move continuously from stroke to stroke with a zero-second glide between strokes. While no glide is held, a 7-squeeze position must be achieved at the end of each stroke cycle.

4. Two-Second Glide Head Up/Two-Second Glide Head Down Drill

Purpose: To enhance breaststroke body position.

Instructions: Swimmers perform the first half of a 25 with the head up and the face facing directly forward. A streamline body position (minus the head) is held for a two-second glide. Upon reaching the halfway point, swimmers switch to full-stroke breaststroke with a seven-squeeze body position held for a two-second glide.

> **Note:** *The drill helps to flatten out swimmers who have*

developed unwanted undulation. As mentioned previously, some swimmers are ideally suited to swimming undulating breaststroke while others are not.

5.   Kick With Board Drill

Purpose: To enhance and condition the breaststroke kick cycle.
Instructions: The drill is performed with a kickboard. Swimmers perform breaststroke kick with the arms fully extended, holding the sides of the kickboard at the midway point or laying the palms on the center of the kickboard. Holding the board in this manner lowers the hips, allowing a heel-led recovery versus a knee-led recovery. A heel-led recovery produces far less drag.

> **Note:** *The drill may also be performed with Speedo Breaststroke Fins.*

6.   Skinny, Fat, In Between Kick Drill

Purpose: To enhance and condition the breaststroke kick cycle.
Instructions: Swimmers perform breaststroke kick with the arms fully extended, holding the sides of the kickboard at the midway point or laying the palms on the center of the kickboard. On the first kick off the wall, a skinny breaststroke kick is performed; on the second, a fat breaststroke kick is performed; on the third, a kick in between the two is performed. Throughout the process swimmers are instructed to identify the kick that feels most propulsive. At the conclusion of the drill, swimmers perform a series of 25s using the kick identified as the most propulsive. Typically the in between kick is chosen.

7.   High Heel Drill

Purpose: To enhance and condition the breaststroke kick cycle.
Instructions: Swimmers perform breaststroke kick on the stomach with the chin resting on the surface and the fully extended arms positioned slightly off the sides of the body. From here the heels draw to the hands. Once contact is made, the propulsive

phase of the kick cycle begins. In a holistic approach, the term *high heel recovery* is used to convey this all-important concept.

> **Note:** *The drill can be performed in two distinct ways. In one the chin rests on the surface. Swimmers performing the drill in this manner must ensure the entire body rises to just below surface level at the conclusion of each kick cycle. Performing the drill in this manner produces a horizontal body position. In the other the head drives downward at the conclusion of each kick cycle to encourage an undulating body action. The head is raised for a breath as the heels draw to the hands. The drill is ideally suited to undulating breaststrokers.*

8.   Kick on Back Drill

Purpose: To enhance and condition the breaststroke kick cycle.
Instructions: Swimmers perform breaststroke kick on the back in a streamline position. Throughout each kick cycle, the quadriceps remain parallel to the surface while the knees remain below the surface. At the completion of each kick cycle, the feet point and hold for a one-second glide to achieve a streamlined horizontal position.

> **Note:** *Another version of the drill involves lying in a horizontal position with the head held in a neutral position. Swimmers grasp the end of a kickboard with both hands, placing it over the knees with the arms fully extended. Placing the kickboard in this position alerts swimmers should the knees break the surface.*

9.   Vertical Kick Drill

Purpose: To enhance and condition the breaststroke kick cycle.
Instructions: Swimmers begin by treading water, transitioning to vertical breaststroke kick with the hands raised above the surface. The quadriceps must remain perpendicular to the surface as the

heels rise toward the butt. Proper posture must be maintained at all times with the head held in a neutral position and the hips in line with the shoulders. Ideally the shoulders should remain out of the water for the duration of the kicking bout.

> **Note:** *For an extra challenge the drill is performed inches away from the wall, ensuring a heel-led recovery. This is a very challenging option reserved for more accomplished junior- and senior-level swimmers.*

10. Eggbeater Drill

Purpose: To enhance and condition the breaststroke kick cycle.

Instructions: Similar to drill nine only the kick is performed by alternating one leg at a time. The feet turn out as in regular breaststroke kick. The eggbeater leg action is similar to peddling a bicycle with the feet turned out.

> **Note:** *Another version of the drill is to perform egg-beater in four different ways over 100 yards/meters. On the first 25 swimmers face forward; on the second swimmers face to the right; on the third swimmers face backward; and on the fourth swimmers face to the left. The body remains as close to vertical at all times with the hands raised above the surface.*

11. Wall-Tracing Drill

Purpose: To enhance the breaststroke arm cycle.

Instructions: Swimmers stand in front of a white sheet of paper attached to a wall with a felt-tipped marker in each hand. From here the arms extend overhead in a breaststroke streamline position with the marker tips placed on the paper. From here swimmers attempt to trace the ideal breaststroke arm cycle as the holistic coach stands nearby to offer corrective feedback. Once mastered the process is repeated only with the eyes closed and using different colored markers. Upon completion the eyes-closed version is compared to the eyes-open version. Ideally both should match.

12. Upside-Down Breaststroke Drill

Purpose: To enhance the breaststroke arm cycle.

Instructions: Swimmers perform full-stroke breaststroke underwater upside-down or on the back. Swimming in this manner provides swimmers with a totally different perspective, allowing them to observe the entire breaststroke arm cycle. Corrective changes are made where needed. The drill is ideal for speeding up the hands as they transition from the scull phase to the recovery phase.

> **Note:** *The drill is well suited to swimmers who pull too far past the shoulders or who pause the hands during the breathing phase.*

13. Pull on Wall Drill

Purpose: To enhance the breaststroke arm cycle.

Instructions: The drill is performed with a kickboard. The feet are placed in the gutter with the legs together and the knees locked out. Both arms are fully extended in front of the shoulders. The palm of one hand is positioned on the kickboard and the other arm is positioned just beneath the kickboard. From here five slow-motion arm cycles are performed with the right arm, followed by five slow-motion arm cycles with the left arm.

> **Note:** *The benefit of the drill is that it provides swimmers with an unequalled opportunity to observe the arm cycle in action and make corrections where needed. It also provides the holistic coach with an opportunity to offer ongoing feedback.*

14. Pull X With Noodle Drill

Purpose: To enhance the breaststroke arm cycle.

Instructions: The drill is performed with a foam noodle.

Swimmers perform the breaststroke arm cycle with a noodle tucked beneath the armpits and the arms remaining in front of the noodle throughout. At no time should the noodle bend or be push backward. The elbows point upward as the arms progress from the sweep phase to the scull phase, as opposed to sliding backward (a common problem in breaststroke). In a holistic approach, the term *elbow popper, not dropper*, is used to convey this all-important concept.

Note: *The drill may also be performed over a lane line with the lane line serving as the noodle.*

15. Pull Drill

Purpose: To enhance and condition the breaststroke arm cycle.
Instructions: The drill is performed with a pull buoy. Swimmers perform the breaststroke arm cycle on a one-second glide with a size-proportionate pull buoy placed between the upper legs. For an additional challenge, an ankle strap may be substituted for the pull buoy. The drill is intended to isolate the arms. Therefore dolphin kick is not permitted. Size-proportionate paddles are optional for junior- and senior-level swimmers. The drill is best performed with a Finis snorkel.

Note: *Another version of the drill involves swimmers performing the breaststroke arm cycle with one dolphin kick per arm cycle. The kick must be executed during the shoot phase. Contrary to popular practice, only one dolphin kick per one arm cycle is permitted, as only one kick per stroke is permitted in full-stroke breaststroke.*

16. Rapid-Fire Drill

Purpose: To enhance and condition the breaststroke arm cycle.
Instructions: Swimmers perform the breaststroke arm cycle in a head-up position on a zero-second glide with the hardest and fastest freestyle kick possible. The kick must remain hard and fast

to encourage a rapid arm cycle, especially as the arms transition from the scull phase to the shoot phase.

> **Note:** *Another version of the drill involves swimmers performing a 25. On the first half the rapid-fire drill is performed. From here swimmers seamlessly transition to full-stroke breaststroke on a zero-second glide. Ideally the same rapid-fire arm action is transferred from the drill to full stroke.*

17. Windshield Wiper Drill

Purpose: To enhance and condition the breaststroke arm cycle.
Instructions: The drill is performed with a pull buoy. Swimmers lie in a facedown floating position with the arms held in a cross position (out from the shoulders) and a size-proportionate pull buoy placed between the upper legs. From here a series of inward and outward sculling actions are performed. During the inward scull, the palms are set at an inward angle of forty-five degrees; during the outward scull, the palms are set at an outward angle of forty-five degrees. The elbows point directly upward throughout the entire sculling process. Three or more sculling actions are performed before a breath is taken. Size-proportionate paddles are added for an additional challenge. The drill is best performed with a Finis snorkel.

18. Shoot Drill

Purpose: To enhance and condition the shoot phase of the breaststroke arm cycle.
Instructions: Swimmers perform a 25 breaststroke pull in a head-up position with one dolphin kick per stroke followed by a 25 breaststroke. Rather than shooting the arms directly forward on the 25 pull, the arms shoot upward and out of the water on a forty-five-degree angle. At the completion of the upward shoot, the arms return to the water in a streamlined position. From here a 25 breaststroke is performed with the goal of transferring the

shooting energy from the drill into full-stroke breaststroke. The arms shoot forward in a straight line just beneath the surface or on the surface when performing full stroke breaststroke.

Note: *The drill is extremely challenging and should only be performed by more accomplished junior- and senior-level swimmers.*

19. Periscope Drill

Purpose: To enhance the shoot phase of the breaststroke arm cycle.

Instructions: Swimmers perform a 25 breaststroke in a head-up position on a one-second glide with the thumbs sticking out of the water throughout the entire shoot phase (similar to a submarine periscope). Sticking the thumbs up in this manner ensures the hands travel forward just beneath the surface as opposed to downward. From here swimmers perform a second 25 breaststroke with the first half in a thumbs-up position and the second half in a thumbs-down position.

Note: *The drill is ideal for swimmers who tend to dive too deeply during the shoot phase.*

20. Lift and Lunge Drill

Purpose: To teach the forward lunge action in breaststroke.

Note: *The term lunge is defined as a sudden forward thrust.*

Instructions: Swimmers perform the breaststroke arm cycle in a head position on a zero-second glide with freestyle kick. As the arms transition from the sweep phase to the scull phase, the shoulders lift (shrug) upward and lunge forward as one unit and in unison with the arms. The lunging action must be performed quickly to achieve the desired result. In a holistic approach, the term *lift and lunge* is used to convey the idea that the breathing cycle and arm cycle must combine to create one explosive action.

> **Note:** *Lunging works best with an undulating style of breaststroke versus a conventional style. In addition the hands must shoot directly forward throughout the lunge as opposed to upward out of the water or downward toward the bottom of the pool.*

21. Tennis-Ball Breathing Drill

Purpose: To enhance the breaststroke breathing cycle.

Instructions: Swimmers perform breaststroke with a tennis ball tucked beneath the chin. Provided the breaststroke arm cycle is performed correctly, the head and shoulders rise naturally, making it unnecessary for the head to move independently. In addition holding the tennis ball in this manner positions the head and upper body in an ideal position, with the eyes facing more downward than forward and the upper body angled more forward.

> **Note:** *In a holistic approach, the term natural breathing spot is used to convey the idea that the upper body rises naturally and at the correct time if the breaststroke pull is performed correctly.*

22. Underwater Breaststroke Transition Drill

Purpose: To enhance breaststroke timing/flow.

Instructions: Swimmers perform a 25 breaststroke with the first three strokes underwater on a zero-second glide. From here swimmers transition seamlessly to full-stroke breaststroke above water on a zero-second glide. Swimming underwater eliminates the breaststroke breathing cycle, allowing for an uninterrupted flow of the arms from the inward scull phase to the shoot phase.

Note: *The drill helps to eliminate the pausing of the hands that is common during the breathing cycle.*

23. Head to Heel Drill

Purpose: To enhance breaststroke timing/flow.

Instructions: Swimmers perform breaststroke over six 25s with the first 25 swum at speed 1 and the sixth 25 swum at speed 6. On each 25 the time lag between the head rise (during the breaststroke breathing cycle) and the heel rise (during the breaststroke kick cycle) is noted. Ideally the time lag between the two should narrow with each 25.

24. MDPS Drill

Note: *MDPS is defined as maximum distance per stroke.*

Purpose: To improve maximum distance per stroke in breaststroke.

Instructions: Swimmers perform a 25 breaststroke with best-form technique at the fastest speed possible while counting strokes. The drill is repeated until the lowest possible stroke count is achieved. For consistency's sake the first stroke is initiated as the head passes underneath the backstroke flags. A diving brick or hockey puck is used to mark the five-yard/meter mark at the bottom of the pool. Beginning the stroke count here creates a consistent twenty-yard/meter course for measurement purposes. For accuracy's sake the fastest speed possible is maintained on each repeat. Upon completion the total number of strokes performed is divided into twenty yards/meters to determine the swimmer's MDPS score.

Note: *To calculate the MDPS score, the total number of strokes is divided into twenty yards/meters. For example if a swimmer performed twelve strokes in twenty yards/*

meters, the MDPS score would be 1.7 yards/meters per stroke.

25. Stroke-Rate Drill

Note: *Stroke rate is defined as the number of stroke cycles performed in one minute.*

In the 100 BR an elite-level female swimmer performs forty-eight or more stroke cycles per minute while an elite-level male swimmer performs fifty-two or more stroke cycles per minute.
Purpose: To enhance breaststroke timing/flow.
Instructions: Swimmers perform a series of 25s breaststroke with best-form technique at the fastest speed possible. Stroke rates are measured using a stopwatch with a stroke-rate function and compared to those of elite-level swimmers. Having a tangible number to strive for can dramatically increase a swimmer's stroke rate. Once an elite-level stroke rate is achieved, swimmers are challenged to maintain it over ever-increasing distances.

Note: *A Finis Tempo Trainer may also be used to increase stroke rate.*

Freestyle Drills
1. Plank on Wall Drill

Note: *The plank position, including the head position, torso, and kick, forms the foundation of freestyle.*

Purpose: To teach freestyle plank position.
Instructions: Swimmers lie in a facedown floating position with the feet in the gutter, the head set in a neutral position, and the eyes facing directly downward. The upper body is fixed in a plank-like position with the arms squeezed against the sides of

the body, the legs together, and the toes pointed.

Note: *To further understand the plank position, picture swimmers lying at attention in the water.*

2. Plank Kick With Rotation Drill

Purpose: To introduce rotation to the freestyle plank position.
Instructions: Swimmers perform freestyle kick in the same plank position achieved on the wall only the entire body (minus the head) rotates forty-five degrees to both sides. Rotation must be smooth, symmetrical, and continuous. In a holistic approach, the term *connect the dots* is used to convey this all-important concept where swimmers imagine having brightly colored dots painted on the shoulders, hips, and ankles. The dots must remain in line and connected as the body rotates from side to side. The drill is best performed with a Finis snorkel.

3. 1-A Plank Kick Drill

Purpose: To integrate the various components of freestyle.
Instructions: Swimmers perform freestyle kick in the same plank position achieved on the wall only with one arm extended in front of the shoulder. The drill introduces four all-important freestyle concepts. The first is *nose number*, where swimmers choose a number between zero and three. A zero-nose number creates a neutral head position with the eyes facing directly downward while a three-nose number creates a head position allowing swimmers to see approximately one stroke length down the pool. The number chosen is based on individual preference. The second is *plank body*, where swimmers attempt to make the upper body feel like a wooden plank. The third is *kick in the box*, where swimmers maintain a tight, symmetrical, continuous kick inside an imaginary box. The width of the box is equal to the

width of the body and the depth of the box is equal to the depth of the body. The fourth is *shoulder-width entry*, where the extended arm is positioned directly in front and in line with the shoulder, similar to the freestyle entry position. The drill is best performed with a Finis snorkel.

4. Butt Squeeze Kick Drill

Purpose: To enhance the freestyle kick cycle.

Instructions: Swimmers perform freestyle kick with the butt squeezed as tightly as possible in plank position. Breathing is to the front, similar to butterfly. Squeezing the butt prevents the knees from bending, encouraging uniformity and whole-leg involvement. In a holistic approach, the term *butt squeeze kick* is used to convey this all-important concept. The drill is best performed with a Finis snorkel.

> **Note:** *Full-stroke freestyle may also be performed using a butt squeeze kick.*

5. Butt Squeeze/No Butt Squeeze Kick Drill

Purpose: To enhance the freestyle kick cycle.

Instructions: Similar to drill four only swimmers squeeze the butt on the first half of each 25 and relax it on the second half. The drill derives the best of drill four while adding greater propulsion through increased knee bend. The amount of knee bend added must not exceed the swimmer's body width and depth. In a holistic approach, the term *kick in the box* is used to convey this all-important concept.

> **Note:** *Swimmers must maintain a continuous kick when breathing.*

6. Streamline Kick Drill

Purpose: To enhance and condition the freestyle kick cycle.

Instructions: Swimmers perform freestyle kick with the arms held in streamline while maintaining a tight, symmetrical, continuous kick. The feet must boil the surface at the completion of each upbeat phase of the kick cycle. To achieve the ideal streamline position, the arms extend fully, the hands are placed one on top of the other with the fingers together and pointed, and the thumb of the top hand wraps around the palm of the bottom hand. Breathing is to the front, similar to butterfly, and kept to a minimum. The drill is best performed with a Finis snorkel.

7. Side Kick Drill

Purpose: To enhance and condition the freestyle kick cycle.

Instructions: Swimmers perform freestyle kick on the side with one arm extended forward of the shoulder. The palm of the extended arm faces downward with the other arm squeezed against the side of the body. The face remains in the water with the bottom ear pressed against the extended arm. The top shoulder, hip, and foot must be positioned directly above the bottom shoulder, hip, and foot. A horizontal body position together with a tight, symmetrical, continuous kick must be maintained throughout. Breathing is to the side, similar to freestyle.

8. Horizontal Kick Drill

Purpose: To enhance and condition the freestyle kick cycle.

Instructions: The drill is performed with a kickboard. Swimmers perform facedown in freestyle kick with the arms fully extended shoulder width apart and the palms positioned at the bottom of the kickboard. The feet remain in the water throughout the entire kicking cycle in order to boil the water, as opposed to splashing the water. Breathing is to the front, similar to butterfly, and kept to a minimum. The drill is best performed with a Finis snorkel.

Note: *Kicking in this manner is the standard method used in a holistic approach as it promotes a horizontal* *body position (considered ideal for freestyle). Kicking with the face out of the water with the hands grasping the top of the kickboard is reserved for power-kick sets only.*

9. Mirror Drill

Purpose: To enhance the freestyle arm cycle.

Instructions: Swimmers perform the freestyle arm cycle in front of a mirror in a forward-leaning position with the chest parallel to the ground. The drill may be performed with or without rotation. The freestyle arm cycle begins slowly at first and then builds to the fastest speed possible with the head remaining in a neutral position throughout. The holistic coach stands nearby to offer corrective feedback. Resistive bands may be used for an additional challenge.

> **Note:** *Swimmers able to perform the correct freestyle arm cycle on land have a much better chance of performing it correctly in the water.*

10. 1-A FR Drill

Purpose: To integrate the various components of freestyle.

Instructions: Similar to drill two only with the addition of one-arm freestyle. Swimmers rotate the entire body (minus the head) toward the right arm as it enters the water and away from the right arm as it exits the water. Ideally the entire body (minus the head) should rotate forty-five degrees to both sides. The left arm remains squeezed against the side of the body throughout. Breathing is to the stroking-arm side. A tight, symmetrical, continuous kick must be maintained at all times. From here the drill is repeated with the left arm. The drill is best performed with a Finis snorkel.

11. Tick Tock Drill

Purpose: To enhance and condition freestyle rotation.

Instructions: The drill is performed with a kickboard. Swimmers perform freestyle pull with a kickboard squeezed tightly between the upper legs. The bottom of the kickboard must be flush with the upper legs so as not to increase drag. As the right arm transitions from pull to push, the left side of the kickboard makes full contact with the surface, and as the left arm transitions from pull to push, the right side of the kickboard makes full contact with the surface. The tick tock action must be equal on both sides. The drill is best performed with a Finis snorkel.

12. 1-10 Drill

Purpose: To enhance the entry phase of the freestyle arm cycle.
Instructions: Swimmers perform a total of ten strokes freestyle beginning with the right arm. Strokes one and two enter inside the shoulders; strokes three and four enter in line with the shoulders; strokes five and six enter slightly outside the shoulders; strokes seven and eight enter slightly wider than strokes five and six; and strokes nine and ten enter slightly wider than strokes seven and eight. Each set of entry numbers must match. In other words strokes one and two must be the same distance inside the shoulders, strokes three and four must be directly in line with the shoulders, and so on. Once complete the holistic coach informs swimmers what pair of numbers resulted in a shoulder-width entry, considered the ideal entry position in freestyle. Typically swimmers are surprised to learn the numbers they choose differ from the ones chosen by the coach.

13. Floating Catch Drill

Purpose: To enhance the catch phase of the freestyle arm cycle.
Instructions: The drill is performed with a pull buoy and foam noodle. Swimmers lie facedown in the water with a size-proportionate pull buoy placed between the upper legs and grasping a noodle with both hands. The hands are placed shoulder width apart with the arms fully extended just beneath the surface.

From here the elbows slowly flex, replicating the catch phase of the freestyle arm cycle. Ideally a ninety-degree angle should form at the completion of the catch with the upper arms parallel to the surface and the forearms and hands perpendicular to the surface. In a holistic approach, the term *perpendicular paddle* is used to convey this all-important concept. The catch is held for three seconds. From here swimmers slowly return to the starting position and repeat. The drill is best performed with a Finis snorkel.

14. 1-A Scull With Pull Buoy Drill

Purpose: To enhance and condition the catch phase of the free-style arm cycle.

Instructions: The drill is performed with a pull buoy. Swimmers place a size-proportionate pull buoy between the upper legs with the right arm positioned in the ideal catch position and the left arm squeezed against the side of the body. From here a sculling action is performed with the right arm. When sculling, the hand and forearm achieve a position perpendicular to the surface and forward of the shoulder. In a holistic approach, the term *perpendicular paddle* is used to convey this all-important concept. Breathing is similar to freestyle and kept to a minimum. From here the drill is repeated with the left arm. The drill is best performed with a Finis snorkel.

> **Note:** *The drill is extremely challenging, as the catch arm is the only source of propulsion. If the elbow drops, swimmers will have difficulty moving forward. In a holistic approach, the term elbow popper, not dropper is used to convey this all-important concept.*

15. Finish Drill

Purpose: To enhance and condition the finish phase of the freestyle arm cycle.

Instructions: The drill is performed with a kickboard. Swimmers perform freestyle pull with a kickboard squeezed tightly between the upper legs. The bottom of the kickboard is positioned flush with the upper legs so as not to increase drag as the body rotates from side to side. As the arm extends backward past the hip to complete the finish, the palm of the hand holds against the side of the kickboard for a count of three seconds. From here the arm initiates the recovery phase. The drill is best performed with a Finis snorkel.

16. Zipper Drill

Purpose: To enhance the recovery phase of the freestyle arm cycle.

Instructions: Swimmers perform freestyle while pretending to have a zipper attached to both sides of the body, running from just below the hip to the armpit. As the arm initiates the recovery phase, the hand grasps the zipper and imitates a zipping action up the side of the body. Once that's complete the arm extends forward of the shoulder in preparation for the entry phase.

> **Note:** *Zipping the side promotes a high-elbow recovery, the most popular form of freestyle recovery.*

17. Three-Second Pause Catch-Up Drill

Purpose: To enhance and condition the freestyle arm cycle.

Instructions: Swimmers perform freestyle kick with the arms fully extended and shoulder width apart. The arms are positioned just beneath the surface with the fingertips facing the other end of the pool. From here a freestyle stroke is performed with the right arm, followed by a freestyle stroke with the left. A three-second pause at the point of entry is added to ensure proper execution. The hands remain shoulder width apart at the point of entry and do not touch at any point. Breathing is every stroke to the stroking-arm side. The drill is best performed with a Finis snorkel.

> **Note:** *The benefit of the drill is that it allows swimmers to focus on one arm at a time while maintaining a continuous kick.*

18. Three-Second Pause Double Catch-Up Drill
Purpose: To enhance the entry phase and finish phase of the freestyle arm cycle.
Instructions: Similar to drill seventeen only swimmers hold for a three-second pause at the point of finish and the point of entry Adding the pause at both points ensures the arm achieves a fully extended position.

19. Kickboard Breathing Drill
Purpose: To enhance the freestyle breathing cycle.
Instructions: Similar to drill three only swimmers hold a kickboard forward of the right shoulder while squeezing the left arm against the side of the body. Breathing is to the non-extended arm side, similar to freestyle. When the swimmer is breathing, the side of the head must remain parallel or near parallel to the surface with the tip of the bottom goggle in contact with the water at all times. In addition the kick must maintain a constant boil throughout the entire breathing cycle.

> **Note:** *If performed correctly the breathing action should be difficult to see from a head-on viewing position. In a holistic approach, the term invisible breathing is used to convey this all-important concept.*

20. No Kickboard Breathing Drill
Purpose: To enhance the freestyle breathing cycle.

Instructions: Similar to drill eighteen only performed without a kickboard. Swimmers must ensure the lead arm (the arm extended forward of the shoulder) remains fully extended and just beneath the surface throughout the entire breathing cycle.

Note: *Dropping the lead arm during the breathing cycle is one of most common stroke faults in freestyle.*

21. People Paddle Drill

Purpose: To integrate the various components of freestyle.

Instructions: Swimmers perform full-stroke freestyle only with an underwater recovery. The arm draws forward beneath the surface, similar to the recovery method used in dog paddle, as opposed to the recovery method used in full-stroke freestyle. The next pull is initiated once the arm achieves a fully extended position forward of the shoulder. The arm must be fully extended at the beginning and end of each pull. In a holistic approach, the term *straight bent straight bent* is used to convey this all-important concept. Breathing is bilateral. The drill contains all of the essential features found in regular freestyle with the exception of an over-water recovery and entry. The drill is best performed with a Finis snorkel.

Note: *The drill promotes a smooth, fully connected, and balanced stroke with arms, torso, and legs working in unison.*

22. Over-Kick Drill

Purpose: To enhance freestyle timing/flow.

Instructions: Swimmers perform a 25 freestyle with a super-fast kick and super-slow arms. This usually requires a few attempts before being mastered. From here the process is repeated beginning with a super-fast kick and super-slow arms transitioning to a super-fast kick with super-fast arms. The drill is best performed with a Finis snorkel.

23. MDPS Drill

> **Note:** *MDPS is defined as maximum distance per stroke.*

Purpose: To improve freestyle stroke efficiency.

Instructions: Swimmers perform a 25 freestyle with best-form technique at the fastest speed possible while counting strokes. The drill is repeated until the lowest possible stroke count is achieved. For consistency's sake the first stroke is initiated as the head passes underneath the backstroke flags. A diving brick or hockey puck is used to mark the five-yard/meter mark at the bottom of the pool. Beginning the stroke count here creates a consistent twenty-yard/meter course for measurement purposes. For accuracy's sake the fastest speed possible is maintained on each repeat. Upon completion the total number of strokes performed is divided into twenty yards/meters to determine the swimmer's MDPS score.

> **Note:** *To calculate the MDPS score, the total number of strokes is divided into twenty yards/meters. For example if a swimmer performed sixteen strokes in twenty yards/meters, the MDPS score would be 1.25 yards/meters per stroke.*

24. Head Up/Head Down Drill

Purpose: To enhance freestyle timing/flow.

Instructions: Swimmers perform a 25 freestyle as fast as possible with the first half swum in a head-up position and the second half swum in a head-down position. The head is held in a neutral position at all times and breathing is not permitted on the second half. The same stroke rate should be maintained in the head-down position as achieved in the head-up position.

Note: *The drill promotes stroke rate over stroke length.*

25. Stroke Rate Drill

Note: *Stroke rate is defined as the number of stroke cycles performed in one minute. In the 100 FR an elite-level female swimmer performs fifty-four or more stroke cycles per minute while an elite-level male swimmer performs fifty or more stroke cycles per minute.*

Purpose: To enhance freestyle timing/flow.

Instructions: Swimmers perform freestyle over a series of 25s with best-form technique at the fastest speed possible. Stroke rates are measured using a stopwatch with a stroke-rate function and compared to those of elite-level swimmers. Having a tangible number to strive for can dramatically increase a swimmer's stroke rate. Once an elite-level stroke rate is achieved, swimmers are challenged to maintain it over ever-increasing distances.

Note: *A Finis Tempo Trainer may also be used to increase stroke rate.*

Kick Sets

As mentioned previously, the kick makes an enormous contribution to each stroke. Although not perfect, the following three-step test can enlighten swimmers on how much the kick contributes to the overall speed of the stroke:

Step 1: Swimmers perform 4 x 25 pull of the same stroke at the fastest speed possible. A size-proportionate pull buoy is used, and adequate rest must be taken between repeats to ensure near-complete recovery. Once complete, the average 25 pull time is calculated.

Note: *Breaststroke pull is performed without butterfly kick or underwater pullout.*

Step 2:   Swimmers perform 4 x 25 full stroke of the same stroke performed in step one at the fastest speed possible. Adequate rest must be taken between repeats to ensure near-complete recovery. Once complete, the average 25 swim time is calculated.

Step 3:   Swimmers subtract the average pull time from the average swim time to determine the contribution made by the kick.

Note: *Ideally the test should be administered on all four strokes and performed frequently to measure the degree and rate of improvement. Accurate records must also be kept to track results from test to test. Given the fact that most swimmers are overly dependent on the arms for speed production, the need to generate additional speed through the legs is paramount. The only exception to the rule is breaststroke, where the kick typically makes a much greater contribution to overall speed, especially in the case of natural breaststrokers. The test also promotes the concept of whole-body swimming, an all-important concept within a holistic approach.*

A second meaningful test is to have swimmers perform a 75 kick of each stroke at the fastest speed possible with sufficient rest between tests. Once complete the 75-kick time is compared to swimmers' best 100-swim time. Ideally they should match or be very close. The closer the match the greater the contribution made by the legs.

Note: *Although this test is not scientifically proven it does encourage greater use of the legs.*

The purpose of kick sets in a holistic approach is threefold: 1) to perfect the technical aspects of each kick cycle, 2) to condition fully the muscles involved in each kick cycle, and 3) to maximize the kicking contribution within each stroke. A technically sound, powerful, and enduring kick is a key to fast swimming. While kick sets typically take longer to complete than other practice sets they are truly worth their weight in gold. Repeat distances range from 25 to 300 yards/meters. Training speeds range from speed 1 to speed 6. Typical kick sets last between five and fifteen minutes for novice-level swimmers, between ten and twenty minutes for junior-level swimmers, and between fifteen and twenty-five minutes for senior-level swimmers. Kick sets may be offered at any point within practice once warm up is complete and repeated more than once. As in all other types of practice sets, the total distance covered is dependent upon swimmers' ability to maintain best-form technique at the desired speed. Technical requirements are emphasized throughout all kick sets. Kick sets for all strokes may be performed using a combination of kicking drills. For more information regarding kicking drills, see Drill Sets in this chapter.

Sample Kick Sets for Butterfly
Novice Level
1. 2(4 x 25 FL K) > Dolphin Drill > 10" @ 25 > 30" Between Sets
2. 2(6 x 25 FL K) > Boom Butt Kick Drill > 10" @ 25 > 30" Between Sets
3. 2(8 x 25 FL K) > Half-Body Kick With Kickboard Drill (Odd 25s) > Whole-Body Kick With Kickboard (Even 25s) > 10" @ 25 > 60" Between Sets

Junior Level

1. 12 x 50 FL K > Whole-Body Kick on Stomach Drill(Odd 50s) > Whole-Body Kick on Back Drill (Even 50s) > 10" @ 50
2. 8 x 75 FL K > Whole-Body Kick With Kickboard Drill (1st 50) > Half-Body Kick With Kickboard Drill (3rd 25) > 15" @ 75
3. 6 x 100 FL K > Two-Way Kick Drill > 20" @ 100

Senior Level

1. 16 x 50 FL K > Streamline Kick on Back Drill > 10" @ 50
2. 8 x 100 FL K > Boom Butt Kick Drill > 15" @ 100
3. 5 x 200 FL K > Two-Way Kick Drill > 30" @ 200

Note: *Intervals or guaranteed amount of rest between repeats may be used in all kick sets. Ultimately the speed and total distance performed is dependent upon swimmers' ability to maintain best-form technique at the desired speed. Adjustments are made to a set should swimmers experience a serious decline in technique or speed.*

Pull Sets

With the exception of breaststroke, the pull is the primary source of propulsion in swimming. Typically swimmers can travel faster with butterfly pull versus butterfly kick, backstroke pull versus backstroke kick, and freestyle pull versus freestyle kick. Therefore the need to isolate and condition the pull from a technical and physical standpoint is absolutely essential.

The purpose of pull sets in a holistic approach is threefold: 1) to perfect the technical aspects of each arm cycle, 2) to condition fully the muscles involved in each arm cycle, and 3) to maximize the pulling contribution in each stroke. Repeat distances typically range from 25 to 300 yards/meters. Training speeds range from speed 1 to speed 6. Typical pull sets last between five and ten minutes for novice-level swimmers, between ten and fifteen minutes for junior-level swimmers, and between fifteen and twenty minutes for senior-level swimmers.

Pull sets may be offered at any point within practice once warm up is complete and repeated more than once. Repeat distances are shorter for novice- and junior-level swimmers to avoid overloading the shoulders. As in all other types of practice sets, the total distance covered is dependent upon swimmers' ability to maintain best-form technique at the desired speed. Technical requirements are heavily emphasized throughout all pull sets.

Paddles are not used at the novice level. Swimmers at the junior and senior levels earn the right to wear paddles based on the ability to maintain best-form technique at the desired speed. Swimmers who butcher their strokes through the use of paddles are not permitted to use them. Paddle size increases as swimmers become stronger and more proficient, beginning with half paddles and progressing to size-proportionate paddles over time. Paddle type, size, and usage vary between strokes. Size-proportionate pull buoys are also used at all levels, as oversized pull buoys distort swimmers' body positions, placing best-form technique in jeopardy.

> **Note:** *Pull sets for junior- and senior-level swimmers may also be performed with bands wrapped around the ankles. Pulling with a band challenges the arms and core a great deal more than pulling with a pull buoy.*

Sample Pull Sets for Freestyle
Novice Level

Pull sets at the novice level are restricted to 25s of all four strokes without paddles. The amount of rest between 25s should be sufficient enough to encourage quality execution. The purpose of pull sets at the novice level is to develop best-form technique in all four strokes while adding strength through a full range of motion. Initially pull sets are performed at speed 1 or speed 2.

Junior Level
1. 3(8 x 25 FR P) > Pull Buoy With Half-Paddles > 10" @ 25 > 30" Between Sets
2. 4(3 x 50 FR P) > Pull Buoy > 15" @ 50 > 30" Between Sets
3. 2(4 x 75 FR P) > Pull Buoy With Half Paddles > 20" @ 75 > 60" Between Sets

Senior Level
1. 24 x 25 FR P > Pull Buoy > 10" @ 25
2. 2(6 x 75 FR P) > Bands With Half Paddles > 15" @ 75 > 45" Between Sets
3. 2(4 x 125 FR P) > Pull Buoy With Full Paddles > 20" @ 125 > 60" Between Sets

Note: *Intervals or guaranteed amount of rest between repeats may be used in all pull sets. Ultimately the speed and total distance performed is dependent upon swimmers' ability to maintain best-form technique at the desired speed. Adjustments are made should swimmers experience a serious decline in technique or speed.*

Challenge Sets

While a typical practice consists of a variety of sets, challenge sets demand the most of swimmers. Repeat distances typically range between 25 and 300 yards/meters. This is due in part to the underlying philosophy of a holistic approach where swimmers are required to hold best-form stroke and turn technique at the desired speed. Repeat distances may be extended beyond 300 should swimmers require a greater challenge provided they meet the technical and speed requirements. At the novice level, repeat distances are limited to 25s, 50s, and 75s. These recommended distances may appear short to some, but limiting the distance dramatically improves technical quality and speed. Training speeds range from speed 1 to speed 6. Typical challenge sets last between five and fifteen minutes for novice-level swimmers, between ten and twenty minutes for junior-level swimmers, and between fifteen and twenty-five minutes for senior-level swimmers. Challenge sets may be offered at any point within practice once warm up is complete and repeated more than once. As in all other types of practice sets, the total distance covered is dependent upon swimmers' ability to maintain best-form stroke and turn technique at the desired speed. Technical requirements are heavily emphasized throughout all challenge sets.

In a holistic approach, swimmers never train to train but rather to prepare for competition. In other words the strokes, turns, and speeds used in training must reflect to one degree or another the strokes, turns, and speeds desired in competition. Challenge sets are standardized and repeated week to week with new sets introduced approximately every three weeks. While some swimmers find this monotonous at times, standardized sets have five major advantages: 1) providing the coach with an effective, consistent, and convenient way to evaluate weekly progress; 2) reducing the amount of explanation time required as swimmers become familiar with the sets through constant repetition; 3) improving set execution as swimmers become better skilled through constant repetition; 4) increasing confidence levels as swimmers are able to track improvements from set to set; and 5) acting as an early warning system for potential overtraining, undertraining, illness, fatigue, stress, or lack of motivation.

Note: *Freestyle is the workhorse of swimming, with swimmers training more of it than any other stroke.*

Breaststroke, on the other hand, is the least trained stroke, with swimmers training less of it than any other stroke (in most cases). Many coaches shy away from breaststroke for a variety of reasons, including the amount of potential stress breaststroke kick places on the knees and how it reduces daily training volumes due to the fact that it's the slowest of all strokes. But how can swimmers excel in breaststroke (or the IM) if they don't train it? In a holistic approach, opportunities to train and master breaststroke abound.

Sample Challenge Sets for Freestyle
Novice Level
1. 16 x 25 FR > Over-Kick Odd 25s > 10" @ 25
2. 10 x 50 FR > No Breathing 1ˢᵗ 2 Cycles off Turn > 15" @ 50
3. 2(4 x 75 FR) > Bilateral Breathing > 10" @ 75 > 45" Rest Between Sets

Junior Level
1. 16 x 50 FR > Head Up FR 1ˢᵗ 25 > 15" @ 50
2. 2(5 x 100 FR) > Breathe @ 5 Even 25s > 20" @ 100 > 1' Rest Between Sets
3. 8 x 150 FR > Breathe 3-5-7 Per 50 > 20" @ 150

Senior Level
1. 2(12 x 50 FR) > Over-Kick Odd 50s > 10" @ 50 > 1' Rest Between Sets
2. 3(5 x 100 FR) > Double Distance Underwater on Even Turns > 15" @ 100 > 1' Rest Between Sets
3. 10 x 200 FR > Head Up FR Odd 25s > Over Kick Even 25s > 30" @ 200

Note: *Intervals or a guaranteed amount of rest between repeats may be used in all challenge sets. Ultimately* *the speed and total distance swum is dependent upon swimmers' ability to maintain best-form stroke and turn technique at the desired speed. Adjustments are made to a set should swimmers experience a serious decline in technique or speed.*

Refocus Sets

Because the ability to focus is key to achieving peak performance in the pool, focused swimmers perform far better than those who are not focused. To improve focus ability, short sets of easy swimming, affirmations, visualization, or meditative breathing are offered at various times throughout practice. Average set length is five minutes or less.

Warm-Down Sets

Providing adequate time for warm-down at the end of practice is extremely challenging to say the least. Research indicates a warm-down lasting up to thirty minutes is required to return lactic acid to resting levels. Given the time restraints of practice, a warm-down such as this is out of the question. As a small compromise, a minimum of five minutes of speed 3 swimming and/or drills is offered at the end of practice for junior- and senior-level swimmers. Research indicates swimmers recover twice as fast when warm-down sets are performed at a medium, continuous pace using the strokes performed in the main set(s), including butterfly. Lactic acid leaves the muscles at a faster rate and metabolizes more quickly. Carbon dioxide is also removed from muscles more rapidly and replaced with oxygen. Swimmers who follow the recommended warm-down procedure perform better practice to practice. As expected, best-form technique is emphasized throughout all warm-down sets. In a holistic approach, sloppy technique is not permitted even during warm-down.

Note: *In a holistic approach, novice-level swimmers perform backstroke, breaststroke, and/or freestyle during warm-down sets depending on the strokes performed in the main set(s), excluding butterfly.*

CHAPTER 5

Dry Land Training

In a holistic approach, the dry side of the physical curriculum is just as important as the wet side. The purpose of the dry side, otherwise known as *Dry Land training*, is fourfold: 1) to facilitate the learning of new skills; 2) to develop superior start, stroke, and turn techniques through increased strength and flexibility; 3) to reduce the risk of swimming-related injuries; and 4) to enhance swimmers' self-images.

> **Note:** *Contrary to popular belief, strength training is not inappropriate or harmful to young swimmers provided the Dry Land program is scientifically sound and executed with safety in mind. This is well-documented and supported by positions from the American Academy of Pediatrics (APP), the American College of Sports Medicine (ACSM), the American Orthopedic Society for Sports Medicine (AOSSM), and the National Strength and Conditioning Association (NSCA).*

⸺ Food for Thought ⸺

When it comes to strength, swimmers fall into one of three categories: 1) those who are stronger than their size, 2) those who are weaker than their size, or 3) those who are somewhere in the middle. Swimmers who are superior in strength and possess essential mental and technical skills rule the pool!

Flexibility also plays a crucial role in swimming success and should not be overlooked. "Decrease your stiffness—increase your swiftness" is an expression I often use to convey its vital importance. To understand the role flexibility and full range of motion play in speed production, simply envision a cheetah in pursuit of its prey or a racehorse at full speed.

Dry land training sessions in a holistic approach are offered at either the beginning or end of practice. Session length is dependent upon time available. A typical session lasts ten to fifteen minutes for novice-level swimmers and fifteen to twenty-five minutes for junior- and senior-level swimmers, although longer sessions may be offered for junior- and senior-level swimmers, time permitting. As one might expect, the complexity and intensity of dry land training progresses from the novice to senior level. All sessions begin with a brief warm up and include dynamic stretching, jumping jacks, jogging in place, or jumping rope.

> **Note:** *If two practices are held in one day, a shortened session of Dry Land training is offered in the morning and a longer session is offered in the afternoon or evening.*

The holistic dry land training curriculum is divided into five sections: 1) strength self-tests, 2) flexibility self-tests, 3) shoulder maintenance exercises, 4) circuits for novice-, junior-, and senior-level swimmers, and 5) stroke-specific strength/flexibility exercises.

> **Note:** *Swimmers are far more likely to commit to a Dry Land training program if limitations in strength or flexibility are known beforehand. To identify potential limitations, the holistic coach conducts a series of strength and flexibility self-tests before initiating the program.*

STRENGTH SELF-TESTS

The following section contains a series of self-tests used to determine swimmers' overall strength in areas critical to peak performance in the pool. All strength self-tests are performed until failure.

Core

Core muscles are defined as the muscles that support the spine through a given range of motion, including the muscles of the stomach, back, and sides. Trained correctly they provide essential core stability and aid in swimming propulsion.

> **Note:** *The first five self-tests are progressive in nature. Once swimmers achieve Self-Test 1, they proceed to Self-Test 2 and so on.*

Self-Test 1
Swimmers lie face up with the legs straight and the arms extended forward of the shoulders. From here a series of sit ups are performed with the legs maintaining constant contact with the ground.

Self-Test 2
Swimmers lie face up with the legs straight and the arms folded across the chest. From here a series of sit ups are performed with the legs maintaining constant contact with the ground.

Self-Test 3
Swimmers lie face up with the legs straight and the hands on the ears. From here a series of sit ups are performed with the legs maintaining constant contact with the ground.

Self-Test 4

Swimmers lie face up with the knees bent ninety degrees and the arms extended forward of the shoulders. From here a series of sit ups are performed with the feet maintaining constant contact with the ground.

Self-Test 5

Swimmers lie face up with the knees bent ninety degrees and the hands placed on the ears. From here a series of sit ups are performed with the feet maintaining constant contact with the ground.

Self-Test 6-A

From a plank position, swimmers raise the right arm to ear level and hold it in place. The hips remain motionless and the back is flat at all times. From here swimmers slowly return to the starting position and repeat on the opposite side.

Self-Test 6-B

From a plank position, swimmers raise the right leg to hip level and hold it in place. The hips remain motionless and the back is flat at all times. From here swimmers slowly return to the starting position and repeat on the opposite side.

Self-Test 6-C

From a plank position, swimmers lift the right arm to ear level and the left leg to hip level and hold it in place. The hips remain motionless and the back is flat at all times. From here swimmers slowly return to the starting position and repeat on the opposite side.

Self-Test 7

Swimmers lie on the right side with the left shoulder, hip, and foot placed over the right shoulder, hip, and foot. From here the right arm draws underneath the upper body with the forearm resting on the ground. From here the body presses into a side plank position and holds in place. A straight line should form along the length of the body from shoulder tip to ankle while the hips remain motionless. From here swimmers slowly return to the starting position and repeat on the opposite side.

Self-Test 8
Swimmers lie face down with the head raised off the ground in a neutral position. From here the arms extend forward of the head, holding in a Y formation, while the hands rotate to a thumbs-up position. From here the legs lift off the ground as high as possible and hold in place. Ideally the height of the legs should equal the height of the arms. From here swimmers slowly return to the starting position.

Upper Body
Self-Test 1
From a plank position, swimmers lift the right hand off the ground, touching the left shoulder. The hips remain motionless and the back is flat at all times. From here swimmers slowly return to the starting position and repeat on the opposite side.

Self-Test 2
From a modified plank position with the knees on the ground, swimmers perform a series of push ups, touching the chest lightly to the ground on each repetition. Shoulders and hips remain in line and parallel to the ground throughout.

Self-Test 3
From a plank position, swimmers perform a series of push ups. The upper arms achieve a parallel-to-the-ground position at the midway point of each repetition. Shoulders and hips remain in

line and parallel to the ground throughout.

Self-Test 4

From a plank position, swimmers perform a series of modified push ups with the upper arms squeezed against the sides of the body and the elbows in a backward-pointing position. Shoulders and hips remain in line and parallel to the ground throughout.

Self-Test 5

To perform this exercise correctly, cables are attached to a wall in front of swimmers at a height of approximately seven feet. From here swimmers grasp the taut cables with both hands. From here the body leans backward to form a forty-five-degree angle with the ground. From here a series of pull ups are performed with the upper arms squeezed against the sides of the body and the elbows in a backward-pointing position.

> **Note:** *The shoulder blades must squeeze together at the top of each pull up.*

Self-Test 6-A

This exercise is performed on a pull up bar. Swimmers grasp the bar with both hands shoulder width apart in a palm-backward position (palms facing the face). From here the arms pull the body upward until the chin clears the bar. From here swimmers slowly return to the starting position.

Self-Test 6-B

This exercise is performed on a pull up bar. Swimmers grasp the bar with both hands shoulder width apart in a palm-backward position (palms facing the face). From here the arms pull the body upward until the chin clears the bar. From here swimmers hold the position for as long as possible. From here swimmers slowly return to the starting position and record the length of time held.

Lower Body

Self-Test 1

The exercise is performed with a chair. Swimmers sit tall in a chair with the right foot on the ground, the left leg extended, and the right knee bent ninety degrees. From here a series of one-legged squats, returning the butt to the chair at the end of each squat, is performed. From here swimmers slowly return to the starting position.

Self-Test 2

The exercise is performed with a chair. Swimmers stand tall in front of a chair, holding a towel spread to shoulder width at shoulder height. From here the arms raise the towel over the shoulders with the arms positioned behind the ears. To ensure proper execution, the towel is held taut between the hands. From here a series of squats is performed, touching the butt to the chair at the end of each squat.

> **Note:** *The heels must remain in contact with the ground at all times.*

Self-Test 3

Swimmers stand tall on a step with the balls of the feet on the edge of the step and the heels hanging over the edge. The knees are placed in a locked out position. From here the right foot rises off the step and a series of calf raises is performed via an upward push through the toes of the left foot. From here swimmers slowly return to the starting position and repeat on the opposite side.

> **Note:** *Upon completion of the self-tests, an accurate assessment of overall strength is determined. Self-tests may be used, in addition to the many strength-promoting exercises outlined in this chapter, to further enhance strength needs.*

FLEXIBILITY SELF-TESTS

The following section contains a series of self-tests used to determine swimmers' overall flexibility in areas critical to peak performance in the pool. A recommended stretch is included with each self-test.

Hamstrings

The term *hamstring* refers to three tendons on the back of the knee. This muscle group plays a major role when driving off a block or wall. In addition it generates propulsion in the butterfly, backstroke, and freestyle kick cycles and assists in the recovery phase of the breaststroke kick cycle. Ideally the quadriceps should be no more than twenty-five percent stronger than the hamstrings. Unfortunately swimming does more to develop quadriceps than hamstrings.

Self-Test Instructions

Swimmers lie face up with the legs together and the arms placed at the sides of the body. From here the right leg lifts as high as possible while the left leg remains straight and in contact with the ground. Ideally a ninety-degree angle should form between the legs. From here swimmers slowly return to the starting position and repeat on the opposite side.

> **Note:** *An inability to perform the self-test as described would indicate limited flexibility of the hamstrings.*

Recommended Stretch

Swimmers lie face up with the right leg bent and the left quadriceps contracted. The knee of the left leg is placed in a locked out position. From here the left leg lifts off the ground, drawing toward the head. As the leg reaches its maximum height, a slight|

pull with the arms is added. The position is held for five seconds or longer once a stretch is felt. From here swimmers slowly return to the starting position and repeat on the opposite side.

Quadriceps/Hip Flexors

The term *quadriceps* refers to four anterior muscles on the front of the thigh. Combined, these muscles contribute to the forceful extension of the knee—a key component in each of the four kicking cycles.

The term *hip flexors* refers to a group of muscles located in the hip area. They contribute to the downbeat phase of the butterfly and freestyle kick cycles, the upbeat phase of the backstroke kick cycle, and the recovery phase of the breaststroke kick cycle.

Self-Test Instructions

Swimmers lie face down with the legs together and the arms placed at the sides of the body. From here the knees bend, drawing the heels to the butt.

> **Note:** *An inability to perform the self-test as described would indicate limited flexibility of the quadriceps/hip flexors.*

Recommended Stretch

Swimmers assume a forward-lunge position by placing the hands on the hips, stepping the right foot forward, and kneeling onto the left knee. The right knee must not extend beyond the toes of the right foot. The position is held for five seconds or longer once a stretch is felt. From here swimmers slowly return to the starting position and repeat on the opposite side.

> **Note:** *For a deeper stretch, the hand pulls the foot upward while the hips push forward.*

Hip Adductors

The term *hip adductors* refers to the large, triangular muscles on the inner thigh. This muscle group is responsible for bringing the legs together during the all-powerful whip phase of the breaststroke kick cycle. Tight or weak hip adductors are susceptible to strain.

Self-Test Instructions

Swimmers lie face up with the legs together and the arms placed at the sides of the body. From here the right leg draws out to the side with the toes pointed upward. Ideally a forty-five-degree angle should form between the legs. From here swimmers slowly return to the starting position and repeat on the opposite side

> **Note:** *An inability to perform the self-test as described would indicate limited flexibility of the hip adductors.*

Recommended Stretch

Swimmers stand tall with the legs apart and the feet spread wider than shoulder width. With the legs straight, the hands reach for the right foot. From here the hands reach for the ground between the feet. From here the hands reach for the left foot. Each position is held for five seconds or longer once a stretch is felt.

Latissimus Dorsi

The term *latissimus dorsi* refers to the broadest and most powerful muscles of the upper back. This muscle group plays a major role in the propulsive phase of each arm cycle. Development of the latissimus dorsi contributes to the stereotypical V shape common among accomplished swimmers.

Self-Test Instructions

Swimmers lie face up with the legs together and the arms placed in a streamline position. From here they attempt to press and hold the entire back and arms against the ground.

Note: *An inability to perform the self-test as described would indicate limited latissimus dorsi flexibility.*

Recommended Stretch

Swimmers kneel down on the ground, sitting on the heels with the knees bent and the toes pointed. From here the chest is placed on the ground with the arms extended forward of the shoulders. The palms are placed flat on the ground with the thumbs together. The position is held for five seconds or longer once a stretch is felt. From here swimmers slowly return to the starting position.

Recommended Stretch

Similar to the previous stretch only the hands slide out to the right while the hips are pushed out to the left.

Recommended Stretch

Similar to the previous stretch only the hands slide out to the left while the hips are pushed out to the right.

Recommended Stretch

Similar to the initial latissimus dorsi stretch only swimmers lift the extended arms off the ground into a streamline position. From here the wrists flex ninety degrees with the fingertips resting on the ground. From here the chest presses downward to experience a deeper stretch. The position is held for five seconds or longer once a stretch is felt. From here swimmers slowly return to the starting position.

Rotator Cuff

The term *rotator cuff* refers to a supporting structure of the shoulder consisting of muscles and tendons that attach the arm to the shoulder joint and enable the arm to move. Injuries of the rotator cuff are extremely common among swimmers due to the repetitive nature of the sport. Proper care of the rotator cuff is critical to a long-term swimming career.

Self-Test Instructions

Swimmers stand tall, raising the right arm over the right shoulder and placing the palm of the right hand on the upper back. From here the left hand reaches behind the lower back with the back of the left hand placed against the lower back. From here the fingertips of the right hand attempt to grasp the fingertips of the left. From here swimmers slowly return to the starting position and repeat on the opposite side.

> **Note:** *An inability to perform the self-test as described would indicate limited flexibility of the rotator cuff muscles.*

Recommended Stretch

Swimmers stand tall and sideways to a wall with the right arm bent ninety degrees. From here the right palm is placed against the wall to serve as an anchor. From here the body rotates away from the wall, holding for five seconds or longer. From here swimmers slowly return to the starting position and repeat on the opposite side.

Recommended Stretch

Swimmers stand tall, holding one end of a standard-length towel in the right hand and placing it behind the right shoulder. From here the left hand grasps the opposite end of the towel with the palm facing outward and the thumb facing upward. From here the right hand gently pulls up on the towel, drawing the left thumb upward along the spine. The position is held for five seconds or longer once a stretch is felt. From here swimmers slowly return to the starting position and repeat on the opposite side.

Pectorals

The term *pectorals* refers to thick, fan-shaped muscles located in the chest. This muscle group adds stroking power to the arms. Tight pectorals can lead to swimming-related shoulder injuries.

Self-Test Instructions

Swimmers stand tall in front of a wall, raising the arms to shoulder level. From here the elbows bend ninety degrees, placing the back of the hands and shoulders against the wall. From here the shoulder blades pinch together while the shoulders and the back of the hands maintain contact with the wall. From here the lower back presses into the wall while maintaining elbow contact. From here a three-inch step is taken away from the wall with the back of the hands, shoulders, and lower back maintaining contact with the wall.

> **Note:** *An inability to perform the self-test as described would indicate limited flexibility of the pectorals.*

Recommended Stretch

Swimmers stand tall in a doorway. From here the arms bend ninety degrees, placing the hands and forearms at shoulder height on the sides of the doorframe. From here a gentle forward step is taken with the right foot. The position is held for five seconds or longer once a stretch is felt. From here swimmers slowly return to the starting position and repeat on the opposite side.

Trunk Rotators

The term *trunk rotators* refers to a number of different muscle groups that wrap around the trunk or midsection. A partial list includes the internal and external oblique muscles, back extensors, and abdominals. Together these muscles provide stability in all four strokes and assist in backstroke and freestyle rotation.

Self-Test Instructions

Swimmers lie face up with the legs extended and the arms placed at the sides of the body. From here the right leg bends, drawing the right foot toward the butt. From here the right knee reaches over the left leg attempting to touch the ground on the opposite side of the left leg. The right shoulder remains in contact with the floor at all times. From here swimmers slowly return to the starting position and repeat on the opposite side.

> **Note:** *An inability to perform the self-test as described would indicate limited flexibility of the trunk rotators.*

Recommended Stretch

The exercise is performed with a medicine ball. Swimmers sit tall on the ground with the knees bent 90 degrees and the feet placed shoulder width apart. From here the hands grasp a medicine ball holding the ball above ground level. From here the body rotates to the right placing the ball as far behind the back as possible. From here the body rotates to the left to pick up the ball. From here swimmers repeat in the opposite direction.

BUTTERFLY, BACKSTROKE, AND FREESTYLE ANKLE FLEXIBILITY

The abilities to dorsi flex and plantar flex the foot have a direct impact on kicking proficiency. *Dorsi flexion* is defined as a foot movement toward the lower leg while *planter flexion* or *toe point* is defined as a foot movement away from the lower leg. Both movements rely heavily on ankle flexibility. Combining these two movements adds propulsion to the butterfly, backstroke, and freestyle kick cycles. In addition adequate plantar flexion assists in the elimination of drag in each of the four kick cycles.

Self-Test Instructions

To measure dorsi flexion, swimmers stand tall on the balls of the feet on the first step of a staircase, with the knees locked out. From here the heels lower to the ground. The closer the heels come to the ground the greater the ability to dorsi flex.

To measure plantar flexion, swimmers sit tall on the ground with the legs extended and the feet together. From here the big toes come as close to the ground as possible without foot separation. The feet should create an arch, forming a straight line from the big toes to the ankles.

Note: *An inability to perform the self-test(s) as described would indicate limited ankle flexibility.*

Recommended Stretch

This exercise is performed with a chair. Swimmers sit tall in a chair with the right leg crossed over the left leg. From here the right foot slowly circles five times in a clockwise direction followed by five times in a counterclockwise direction. From here swimmers slowly return to the starting position and repeat on the opposite side.

Note: *The ankles must circle through a full range of motion.*

BREASTSTROKE ANKLE FLEXIBILITY

Ideally swimmers should be able to turn the feet out and in with ease. Full outward rotation facilitates a better catch at the top of the kick while full inward rotation facilitates a better finish and greater propulsion at the bottom of the kick. Swimmers who are unable to turn the feet out to a ninety-degree angle are forced to spread the knees wider than the recommended amount to facilitate the ideal foot catch. Unfortunately this increased knee spread creates additional drag and may cancel out any potential benefit. Improvements in outward and inward ankle rotation result in increased levels of propulsion.

Self-Test Instructions

Swimmers sit tall with the back placed against a wall. From here the feet are placed together with toes pointed directly upward. With heels together, the feet spread as far apart as possible. Ideally both feet should achieve a forty-five-degree angle or greater.

> **Note:** *An inability to perform the self-test as described would indicate limited ankle flexibility.*

Recommended Stretch

Swimmers sit tall with the legs crossed, cupping the right foot with both hands. From here the foot gently rotates so the sole faces inward toward the stomach. From here the right foot is pulled gently toward the stomach. A stretch of thirty seconds or longer is held once a stretch is felt. From here swimmers slowly return to the starting position and repeat on the opposite side.

> **Note:** *Upon completion of the self-tests, an accurate assessment of overall flexibility is determined. Self-tests may be used to enhance flexibility needs further.*

YOGA FOR SWIMMERS

The practice of yoga is the perfect match for the sport of competitive swimming as both draw upon the entire body. When I first began the practice of yoga I was amazed by the many similarities between the two. For example the popular posture downward dog instantly reminded me of the all-important chest press in butterfly. I was also amazed by how yoga strengthens and stretches the body while relaxing the mind.

> **Note:** *There are a multitude of yoga postures that relate to swimming postures.*

Yoga is gentle on swimmers' joints, forgiving of injuries, and deeply relaxing. It's the perfect complement to in-water training, developing strength and flexibility through time-tested postures. In addition yoga postures encourage a full range of motion, promoting supple and extended muscles as opposed to tight and compacted muscles. Extended muscles allow swimmers to achieve maximal extension through each of the four arm cycles and the four kick cycles, generating greater overall propulsion. In a holistic approach, the practice of yoga is highly regarded and taught at the novice, junior, and senior levels with various yoga postures intermixed with conventional stretching exercises.

> **Note:** *For like-minded coaches, I highly recommend Yoga for Swimmers with Barbara Won. Available in DVD format.*

SHOULDER MAINTENANCE EXERCISES

A swimmer has a greater than sixty percent chance of experiencing a shoulder-related injury sometime in his or her swimming career. While there are many contributing factors, the five main culprits are: 1) improper stroke mechanics, 2) excessive yardage, 3) weak shoulder-related musculature, 4) prolonged periods of excessive training, and 5) over-training a particular stroke or a component of a particular stroke. As a precautionary measure, the following shoulder strengthening exercises are performed every other day. The number of repetitions is subject to the swimmer's age, skill level, and time available.

External Rotation With Bands

The exercise is performed with a band attached to a wall at hip level. Swimmers stand tall, sideways to a wall, with the left side facing the wall. From here the right hand, farthest from the wall, grasps the taut band. From here the right elbow bends ninety degrees, pressing into the side of the body. The right forearm rests on the stomach with the right thumb pointing upward. From here the right arm pulls away from the stomach via outward shoulder rotation. A ninety-degree elbow bend is maintained throughout, while the elbow remains pressed against the side of the body. From here swimmers slowly return to the starting position and repeat on the opposite side.

V-Ups

Swimmers stand tall, grasping a pair of one to three pound dumbbells in each hand with the elbows straight and the arms at the sides of the body. From here the arms raise to shoulder level on a forty-five-degree angle with the thumbs facing upward, forming a V shape upon completion. The shoulders must be held back throughout the raising and lowering of the arms. From here swimmers slowly return to the starting position.

> **Note:** *The amount of weight selected is dependent upon the swimmer's strength and skill level.*

Rowing Retraction With Bands

The exercise is performed with a band attached to a wall at shoulder level. Swimmers stand tall, facing a wall. From here the hands grasp the taut band, pulling backward via a squeezing together of the shoulder blades. Once complete, the elbows bend backward to complete the pulling action. From here swimmers slowly return to the starting position.

T-Y on Floor

Swimmers lie facedown with the legs together. From here the arms extend directly out from the shoulders, with the palms flat on the ground. At this point the body resembles the letter T. From here the arms raise off the ground via a squeezing of the shoulder blades while the head remains in contact with the ground. From here the arms are placed into a Y position with the thumbs facing upward. From here the arms raise off the ground to ear level via an upward shoulder shrug while the head remains in contact with the ground.

> **Note:** *Once perfected, both exercises are progressed to a stability ball with the chest resting on the ball and the feet in contact with the ground.*

Circuits for Novice-, Junior-, and Senior-Level Swimmers

Circuits are a popular form of Dry Land training within a holistic approach. Each circuit is divided into separate sections, including: front core, back core, upper body, lower body, and stretches. In addition circuits are divided into circuit A or circuit B for novice-, junior-, and senior-level swimmers with circuits alternated if desired. Typically circuits for novice-level swimmers last up to fifteen to twenty minutes, while circuits for junior- and senior-level swimmers last up to twenty-five to thirty minutes. The types of exercises and number of repetitions performed are subject to the swimmer's age, skill level, and time available. See the Dry Land Training Glossary at the end of this chapter for a detailed explanation of each recommended exercise.

Novice Circuit A
Front Core
- Chair Crunch > 1 x 10
- Scissors > 1 x 10
- Half Sit Up > 1 x 10
- Streamline Crunch > 1 x 10

- Half Jackknife Crunch > 1 x 10

Back Core
- Plank > Shoulder Protraction/Retraction > 2 x 10
- Plank > Knee to Elbow With Alternating Legs > 2 x 10
- Plank > Table to Plank to Hands to Elbows > 2 x 10

Lower Body
- Chair Squat > 2 x 10

Back Core
- Plank > Elbows > Hold 30" > 2 x
- Plank > Right Side > Hold 30" > 2 x
- Plank > Left Side > Hold 30" > 2 x

Lower Body
- Standing Lunge > 10 Each Side

Back Core
- Plank > Touch Opposite Hand > 2 x 10
- Plank > Touch Opposite Shoulder > 2 x 10
- Plank > Alternating Arms to Ceiling > 2 x 10

Stretches
- Lunge Stretch > 3 Each Side
- Hamstring Stretch > 3 Each Side
- Child Pose Stretch > 3 x
- Wall Stretch > 3 x
- Towel Shoulder Stretch > 3 Each Side

Novice Circuit B
Front Core
- Overhead Crunch With Med Ball > 1 x 10
- Russian Twist (Feet Down) With Med Ball > 1 x 10
- Chair Crunch > 1 x 10

- Sit Up With Hands on Ears > 1 x 10
- Streamline Crunch > 1 x 10

Lower Body
- Sideways Step Up > 10 Each Leg

Upper Body
- Seated Row With Band > 2 x 10
- Straight Arm Pull (On Back) With Band > 10 Each Arm
- Knee Push Up > 2 x 10
- 45-Degree Pull Up With Cables > 2 x 10

Lower Body
Single-Leg Dead Lift > 10 Each Leg

Stretches
- Lunge Stretch > 3 Each Side
- Hamstring Stretch > 3 Each Side
- Child Pose Stretch > 3 x
- Wall Stretch > 3 x
- Towel Leg Stretch > 3 Each Side

Junior Circuit A
Front Core
- Chair Crunch > 1 x 15
- Bicycles > 1 x 15
- 90-Degree Toe Touch > 1 x 15
- Crunch Position With Scissors > 1 x 15
- Sit Up With Arms at Head > 1 x 15
- Streamline Sit Up > 1 x 15
- Rotations > 1 x 15

- Half Jackknife Crunch > 1 x 15

Back Core
- Plank > Shoulder Protraction/Retraction > 2 x 15
- Plank > Knee to Elbow With Alternating Legs > 2 x 15
- Plank > Table to Plank to Hands to Elbows > 2 x 15
- Plank > Leg Backward > 15 Each Leg
- Plank > Arm Forward > 15 Each Leg

Lower Body
- Forward Step Up > 15 Each Leg
- Sideways Step Up > 15 Each Leg

Back Core
- Plank > Elbows > Hold 1' > 2 x
- Plank > Right Side > Hold 1' > 2 x
- Plank > Left Side > Hold 1' > 2 x

Lower Body
- Chair Squat With Med Ball > 2 x 15
- Walking Lunge With Med Ball > 2 x 15

Back Core
- Plank > Touch Opposite Hand > 2 x 15
- Plank > Touch Opposite Shoulder > 2 x 15
- Plank > Knee to Elbow With Alternating Legs > 2 x 15
- Plank > Alternating Arms to Ceiling > 2 x 15
- Plank > Swimmers > 15 Each Arm

Stretches
- Lunge Stretch > 4 Each Side
- Hamstring Stretch > 4 Each Side
- Child Pose Stretch > 4 x
- Wall Stretch > 4 x
- Towel Stretch > 4 Each Side

- Shoulder External Rotation Stretch > 4 Each Side
- Trunk Rotation Stretch > 4 Each Side
- Cobra > 4 x

Junior Circuit B
Front Core
- Overhead Sit Up With Med Ball > 1 x 15
- Russian Twist (Feet Up) With Med Ball > 1 x 15
- Overhead Crunch (Leg Lift) With Med Ball > 1 x 15
- Chair Crunch > 1 x 15
- Bicycles > 1 x 15
- Half Jackknife Crunch > 1 x 15
- Bent Leg Sit Up With Arms Folded > 1 x 15
- Streamline Sit Up > 1 x 15

Lower Body
- Sideways Step Up > 15 Each Leg
- Sideways Step Down With Floor Touch > 15 Each Leg

Upper Body
- Standing Row With Band > 2 x 15
- Straight Arm Pull (On Back) w/Band > 2 x 15
- Single Arm Row With Band > 15 Each Side
- Push Up > 2 x 10-15
- 45-Degree Pull Up With Cables > 2 x 15
- Pull Up With Superband > 2 x 15

Lower Body
- Single-Leg Dead Lift > 15 Each Leg
- Single-Leg Bridge > 15 Each Leg

Stretches
- Lunge Stretch > 4 Each Side
- Hamstring Stretch > 4 Each Side

- Piriformis Stretch > 4 Each Side
- Wall Stretch > 4 x
- Towel Shoulder Stretch > 4 Each Side
- Shoulder External Rotation Stretch > 4 Each Side
- Trunk Rotation Stretch > 4 Each Side
- Inner Thigh Stretch > 4 x

Senior Circuit A
Front Core
- Chair Crunch > 1 x 20
- Bicycles > 1 x 20
- 90-Degree Toe Touch > 1 x 20
- Crunch Position With Scissors > 1 x 20
- Sit Up With Hands on Ears > 1 x 20
- Half Sit Up With Arm Clap > 1 x 20
- Streamline Sit Up > 1 x 20
- Rotations > 1 x 20
- 45-Degree Jackknife > 1 x 20
- Choice (from above) > 1 x 20

Back Core
- Plank > Shoulder Protraction/Retraction > 2 x 20
- Plank > Knee to Elbow With Alternating Legs > 2 x 20
- Plank > Table to Plank to Hands to Elbows > 2 x 20
- Plank > Push Up or Knee Push Up > 2 x 20
- Plank > Leg Backward > 20 Each Leg
- Plank > Arm Forward > 20 Each Arm

Lower Body
- Chair Squat With Med Ball > 2 x 20
- Forward Step Up > 20 Each Leg
- Sideways Step Up > 20 Each Leg

Back Core
- Plank > Elbows > Hold 2' > 2 x

- Plank > Right Side > Hold 2' > 2 x
- Plank > Left Side > Hold 2' > 2 x

Lower Body
- Walking Lunge With Med Ball > 2 x 20

Back Core
- Plank > Arm Forward > 20 Each Arm
- Plank > 90-Degrees > 20 Each Arm
- Plank > Knee to Elbow With Alternating Legs > 2 x 20
- Plank > Alternating Arms to Ceiling > 2 x 20
- Plank > Opposites > 2 x 20
- Plank > Swimmers > 20 Each Arm

Stretches
- Lunge Stretch > 5 Each Side
- Hamstring Stretch > 5 Each Side
- Child Pose Stretch > 5 x
- Wall Stretch > 5 x
- Towel Stretch > 5 x
- Shoulder External Rotation Stretch > 5 Each Side
- Trunk Rotation Stretch > 5 Each Side
- Cobra > 5 x

Senior Circuit B
Front Core
- Overhead Sit Up With Med Ball > 1 x 20
- Russian Twist (Feet Up) With Med Ball > 1 x 20
- Overhead Crunch (Leg Lift) With Med Ball > 1 x 20
- Chair Crunch > 1 x 20
- Bicycles > 1 x 20
- Half Jackknife Crunch > 1 x 20
- 90-Degree Toe Touch > 1 x 20
- Sit Up With Arms at Side > 1 x 20
- Streamline Sit Up > 1 x 20

- Choice (from above) > 1 x 20

Lower Body
- Sideways Step Up > 20 Each Leg
- Sideways Step Down With No Floor Touch > 20 Each Leg

Upper Body
- Standing Row (Squat Position) With Band > 2 x 20
- Push Up > 2 x 20
- Single Arm Pull With Band > 2 x 20
- Plank > Freestyle With Band > 20 Each Side
- Knee Push Up > 2 x 20
- 30-Degree Pull Up With Cables > 2 x 20
- Pull Up With Superbands > 2 x 20
- Tricep Push Up > 2 x 20

Lower Body
- Single-Leg Dead Lift > 20 Each Leg
- Single-Leg Bridge > 20 Each Leg

Stretches
- Lunge Stretch > 5 Each Side
- Hamstring Stretch > 5 Each Side
- Piriformis Stretch > 5 Each Side
- Child Pose Stretch > 5 x
- Towel Leg Stretch > 5 Each Side
- Shoulder External Rotation Stretch > 5 Each Side
- Trunk Rotation Stretch > 5 Each Side
- Inner Thigh Stretch > 5 x

Swim-Specific Strength and Flexibility Exercises

While circuits are the most efficient means to train a large group of swimmers, the holistic coach may prefer to have swimmers perform stroke-specific strength and flexibility exercises based on individual needs. For example exercises listed under Butterfly Flexibility could be used with swimmers lacking the necessary flexibility for butterfly, or the exercises listed under Start and Turn Strength could be used with swimmers lacking explosiveness off the block and walls. See the Dry Land Training Glossary at the end of this chapter for a detailed explanation of each exercise.

Butterfly Core Strength
- Plank > Arm Forward
- Plank > Leg Backward
- Sit Up With Med Ball
- Streamline Crunch

Butterfly Propulsive Strength
- Power Squats
- Single Arm Pull With Band
- Tricep Push Up
- 45-Degree Pull Up With Rings or Cables

Butterfly Flexibility
- Child Pose Streamline on Fingertips
- Child Pose With Hands on Table
- Cobra
- Core Hip Stretch

Backstroke Core Strength
- Back Kick
- Free Kick
- Front Tucks
- 90-Degree Toe Touch

Backstroke Propulsive Strength
- Single Arm Pull With Band

- Tricep Push Up
- Standing Lunge
- Straight-Leg Raises

Backstroke Flexibility
- Doorway Stretch
- Child Pose Stretch (Right)
- Child Pose Stretch (Left)
- Lunge Stretch

Breaststroke Core Strength
- Crunch With Feet Lift
- Plank > Knee to Elbow
- Plank > Knee to Elbow With Alternating Legs
- Single-Leg Lowering

Breaststroke Propulsive Strength
- Leapfrog Jump
- Knee Push Up
- Plank > Down and Up
- Squat With Med Ball

Breaststroke Flexibility
- Back Bridge
- Breaststroke Streamline
- Rocking Horse Stretch
- Child Pose Streamline on Fingertips

Freestyle Core Strength
- Half Jackknife Crunch
- Overhead Sit Up With Med Ball
- Single Arm Press With Rotation With Band
- Russian Twist (Feet Up) With Med Ball

Freestyle Propulsive Strength
- Plank > Freestyle With Band
- Plank > Perpendicular Paddle
- Push Up
- Tricep Push Up

Freestyle Flexibility
- Doorway Stretch
- Child Pose Stretch (Left)
- Child Pose Stretch (Right)
- Rocking Horse Stretch

Start and Turn Strength
- Lunge Jump
- Power Step Up
- Squat Jump
- Single-Leg Dead Lift

DRY LAND TRAINING GLOSSARY

The following glossary outlines more than 100 strength and flexibility exercises performed in the novice-, junior-, and senior-level dry land training circuits. Self-test exercises for strength and flexibility, ankle felxibility exercises for the four strokes, and shoulder maintenence exercises are outlined on their respective pages.

Back Bridge
Swimmers lie face up with the knees bent ninety degrees, the feet spread shoulder width apart, and the palms placed next to the ears. From here the body presses into a bridge position, holding for five seconds or longer. From here swimmers slowly return to the starting position.

Back Kick
Swimmers lie face up, leaning back on the elbows with the legs straight. From here the legs rise six inches off the ground with the toes pointed. From here swimmers perform a series of straight-leg backstroke kicks.

Bicycles
Swimmers lie face up with the knees bent forty-five degrees and the palms placed next to the ears. From here a series of slow bicycling motions are performed, touching the right knee to the left elbow and the left knee to the right elbow.

Bent-Leg Sit Up With Arms Folded
Swimmers lie face up with the knees bent ninety degrees and the arms folded across the chest. From here the upper body rises upward off the ground while the feet maintain contact with the ground. From here swimmers slowly return to the starting position.

Bent Row With Dumbbells
The exercise is performed with a pair of dumbbells. Swimmers bend forward at the waist with the knees slightly bent, the chest parallel to the floor, and the arms extended with a dumbbell in each hand. From here the elbows bend, drawing the dumbbells toward the chest. From here swimmers slowly return to the starting position.

Breaststroke Streamline
Swimmers lie face up in a streamline position with the back pressed to the ground and the thumbs squeezed together. The position is held for five seconds or longer once a stretch is felt.

Chair Crunch
Swimmers lie face up with the knees bent ninety degrees, feet raised off the ground and palms next to the ears. From here the

head and shoulders curl upward; the elbows touch the knees and the knees touch the elbows. From here swimmers slowly return to the starting position.

Chair Squat
The exercise is performed with a chair. Swimmers stand tall in front of a chair with the feet shoulder width apart and the arms in front of the shoulders at shoulder height. From here the butt gently lowers as close to the chair as possible without touching. The back remains straight, the knees in line with the feet. From here swimmers slowly return to the starting position.

Chair Squat With Med Ball
Similar to Chair Squat only a medicine ball is held at chest level.

Child Pose Streamline on Fingertips
Similar to Child Pose Stretch only the wrists bend ninety degrees in order to rest on the fingertips. From here the chest presses downward. The position is held for five seconds or longer once a stretch is felt. From here swimmers slowly return to the starting position.

> **Note**: *Resting on the fingertips allows for a deeper chest stretch.*

Child Pose Stretch
Swimmers kneel on the ground with the knees shoulder width apart. From here the heels draw toward the butt while the arms extend into a streamline position. From here the palms and forehead lower to the ground while the chest presses downward. The position is held for five seconds or longer once a stretch is felt. From here swimmers slowly return to the starting position.

Child Pose Stretch (Left)
Similar to Child Pose Stretch only the hands slide out to the left while the hips push out to the right. The position is held for five

seconds or longer once a stretch is felt. From here swimmers slowly return to the starting position.

Child Pose Stretch (Right)
Similar to Child Pose Stretch only the hands slide out to the right while the hips push out to the left. The position is held for five seconds or longer once a stretch is felt. From here swimmers slowly return to the starting position.

Child Pose With Hands (On Table)
Similar to Child Pose Stretch only swimmers slide both hands across the top of a table, pressing the chest downward. The position is held for five seconds or longer once a stretch is felt. From here swimmers slowly return to the starting position.

Cobra
Swimmers lie face down with the legs straight and the palms on the ground beneath the shoulders. From here the head tilts backward, arching the spine. As the head tilts, the arms extend fully. The position is held for five seconds or longer once a stretch is felt. From here swimmers slowly return to the starting position.

Core Hip Stretch
Swimmers lie facedown with the knees bent. From here the hands grasp the feet, pulling the heels toward the butt with the knees squeezed together. The position is held for five seconds or longer once a stretch is felt. From here swimmers slowly return to the starting position.

Crunch Position With Scissors
Swimmers assume a crunch position with the legs straight. From here the legs rise approximately six inches off the ground. From here the right leg lowers slowly to slightly off ground level while the left leg remains in position. From here the right leg slowly returns to the starting position. From here the left leg lowers slowly to slightly off ground level while the right leg remains

in position. From here the left leg slowly returns to the starting position.

Crunch With Feet Lift

Swimmers lie face up with the knees bent ninety degrees and the hands next to the ears. From here the elbows draw to the knees. At the point of contact the feet lift off the ground, pulling the knees toward the chest. From here swimmers slowly return to the starting position.

Doorway Stretch

Swimmers stand tall inside a doorway with the arms at shoulder height and bent ninety degrees. From here the hands and forearms press against the outside of the doorframe. From here the right foot steps forward. The position is held for five seconds or longer once a stretch is felt. From here swimmers slowly return to the starting position and repeat on the opposite side.

Double-Leg Lowering

Swimmers lie face up with the legs raised ninety degrees off the ground and the arms at the sides of the body. From here the legs slowly lower to the ground. The lowering process continues as long as the back remains flat on the ground. From here swimmers slowly return to the starting position.

Double Leg Pike

Swimmers lie face up with the legs straight and the arms at the sides of the body. From here the legs raise ninety degrees off the ground while the hands reach to the feet in a crunch-like fashion. From here swimmers slowly return to the starting position.

Forward Step Up

Swimmers stand tall in front of a bench with the feet shoulder width apart. From here the right foot steps onto the bench with the right leg driving the body upward. From here the right foot returns to the ground. From here the left foot steps onto the bench with the left leg driving the body upward.

Free Kick

Swimmers assume a plank position. From here the right leg lifts off the ground with the toes pointed. From here the right leg rapidly lowers and rises, simulating a freestyle kicking action. From here the left leg lifts off the ground with the toes pointed. From here the left leg rapidly lowers and rises, simulating a freestyle kicking action.

Front Tuck

Swimmers sit tall with the knees bent ninety degrees. From here the arms wrap around the legs as the body balances on the butt with the feet off the ground. From here the arms open while the legs extend outward. Balance must be maintained throughout. From here swimmers slowly return to the starting position.

Half Jackknife Crunch

Swimmers lie face up with the legs straight. From here the right arm extends behind the head with the left arm at the side of the body. From here the right arm and the left leg lift off the ground simultaneously. From here the right hand touches the left foot. From here swimmers slowly return to the starting position and repeat on the opposite side.

Half Sit Up

Swimmers sit tall with the legs straight and the hands next to the ears. From here the upper body slowly lowers to the halfway point. From here swimmers slowly return to the starting position.

Half Sit Up With Hold
Swimmers sit tall with the legs straight. From here the arms extend in front of the shoulders at shoulder height. From here the upper body slowly lowers to the halfway point and hold in place. From here the extended arms rise over the head into a streamline position. From here swimmers slowly return to the starting position.

Half Sit Up With Arm Clap
Swimmers sit tall with the legs straight. From here the arms extend in front of the shoulders at shoulder height. From here the upper body slowly lowers to the halfway point and hold in place. From here the right arm crosses over the left arm and the left arm crosses over the right arm in clapping fashion.

Half Sit Up With Rotation
Swimmrs sit tall with the legs straight. From here the upper body slowly lowers to the halfway point. From here the hands clasp together. From here the body rotates from side to side.

Hamstring Stretch
Swimmers lie face up with the legs together. From here the right leg raises off the ground. From here the hands grasp the back of the upper right leg, pulling to a ninety-degree angle with the knee slightly bent. From here the right leg slowly straightens. The position is held for five seconds or longer once a stretch is felt. From here swimmers slowly return to the starting position and repeat on the opposite side.

Inner Thigh Stretch
Swimmers sit tall with the legs together and the knees bent ninety degrees. From here the knees spread apart with the soles of the feet placed together. From here the forearms gently press the knees toward the ground. The position is held for five seconds or longer once a stretch is felt. From here swimmers slowly return to the starting position.

Knee Push Up
Similar to a standard push up only performed on the knees.

Leapfrog Jump
Swimmers assume a squatting position with the back angled forty-five degrees and the hands touching the ground. From here a forward leap is performed. From here swimmers slowly return to the starting position.

Lunge Jump
Swimmers start in a lunge position with the right leg forward and the left leg back. From here the right foot aligns over the right ankle. From here the left heel is positioned slightly off the ground. From here the left arm swings forward and the right arm swings backward as the legs jump into the opposite lunge position. From here swimmers slowly return to the starting position and repeat on the opposite side.

Lunge Stretch
Swimmers kneel on the right knee with the right leg bent ninety degrees. From here the right foot aligns over the right ankle. From here the hips push forward to stretch the hip and thigh of the left leg. The position is held for five seconds or longer once a stretch is felt. From here swimmers slowly return to the starting position and repeat on the opposite side.

Modified Scissor
Swimmers lie face up with the legs straight and the arms at the sides of the body. From here the right leg raises approximately six inches off the ground. From here the hands reach forward, grasping the right ankle. From here swimmers slowly return to the starting position and repeat on the opposite side.

Overhead Crunch With Med Ball
The exercise is performed with a medicine ball. Swimmers lie face

up with the legs straight, holding the medicine ball behind the head with the arms extended. From here the arms lift the ball off the ground as the head and shoulders raise off the ground too. From here swimmers slowly return to the starting position.

Overhead Crunch (Leg Lift) With Med Ball

The exercise is performed with a medicine ball. Swimmers lie face up with the legs straight, holding the medicine ball behind the head with the arms extended. From here the arms lift the ball off the ground as the right leg raises. From here the right shin touches the ball directly above the waist. From here swimmers slowly return to the starting position and repeat on the opposite side.

Overhead Sit Up (Throw) With Med Ball

The exercise is performed with a medicine ball and a partner. The swimmer lies face up with the legs straight, holding the medicine ball behind the head with the arms extended. From here the upper body rises off the ground while the feet maintain contact with the ground. As the upper body rises, the arms throw the ball to an awaiting partner. Upon reaching the top, the partner tosses the ball back to the awaiting swimmer. From here the swimmer slowly returns to the starting position.

Overhead Sit Up With Med Ball

The exercise is performed with a medicine ball. Swimmers lie face up with the legs straight, holding the medicine ball behind the head with the arms extended. From here the upper body curls into a sit up. From here swimmers slowly return to the starting position.

Piriformis Stretch

Swimmers lie face up with the legs crossed as if sitting in a chair. From here both hands grasp the back of the leg. From here the hands pull the knee forward toward the chest. This position is held for five seconds or longer once a stretch is felt. From here swimmers slowly return to the starting position and repeat on the opposite side.

Plank > Alternating Arms to Ceiling
Swimmers assume a plank position. From here the right arm lifts to the ceiling. From here swimmers slowly return to the starting position and repeat on the opposite side.

Plank > Arm Forward
Swimmers assume a plank position. From here the right arm lifts to ear level. From here swimmers slowly return to the starting position and repeat on the opposite side.

Plank > 90 Degrees
Swimmers assume a plank position. From here the right arm lifts sideways to ninety degrees. From here swimmers slowly return to the starting position and repeat on the opposite side.

Plank > Down and Up
Swimmers assume a plank position. From here the right elbow touches the ground. From here swimmers slowly return to the starting position and repeat on the opposite side.

Plank > Elbows
Swimmers assume a plank position on the elbows rather than the hands.

Plank > Freestyle With Band
The exercise is performed with a band attached to a wall at shoulder level. Swimmers assume a plank position. From here the right hand grasps the taut band. From here the right arm extends in front of the right shoulder, similar to the entry phase of the freestyle arm cycle. From here the arm pulls backward past the hip, simulating the correct catch/finish phase of the freestyle arm

cycle. From here swimmers slowly return to the starting position and repeat on the opposite side.

Plank > Hand to Elbow
Swimmers assume a plank position, touching the right hand to the left elbow. From here swimmers slowly return to the starting position and repeat on the opposite side.

Plank > Head Up Push Up
Similar to Plank > Push Up only with the head tilted upward.

Plank > Knee to Elbow
Swimmers assume a plank position, touching the right knee to the right elbow. From here swimmers slowly return to the starting position and repeat on the opposite side.

Plank > Knee to Elbow With Alternating Legs
Similar to Plank > Knee to Elbow only the right knee touches the left elbow and the left knee touches the right elbow in an alternating fashion.

Plank > Leg Backward
Swimmers assume a plank position, lifting the right leg to hip level. From here swimmers slowly return to the starting position and repeat on the opposite side.

Plank > Opposites
Swimmers assume a plank position, lifting the right arm to ear level and left leg to hip level. From here swimmers slowly return to the starting position and repeat on the opposite side.

Plank > Perpendicular Paddle
Similar to Plank > Freestyle With Band only swimmers work the catch phase of the freestyle arm cycle.

Plank > Push Up

Swimmers assume a plank position. From here a push up with the upper arms squeezed against the sides of the body is performed. The elbows assume a pointed-backward position throughout.

Plank > Shoulder Protraction/Retraction

Swimmers assume a plank position and move the shoulders forward and backward.

Plank > Side (Right/Left)

Swimmers lie on the right side with the left shoulder, hip, and ankle over the right shoulder, hip, and ankle. From here the right arm draws underneath the body with the forearm resting on the ground. From here the body presses into a side plank position. From here swimmers slowly return to the starting position and repeat on the opposite side.

Plank > Swimmers

Swimmers assume a plank position. From here a straight-arm butterfly recovery is performed both forward and backward with the right arm. From here a straight-arm butterfly recovery is performed both forward and backward with the left arm.

Plank > Table to Plank to Hands to Elbows

Swimmers assume a modified plank position with the knees on the ground before moving to a standard plank position. From here the body assumes a second modified plank position with the elbows on the ground. From here swimmers slowly return to the starting position.

Plank > Touch Opposite Hand

Swimmers assume a plank position. From here the right hand touches the left hand then the left hand touches the right hand.

Plank > Touch Opposite Shoulder

Swimmers assume a plank position. From here the right hand touches the left shoulder. From here the left hand touches the right shoulder.

Power Squat

The exercise is performed with a chair. Swimmers stand tall in front of a chair with the feet shoulder width apart and the arms in a streamline position. From here the butt slowly lowers as close to the chair as possible without touching. The back remains straight with the knees in line with the feet. From here the legs drive upward as the body assumes a streamline position. From here swimmers slowly return to the starting position.

Power Step Up

Swimmers stand tall, placing the right foot on a step. From here the body drives upward through the right leg, landing the right foot on the step above. From here swimmers slowly return to the starting position and repeat on the opposite side.

Pull Up With Superband

The exercise is performed with a Superband with one end attached to the center of the pull up bar and the other end tied to form a noose. Swimmers grasp the bar with both hands shoulder width apart in a palm-backward position (palms facing the face). From here the knee is inserted into the noose. At this point the Superband is stretched to the max and ready to assist pulling the body upward. From here the arms pull the body upward until the chest makes contact with the bar. The head is held in a neutral position with the shoulders back. As the arms pull, the elbows point outward. From here swimmers slowly return to the starting position.

Note: A Superband is an extra-long resistive band used for a variety of physical training purposes including assisted pull ups and chin-ups.

Push Up
Swimmers lie face down with the legs straight, the hands placed underneath the shoulders, toe tips resting on the ground, and the head held in a neutral position. From here the arms press the body into a plank position. From here the arms lower the body to three inches off the ground. From here swimmers slowly return to a plank position.

Rocking Horse Stretch
Swimmers lie facedown with the knees bent. From here the hands grasp the ankles as the head, chest, and thighs lift off the ground. The position is held for five seconds or longer once a stretch is felt. From here swimmers slowly return to the starting position.

Rotations
Swimmers sit tall with the knees bent ninety degrees and the feet off the ground. From here the hands clasp as the body rotates from side to side.

Rotational Lunge With Med Ball
Similar to Standing Lunge only with the medicine ball held at chest level. Swimmers stand tall, stepping forward with the right foot while rotating the upper body fully to the left. From here swimmers slowly return to the starting position and repeat on the opposite side.

Russian Twist (Feet Down) With Med Ball
The exercise is performed with a medicine ball. Swimmers sit tall with the knees bent ninety degrees and the feet slightly apart, holding a medicine ball above ground level. From here the upper body rotates from side to side, touching the ball to the ground on both sides.

Russian Twist (Feet Up) With Med Ball
Similar to Russian Twist (Feet Down) With Med Ball only the feet are held off the ground.

Seated Row With Band
The exercise is performed with a band attached to a wall at shoulder level. Swimmers sit tall with the legs straight. From here the hands grasp a taut band in a thumbs-up position. From here the elbows bend ninety degrees, pulling the handles back toward the chest. From here the shoulder blades squeeze together as the pull nears completion. From here swimmers slowly return to the starting position.

Scissors
Swimmers lie face up with the legs straight and the arms at the sides of the body. From here the legs raise off the ground approximately three inches. From here the right leg rises an additional three inches above the left. From here the right leg lowers until even with the left. From here swimmers slowly return to the starting position and repeat on the opposite side.

Shoulder External Rotation Stretch
Swimmers stand tall with the right side of the body next to a wall. From here the right arm bends ninety degrees and the right palm is placed against the wall. From here the body rotates away from the wall. The position is held for five seconds or longer once a stretch is felt. From here swimmers slowly return to the starting position and repeat on the opposite side.

Sideways Step Down With Floor Touch
Swimmers stand tall and sideways on a bench. From here the right foot lowers to the ground until the right hand makes contact with the ground. From here swimmers slowly return to the starting position and repeat on the opposite side.

Sideways Step Down With No Floor Touch
Similar to Sideways Step Down With Floor Touch only the hand does not touch the ground.

Sideways Step Up
Swimmers stand tall with the right side of the body next to a bench. From here the right foot steps onto the bench as the left leg pushes upward to full extension. From here swimmers slowly return to the starting position and repeat on the opposite side.

Sideways Step Up With Med Ball
Similar to Sideways Step Up only a medicine ball is held at chest level.

Single Arm Press With Rotation With Band
The exercise is performed with a band attached to a wall at shoulder level. Swimmers stand tall, grasping the taut band with the right hand at shoulder level. The left foot faces away from the wall in a lunge position. From here the body rotates away from the wall while the right arm extends. From here swimmers slowly return to the starting position and repeat on the opposite side.

Single Arm Pull With Band at Hip Level
The exercise is performed with a band attached to a wall at hip level. Swimmers bend forward at the waist until the chest is parallel to the floor while grasping the taut band with the right hand. From here the right arm extends in front of the right shoulder, simulating the entry phase of the freestyle arm cycle. From here the right arm pulls past the right hip, simulating the correct catch/finish phase of the freestyle arm cycle. From here swimmers slowly return to the starting position and repeat on the opposite side.

Single Arm Row With Band at Shoulder Level

The exercise is performed with a band attached to a wall at shoulder level. Swimmers stand tall, extending the right arm to shoulder level until the right shoulder is directly under the chin. From here the right hand grasps the taut band in a thumbs-up position. From here the hips rotate to the right while the band is pulled backward through the right arm. As the arm pulls, the right elbow bends. From here swimmers slowly return to the starting position and repeat on the opposite side.

Single Leg Bridge
Swimmers lie face up with the legs straight. From here the right leg bends ninety degrees and the right foot remains on the ground. From here the hips rise off the ground through the right leg. A straight line should form from the ankle of the left foot to the left shoulder. From here swimmers slowly return to the starting position and repeat on the opposite side.

Single Leg Bridge With Therapy Ball
The exercise is performed with a fifty-five-centimeter therapy ball. Swimmers lie face up with the legs straight. From here the right leg rises and the right heel is placed on the therapy ball. From here the left leg bends ninety degrees. From here the hips rise upward through the right leg. From here swimmers slowly return to the starting position and repeat on the opposite side.

Single Leg Dead Lift
Swimmers stand tall, balanced on the right leg. From here the left hand touches the ground without rounding the back. From here swimmers slowly return to the starting position and repeat on the opposite side.

Single Leg Lowering
Similar to Double Leg Lowering only the legs alternate one at a time.

Sit Up With Arms at Side

Swimmers lie face up with the legs straight and the arms at the sides of the body. From here the upper body curls into a sit up position while the legs maintain contact with the ground. From here swimmers slowly return to the starting position.

Sit Up With Arms Extended

Swimmers lie face up with the legs straight and raise the arms directly above the shoulders. From here the upper body curls into a sit up position while the legs maintain contact with the ground. From here swimmers slowly return to the starting position.

Sit Up With Hands on Ears

Swimmers lie face up with the legs straight and the hands on the ears. From here the upper body curls into a sit up position while the legs maintain contact with the ground. From here swimmers slowly return to the starting position.

Sit Up With Med Ball

The exercise is performed with a medicine ball. Swimmers lie face up with the legs straight while holding a medicine ball at chest level. From here the upper body curls into a sit up while the legs maintain contact with the ground. From here swimmers slowly return to the starting position.

Squat Jump

Swimmers stand tall with the feet shoulder width apart and the arms at the sides of the body. From here the body slowly lowers into a squat position while the arms draw behind the hips. From here the arms throw into a streamline position as the legs drive upward. From here swimmers slowly return to the starting position.

Squat With Med Ball

The exercise is performed with a medicine ball. Swimmers stand tall, holding a medicine ball at chest level with the upper arms squeezed against the sides of the body. From here the ball lowers to the ground through a bending of the knees. From here the hands lift the ball off the ground, thrusting upward into full extension. From here swimmers slowly return to the starting position.

Standing Lunge
Swimmers stand tall with the feet together and the hands clasped behind the head. From here the right foot steps forward as both knees bend. At this point the right knee is positioned directly over the right ankle with the left knee and heel positioned slightly off the ground. From here the left knee pushes to full extension while the right foot returns to the starting position. From here swimmers slowly return to the starting position and repeat on the opposite side.

Standing Row With Band
The exercise is performed with a band attached to a wall at shoulder level. Swimmers grasp the taut band with both hands in a thumbs-up position. From here the elbows bend ninety degrees, pulling the handles back toward the chest. From here the shoulder blades squeeze together as the pull nears completion. From here swimmers slowly return to the starting position.

Step Up
Swimmers stand tall in front of a bench with the feet shoulder width apart and the arms at the sides of the body. From here the right foot steps up on the bench followed by the left. From here the right foot steps down from the bench followed by the left.

Straight Arm Pull (on Back) With Band
The exercise is performed with a band attached to a wall directly behind the head. Swimmers lie face up with the legs straight. From here the hands grasp the taut band and pull it over the

shoulders to the ground. From here swimmers slowly return to the starting position.

Straight Arm Pull With Band

The exercise is performed with a band attached to a wall at shoulder level. Swimmers stand tall with the feet shoulder width apart. From here the upper body bends forward until the chest is parallel to the ground. From here the arms extend forward of the shoulders. From here the hands grasp the taut band. From here the arms pull the bands to the thighs. From here swimmers slowly return to the starting position.

Straight Leg Raise

Swimmers lie face up with the legs straight. From here the right leg bends ninety degrees while the left leg remains straight. From here the left leg lifts six inches off the ground. From here the left leg lowers to slightly off ground level. Throughout the sequence the left leg remains off the ground. From here swimmers slowly return to the starting position and repeat on the opposite side.

> **Note:** *Ankle weights may be added for an additional challenge.*

Streamline Crunch

Swimmers lie face up in a streamline position. From here the upper body curls into a crunch position with the arms, head, and shoulder blades off the ground. From here swimmers slowly return to the starting position.

Streamline Sit Up

Swimmers lie face up in a streamline position. From here the upper body curls into a sit up position. From here swimmers slowly return to the starting position.

Towel Leg Stretch

The exercise is performed with a towel. Swimmers sit tall with the legs straight and place the rolled towel under the ball of the right foot. From here the hands grasp the towel at both ends and pull it toward the chest. The position is held for five seconds or longer once a stretch is felt. From here swimmers slowly return to the starting position and repeat on the opposite side.

Towel Shoulder Stretch

The exercise is performed with a towel. Swimmers stand tall, holding a towel above the right shoulder with the right hand. From here the towel is lowered behind the back. From here the left hand grasps the other end of the towel behind the lower back. From here the right arm extends, pulling the left hand upward along the spine. The position is held for five seconds or longer once a stretch is felt. From here swimmers slowly return to the starting position and repeat on the opposite side.

Tricep Push Up

Swimmers lie facedown with the legs straight. From here the hands are placed underneath the shoulders with the toe tips resting on the ground. From here the head is placed and held in a neutral position. From here the upper arms squeeze against the sides of the body with the elbows pointing backward. From here the arms press the body upward into a plank position. From here the arms lower the body to three inches off the ground before returning to a plank position.

Trunk Rotation Stretch

Swimmers lie face up with the knees bent ninety degrees, the feet flat on the ground, and the arms positioned away from the sides of the body. From here the legs rotate to the right, touching the outside of the right knee to the ground. The position is held for five seconds or longer once a stretch is felt. From here swimmers slowly return to the starting position and repeat on the opposite side.

Walking Lunge
Similar to Standing Lunge only swimmers step forward on each lunge rather than returning to the original starting position.

Walking Lunge With Med Ball
Similar to Walking Lunge only the medicine ball is held at chest level.

Wall Stretch
Swimmers stand tall with the back against the wall. From here the arms raise above the head to full extension. From here the hands (knuckle side) press against the wall. The position is held for five seconds or longer once a stretch is felt. From here swimmers slowly return to the starting position.

30-Degree Pull Up With Cables
The exercise is performed with suspension cables attached to a wall approximately seven feet above the ground. Swimmers stand tall, grasping the cables with both hands in a thumbs-up position. From here the feet step back until the arms are fully extended. At this point the body is positioned at a thirty-degree angle relative to the ground. From here the arms pull the body upward. As the arms pull, the upper arms squeeze against the sides of the body with the elbows pointing backward. From here the shoulder blades squeeze together as the pull nears completion. From here swimmers slowly return to the starting position.

45-Degree Jackknife
Swimmers lie face up in a streamline position. From here the arms and legs raise off the ground and the fingertips touch the toe tips. From here swimmers slowly return to the starting position.

45-Degree Pull Up With Cables
Similar to Thirty-Degree Pull Up With Cables only the body angles forty-five degrees.

90-Degree Toe Touch
Swimmers stand tall with the arms extended overhead. From here the upper body leans forward, touching the fingertips to the toe tips. If necessary the knees may bend slightly. The position is held for five seconds or longer once a stretch is felt. From here swimmers slowly return to the starting position.

A BIG THANK YOU!

I wish to thank Cheryl Blenk for providing much of the content in this chapter. In addition to being a part-time member of the Peak Performance Swim Camp coaching staff, Cheryl has spent more than twenty years working in the health-care and fitness industries. She is a certified athletic trainer as well as a certified strength and conditioning specialist and a USA Triathlon coach. Cheryl has worked at some of the most prestigious health facilities including: Hospital for Special Surgery, The New York Athletic Club, Chelsea Piers, and La Palestra. Her knowledge and expertise in sports medicine combined with her experience as a lifetime competitive swimmer and coach gives her a keen understanding of the unique approach needed to attain the competitive edge in swimming. Cheryl owns a fitness consulting business in New York and travels throughout the United States and abroad designing strength and conditioning programs for athletes.

Note: *For further information on these exercises or to purchase programs and/or equipment, go to the Swimming Triangle website at www.swimmingtriangle.com*

THE NATIONAL TRAINING CENTER

As an alternative to the dry land training programs outlined above, coaches, parents, and swimmers may wish to contact the Human Performance Lab at the National Training Center in Clermont, Florida, for individualized fitness testing. The director of the lab is Carol Kneller (who has a master's degree in athletic training). Staff members include Sharylynne Rivera (master's degree in exercise physiology) and Misty Becerra (bachelor's degree in exercise science). Swimmers traveling to NTC undergo a battery of tests geared to pinpointing fitness deficiencies relative to swim-specific strength and flexibility. Once deficiencies are identified, a personalized dry land program is put in place. Each program includes a step-by-step video presentation of recommended exercises created to ensure proper execution and reduce the risk of injury

> **Note:** *The National Training Center is a 300-acre sport, health, and fitness center geared to assisting athletes (of all sports) in achieving peak performance. Many world-class athletes call NTC home. The facilities include: a 70-meter x 25 yard outdoor pool; a 37,000 square foot fitness center; a 400-meter high-tech track; and multipurpose athletic fields. A full-fledged hospital is located next to NTC and first-class hotel accommodations border the campus. Clermont is located twenty minutes west of Orlando and only fifteen minutes from Disney World, Universal Studios, and SeaWorld. NTC is also home to Peak Performance Swim Camp. The facility is a great training camp destination for all sports. For further information contact NTC at 888-841-7995 or go to www.usantc.com.*

CHAPTER 6

The Holistic Funnel

The title of this chapter clearly conveys its purpose. Now that the mental, technical, and physical curricula are in place, the holistic coach is challenged to implement an approach that incorporates all three in one practice. This is by no means an easy feat, as they key objectives of each curriculum must be ever present. To assist the holistic coach in this endeavor, sample practices for novice-, junior-, and senior-level swimmers are provided below. Although practices differ from level to level, they all share a holistic theme.

> **Note:** *Mental conditioning concepts are typically presented in a chalk-talk format at the beginning of practice or used as themes throughout practice.*

For sample purposes one-hour practice sessions for novice level, one and a half hour practice sessions for junior level, and two-hour practice sessions for senior level are presented. Sample practices may be adjusted should the amount of time dedicated to practice differ. Additional samples are posted on *The Swimming Triangle* website at www.swimmingtriangle.com.

> **Note:** *As mentioned previously some coaches will find the junior- and senior-level practice examples relatively easy, but two important factors must be considered. In a holistic approach, best-form stroke and turn technique*

is required throughout the entire practice (initially reducing yardage totals), and the average speeds per 25 are typically faster than those found in a conventional or garbage-yardage approach.

Detailed information regarding training methodologies, practice structure, and practice sets appear in Chapter 4. Sample dry land training circuits, as cited below, are outlined in Chapter 5. Explanations of the practice terminology used in the sample novice-, junior-, and senior-practices are listed in the Practice Glossary immediately following this section.

Note: *Although not ideal, a home version dry land training program is recommended for swimmers should time not be available during regular practice hours. In that case the holistic coach will test swimmers periodically to ensure compliance.*

NOVICE-LEVEL PRACTICE

The speed of each set presented below is determined by the swimmers' ability to maintain best-form stroke technique throughout. Although most swimmers could easily perform these sets at a much faster pace, they are not permitted to do so unless best-form stroke technique is exhibited. For sample purposes all sets begin at speed 1 or speed 2. The six-speed training concept is used exclusively in all sample novice practices.

Sample 1
- Dry Land Training: Novice Circuit A
- 5' Mental: *101 Winning Ways* > Page 41
- 15' Warm Up: 1-4 Front Start Progression
- 15' Technical: FL > 25s > Speed 1 or Speed 2 > FL Body Position

- 15' Challenge: FL > 25s > Speed 2 or Higher > Odd 25s > FL > Breathe @ 2 > Even 25s > FR > Breathe @ 3
- 10' Kick: BK > 25s > Speed 2 or Higher > Streamline Kick on Back Drill > Butt Squeeze Kick > Boil Water

Sample 2
- Dry Land Training: Novice Circuit B
- 5' Mental: *101 Winning Ways* > Page 21
- 10' Warm Up: 1-3 FR Turn Progression
- 10' Drill: FR > 25s > Speed 2 or Higher > People Paddle Drill
- 10' Pull: FR > 25s > Speed 2 or Higher > Breathe @ 3 > Size Proportionate Pull Buoy > No Paddles
- 10' Challenge: FR > 25s > Speed 2 or Higher > Breathe @ 3 > Streamline Stance Off Walls > Breakout Timing
- 5' Recover/Refocus/Review: Meditative Breathing
- 10' Challenge: FR > 25s > Speed 2 or Higher > Breathe @ 3 > Streamline Stance off Walls > Breakout Timing

Sample 3
- Dry Land Training: Novice Circuit A
- 5' Mental: *101 Winning Ways* > Page 43
- 10' Warm Up: 1-3 BR Turn Progression
- 15' Technical: BK > 25s > Speed 1 or Speed 2 > 1-4 BK Arm Cycle
- 15' Kick: FL > 25s > Speed 2 or Higher > Odd 25s > Whole-Body Kick Drill > Even 25s > Half Body Kick Drill
- 15' Challenge: BK > 25s > Speed 2 or Higher > Cup Head > Body Whip > Breakout Timing > Flat Back Finish

Sample 4
- Dry Land Training: Novice Circuit B

- 5' Mental: *101 Winning Ways* > Page 59
- 15' Warm Up: 1-4 BK Start Progression
- 10' Drill: BR > 25s > Speed 2 or Higher > 7-Squeeze > 1" Glide
- 10' Pull: BK > 25s > Speed 2 or Higher > Size-Proportionate Pull Buoy > No Paddles
- 10' Challenge: FR > 25s > Speed 2 or Higher > Odd 25s > Minimal Kick > Even 25s > Maximal Kick
- 5' Recover/Refocus/Review: Review Freestyle Kick Focus Points
- 10' Challenge: FR > 25s > Speed 2 or Higher > Odd 25s > Minimal Kick > Even 25' > Maximal Kick

Sample 5
- Dry Land Training: Novice Circuit A
- 5' Mental: *101 Winning Ways* > Page 85
- 10' Warm Up: 1-3 FR Turn Progression
- 15' Technical: BR > 25s > Speed 1 or Speed 2 > 1-3 BR Kick Cycle
- 15' Challenge: BR > 25s > Speed 2 or Higher > 7-Squeeze > 2" Glide > I-Y-Elbows High
- 15' Kick: FR > 25s > Speed 2 or Higher > Side Kick Drill > Alternate Sides @ 25

Sample 6
- Dry Land Training: Novice Circuit B
- 5' Mental: *101 Winning Ways* > Page 73
- 10' Warm Up: 1-3 BK Turn Progression
- 15' Technical: FR > 25s > Speed 1 or Speed 2 > 1-2 FR Breathing Cycle
- 15' Challenge: FL > 25s > Speed 2 or Higher > Odd 25s > FL > Even 25s > 1A FL Side/Front Drill
- 15' Kick: BR > 25s > Speed 2 or Higher > Hold Board Midway With Face Out > High Heels > W > Snap Butt

Sample 7

- Dry Land Training: Novice Circuit A
- 5' Mental: *101 Winning Ways* > Page 53
- 10' Warm Up: 1-4 Front Start Progression
- 10' Drill: BK > Speed 2 or Higher > 25s > Streamline Kick on Back Drill > Butt Squeeze Kick > Boil Water
- 10' Pull: FR > Speed 2 or Higher > Breathe @ 3 > Size-Proportionate Pull Buoy > No Paddles > Full Extension/Full Finish > Equal Hip Rotation
- 10' Challenge: FR > 25s > Speed 2 or Higher > MDPS
- 5' Recover/Refocus/Review: 100 BK > Best-Form Technique
- 10' Challenge: FR > 25s > Speed 2 or Higher > MDPS

Sample 8

- Dry Land Training: Novice Circuit B
- 5' Mental: *101 Winning Ways* > Page 39
- 10' Warm Up: 1-3 FR Turn Progression
- 15' Technical: FL > 25s > Speed 1 or Speed 2 > 1-2 FL Kick Cycle
- 15' Kick: FR > 25s > Speed 2 or Higher > Horizontal Kick Drill > To, Not Through > 3-5 Knee Bend
- 15' Challenge: BK > 25s > Speed 2 or Higher > Odd 25s > Minimal Kick > Even 25s > Maximal Kick

Sample 9

- Dry Land Training: Novice Circuit A
- 5' Mental: *101 Winning Ways* > Page 35
- 10' Warm Up: 1-3 FL Turn Progression
- 10' Drill: FL > 25s > Speed 2 or Higher > 1A FL Side/ Front Drill
- 10' Pull: BR > 25s > Speed 2 or Higher > 7-Squeeze > 1" Glide > Size-Proportionate Pull Buoy > No Paddles
- 10' Challenge: FR > 25s > Speed 2 or Higher > Odd 25s > Breathe Right Side Only > Even 25s > Breathe

Left Side Only
- 5' Recover/Refocus/Review: Meditative Breathing
- 10' Challenge: FR > 25s > Speed 2 or Higher > Odd 25s > Breathe Right Side Only > Even 25s > Breathe Left Side Only

Sample 10
- Dry Land Training: Novice Circuit B
- 5' Mental: *101 Winning Ways* > Page 13
- 15' Warm Up: 1-4 BK Start Progression
- 10' Technical: BK > 25s > Speed 1 or Higher > BK Body Position
- 15' Challenge: BR > 25s > Speed 2 or Higher > Odd 25s > 7-Squeeze > 3" Glide > Even 25s > 7-Squeeze > 0" Glide > 2 + 3 = 1 > Breakout Timing
- 15' Kick: FL > 25s > Speed 2 or Higher > Streamline Kick on Back Drill > Butt Squeeze Kick > Boil Water

Note: *The mental concepts for the novice-level practices come from my first book,* 101 Winning Ways, *available for purchase through the Peak Performance Swim Camp website at www.swimcamp.com.*

JUNIOR-LEVEL PRACTICE
The speed of each set presented below is determined by the swimmers' ability to maintain best-form stroke and turn technique throughout. Although most swimmers could easily perform these sets at a much faster pace, they are not permitted to do so unless best-form stroke and turn technique is exhibited. For sample purposes all sets begin at speed 2. Typically junior-level swimmers of lesser ability begin most Drill Sets at speed 2 or speed 3 and Challenge Sets/Kick Sets at speed 3 or speed 4, while junior-level swimmers of greater ability begin most Drill Sets at speed 3 and Challenge Sets/Kick Sets at speed 4 or speed 5.

Note: *Unlike the novice level, junior-level practices use a combination of six-speed training and touch times.*

Sample 1

- Dry Land Training: Junior Circuit A
- 10' Mental: Shared Responsibility > See Mental Curriculum
- 10' Warm Up: FL/BK Finishes
- 15' Kick: FR > 50s > Speed 2 or Higher > Horizontal Kick Drill > To, Not Through
- 20' Challenge: FR > 100s > Using Touch Times > Breathe @ 3 > MDPS
- 10' Kick: BK > 25s > Speed 2 or Higher > 3-5 Knee Bend > Boil Water
- 10' Pull: BK > 75s > Speed 2 or Higher > Size Proportionate Pull Buoy > No Paddles
- 15' Challenge: BK > 100s > Using Touch Times > Cup Head > Windmill Arms

Sample 2

- Dry Land Training: Junior Circuit B
- 5' Mental: *101 Winning Ways* > Page 83
- 20' Warm Up: Front Starts
- 15' Technical: FR Arm Cycle > FR Kick Cycle > Build 25s
- 25' Challenge: FR > 200s > Using Touch Times > Breathe @ 3 > Flutter Not Sputter
- 10' Drill: FL > 25s > Speed 2 or Higher > 1A FL Front/Front Drill
- 15' Challenge: FL > 25s > Speed 2 or Higher > Breathe @ 2 > Body Whip

Sample 3

- Dry Land Training: Junior Circuit A
- 10' Mental: Risk Taking > See Mental Curriculum
- 15' Warm Up: FL/BR Turns

- 20' Kick: FR > 100s > Speed 2 or Higher > Horizontal Kick Drill > To, Not Through
- 10' Pull: FR > 50s > Speed 2 or Higher > Size Proportionate Pull Buoy > No Paddles
- 15' Challenge: FR > 125s > Speed 2 or Higher > Breathe @ 5
- 5' Recover/Refocus/Review: Review Freestyle Focus Points
- 15' Challenge: FR > 125s > Speed 2 or Higher > Breathe @ 5

Sample 4

- Dry Land Training: Junior Circuit B
- 10' Mental: Commitment > See Mental Curriculum
- 20' Warm Up: BK Starts
- 15' Drill: FR > 50s > Speed 2 or Higher > 3" Pause C/U Drill > Breath @ Stroke > Parallel Breathing > Flutter Not Sputter
- 20' Challenge: FR > 100s > Using Touch Times > Breathe @ 3 > Almost C/U Timing
- 10' Kick: BR > 50s > Speed 2 or Higher > Hold Board Midway With Face Out > High Heels > W
- 15' Challenge (15'): BR > 75s > Using Touch Times > 7-Squeeze > 1" Glide

Sample 5

- Dry Land Training: Junior Circuit A
- 10' Mental: The 10 Keys > See Mental Curriculum
- 15' Warm Up: BK/FR Turns
- 10' Kick: FR > 75s > Speed 2 or Higher > Side Kick Drill

- 10' Pull: FR > 50s > Speed 2 or Higher > The 4 Lines > Nose Numbers
- 20' Challenge: FR > 150s > Speed 2 or Higher > The 4

Lines > Nose Numbers
- 10' Technique: FL Arm Cycle > Plus Build 25s Maintaining Technique
- 15' Challenge: FL > 50s Speed 2 or Higher > 1st 25 > Full Stroke > 2nd 25 >
- 2 + 2 + 2 FL Drill

Sample 6

- Dry Land Training: Junior Circuit B
- 10' Mental: Resist the Urge to Be Average > See Mental Curriculum
- 10' Warm Up: BR/FR Finishes
- 15' Kick: FR > 150s > Speed 2 or Higher > Horizontal Kick Drill > Boil Water
- 20' Challenge: FR > 200s > Using Touch Times > Breathe @ 3 > MDPS
- 10' Kick: BR > 100s > Speed 2 or Higher > Hold Board Midway With Face Out > W > Snap Finish
- 10' Pull: BR > 25s > Speed 2 or Higher > Size-Proportionate Pull Buoy > No Paddles > I-Y-Elbows High
- 15' Challenge: BR > 50s > Using Touch Times > 1st 25 > 7-Squeeze > 1" Glide > 2nd 25 > 7-Squeeze > 0" Glide

Sample 7

- Dry Land Training: Junior Circuit A
- 5' Mental: *101 Winning Ways* > Page 81
- 20' Warm Up: Front Starts
- 25' Challenge: FR > 100s > Using Touch Times > Breathe @ 3 > The 3 Lines
- 10' Drill: BK > 50s > Speed 2 or Higher > 1A BK > 1-4 BK Arm Cycle > Roll In/Roll Out
- 15' Challenge: BK > 50s > Speed 2 or Higher > Seamless Turns > Breakout Timing
- 15' Kick: BK > 25s > Speed 2 or Higher > Streamline

Kick on Back Drill > 3-5 Knee Bend > Boil Water

Sample 8

- Dry Land Training: Junior Circuit B
- 10' Mental: Think Positive > See Mental Curriculum
- 15' Warm Up: IM Turns
- 20' Kick: FL > 75s > Speed 2 or Higher > 2-Way Kick on Side Drill
- 10' Drill: FL > Speed 2 or Higher > FL Arms With FR Kick Drill > Breathe @ Stroke
- 15' Challenge: FR > 125s > Speed 2 or Higher > ½ Breathe > ½ No Breathe
- 5' Recover/Refocus/Review: 200 BK > Best-Form Technique
- 15' Challenge: FR > 125s > Speed 2 or Higher > ½ No Breathe > ½ Breathe

Sample 9

- Dry Land Training: Junior Circuit A
- 10' Mental: Confidence > See Mental Curriculum
- 20' Warm Up: BK Starts
- 15' Technical: FR Arm Cycle > Plus Build 25s Maintaining Technique
- 20' Challenge: FR > 200s > Using Touch Times > Supersize > Power Triangle > Streamline Stance Off Walls
- 10' Kick: FR > 75s > Speed 2 or Higher > Hold Top Of Board With Face Out > To, Not Through
- 15' Challenge: FR > 100s > Using Touch Times > Supersize > Power Triangle > Streamline Stance Off Walls

Sample 10

- Dry Land Training: Junior Circuit B

- 10' Mental: Role Models > See Mental Curriculum
- 15' Warm Up: FL/BK/BR/FR Turns
- 10' Kick: FR > 100s > Speed 2 or Higher > Parallel Breathing With Kickboard Drill
- 10' Pull: FR > 25s > Speed 2 or Higher > Tick Tock Finish Drill > Breathe @ 3 > Equal Rotation
- 20' Challenge: FR > 50s > Speed 2 or Higher > Breathe @ 3 > Parallel Breathing > Flutter Not Sputter
- 10' Drill: FL > 25s > Speed 2 or Higher > FL Arms With No Kick Drill > Breathing @ Stroke > Chest Press > 1-2 FL Breathing Cycle
- 15' Challenge: FL > 50s > Speed 2 or Higher > Chest Press > 1-2 FL Breathing Cycle

SENIOR-LEVEL PRACTICE

The speed of each set is determined by the swimmers' ability to maintain best-form stroke and turn technique throughout. Although most swimmers could easily perform these sets at a much faster pace, they are not permitted to do so unless best-form stroke and turn technique is exhibited. For sample purposes all sets in these begin at speed 2 or higher. Typically senior-level swimmers of lesser ability begin most Drill Sets at speed 2 or speed 3 and Challenge Sets/Kick Sets at speed 3 or speed 4 while senior-level swimmers of greater ability begin most Drill Sets at speed 3 and Challenge Sets/Kick Sets at speed 4 or speed 5.

Note: *Unlike the novice level, senior-level practices use a combination of six-speed training and touch times.*

Sample 1
- Dry Land Training: Senior Circuit A
- 10' Mental: The 5 Ps > See Mental Curriculum
- 15' Warm Up: FR Turns
- 15' Kick: FR > 100s > Speed 2 or Higher > Odd 25s

> Horizontal Kick Drill > Even 25s > Hold Top Of Board With Face Out
- 15' Drill: FR > 75s > Speed 2 or Higher > 50 > 6-Kick Switch Drill > Breathe Both Sides + 25 FR > Breathe @ 3 > Full Extension/Full Finish > Flutter Not Sputter
- 25' Challenge: FR > 300s > Using Touch Times > Water Height > Boil Water > No Breathing 1st Stroke Cycle Off Walls
- 15' Drill: IM > 50s > Speed 2 or Higher > 1st 50 > 1A FL Drill > 2nd 50 > 1A BK Drill > 3rd 50 > BR Pull With FR Kick Drill > 4th 50 > 1A FR Drill > Full Extension/Full Finish
- 25' Challenge: IM > 200s > Speed 2 or Higher > Supersize > Seamless Turns

Sample 2
- Dry Land Training: Senior Circuit B
- 10' Mental: Power of Passion > See Mental Curriculum
- 15' Warm Up: Front Starts
- 20' Challenge: FR > 100s > Using Touch Times > The 4 Lines
- 5' Recover/Refocus/Review: Meditative Breathing
- 20' Challenge: FR > 100s > Using Touch Times > The 4 Lines
- 15' Kick: FL > 75s > Speed 2 or Higher > Whole Body Kick Drill
- 15' Drill: FL > 50s > Speed 2 or Higher > 1A FL Front/ Side Drill > 3-4 Knee Bend > 1st Kick > 4-5 Knee Bend > 2nd Kick
- 20' Challenge: FL > 100s > Using Touch Times > 1-4 FL Arm Cycle

Sample 3

- Dry Land Training: Senior Circuit A
- 10' Mental: Focus > See Mental Curriculum
- 15' Warm Up: IM Turns
- 10' Technical: FL > Speed 2 or Higher > Arm Timing > Kick Timing > Breathing Timing
- 25' Challenge: IM > 200s > Speed 2 or Higher > Seamless Swimming > Seamless Turns > Breakout Timing
- 20' Drill: FR > 100s > Speed 2 or Higher > People Paddle Drill > Breathe @ 3
- 25' Challenge: FR > 400s > Using Touch Times > The 4 Lines > Streamline Stance Off Walls
- 15' Kick: FR > 300s > Speed 2 or Higher > 1st 150 > Side Kick Drill > 2nd 150 Horizontal Kick Drill

Sample 4

- Dry Land Training: Senior Circuit B
- 10' Mental: Delayed Gratification > See Mental Curriculum
- 20' Warm Up: BK Starts
- 15' Challenge: IM order > 25s > Speed 2 or Higher > Focus Starts/Finishes
- 25' Challenge: FR > 150s > Speed 2 or Higher > Even Speed > Streamline Stance Off Walls > Breakout Timing
- 20' Kick: BR > 75s > Speed 2 or Higher > Streamline Kick on Back Drill > FFF
- 15' Drill: BR > 75s > Speed 2 or Higher > 1st 50 > BR P With FR K Drill > 3rd 25 > 7-Squeeze > 0" Glide
- 15' Challenge: BR > 100s > Speed 2 or Higher > Odd 25s > 2 Pull Outs Off Wall > Even 25s > 3 Pull Outs Off Wall

Sample 5

- Dry Land Training: Senior Circuit A
- 10' Mental: Get Real > See Mental Curriculum
- 10' Warm Up: BR Turns
- 10' Drill: FR > 100s > Speed 2 or Higher > Odd 25s > Zipper Drill > Breathe @ 3 > Even 25s > FR > Breathe @ 3 > Match Recovery Arms
- 25' Challenge: FR > 200s > Speed 2 or Higher > Odd @ 25s > FR > Breathe @ 3 > Even 25s > Fast Kick/Slow Arms Drill > Breathe @ 3
- 15' Kick: FL > 25s > Speed 2 or Higher > 3-4 Knee Bend > 1st Kick > 4-5 Knee Bend > 2nd Kick
- 20' Challenge: FL > 75s > Speed 2 or Higher > 1st 25 > FL > Breathe @ 3 > 2nd 25 > FR > Breathe @ 3 > 3rd 25 > FL > Breathe @ 3
- 15' Pull: BK > 125s > Speed 2 or Higher > Size Proportionate Pull Buoy > Paddles > Cup Head > Equal Rotation > FFF
- 15' Challenge: BK > 75s > Speed 2 or Higher > 5" Rule

Sample 6

- Dry Land Training: Senior Circuit B
- 10' Mental: Competitiveness > See Mental Curriculum
- 15' Warm Up: BK Turns
- 15' Kick: BK > 100s > Speed 2 or Higher > Streamline Kick on Back Drill > Cup Head > Boil Water
- 15' Drill: BK > 50s > Speed 2 or Higher > 1A BK With Pull Buoy in Armpit Drill > Roll In/Roll Out
- 25' Challenge: BK > 200s > Using Touch Times > Seamless Turns > Streamline Stance Off Walls > 5" Rule
- 15' Drill: BR > 50s > Speed 2 or Higher > BR P With Pull Buoy Drill > No FL K > 3-S Pull
- 25' Challenge: IM > 300s > Speed 2 or Higher > MDPS

Sample 7

- Dry Land Training: Senior Circuit A
- 10' Mental: Good Pain Versus Bad Pain > See Mental Curriculum
- 15' Warm Up: Front Starts
- 20' Challenge: FR > 300s > Using Touch Times > MDPS > 1st 150 > Minimal Kick > 2nd 150 > Maximal Kick
- 5' Recover/Refocus/Review: 200 BK > Best-Form Technique
- 20' Challenge: FR > 300s > Using Touch Times > MDPS > 1st 150 > Minimal Kick > 2nd 150 > Maximal Kick
- 15' Kick: BR > 50s > Speed 2 or Higher > High Heel Drill > 10 Knee Bend
- 15' Drill: BR > 25s > Speed 2 or Higher > ½ Shoot Drill > ½ BR
- 20' Challenge: BR > 100s > Using Touch Times > 1st 50 > 7-Squeeze > 1" Glide > 2nd 50 > 7-Squeeze > 0" Glide

Sample 8

- Dry Land Training: Senior Circuit B
- 10' Mental: Near Perfection > See Mental Curriculum
- 15' Warm Up: IM Turns
- 10' Technical: BR > Speed 1 or Speed 2 > 3-S Pull
- 25' Challenge: IM > 200s > Speed 2 or Higher > Seamless Swimming > Seamless Turns
- 20' Drill: FR > 100s > Speed 2 or Higher > 6-Kick Switch Drill > Breathe Both Sides
- 20' Challenge: FR > 50s > Speed 2 or Higher > Supersize > Flutter Not Sputter
- 20' Kick: FR > 25s > Speed 2 or Higher > Streamline Kick on Front Drill > 2 Breaths or Less @ 25

Sample 9

- Dry Land Training: Senior Circuit A
- 10' Mental: Patience > See Mental Curriculum
- 20' Warm Up: BK Starts

- 15' Challenge: IM > 25s > Speed 2 or Higher > Focus Starts/Finishes
- 25' Challenge: FR > 400s > Speed 2 or Higher > Odd 100s > Breathe @ 3 > Even 100s > Breathe @ 5 > 0-3 Nose Number > Full Extension/Full Finish
- 20' Kick: FL > 50s > Speed 2 or Higher > Streamline Kick on Back Drill > To, Not Through
- 15' Drill: FL > 50s > Speed 2 or Higher > 1A FL Front/Front Drill > Full Extension/Full Finish
- 15' Challenge: FL > 50s > Speed 2 or Higher > 1st 25 > No Breathing Last 3 Strokes Into Wall > 2nd 25 > No Breathing Last 5 Strokes Into Wall

Sample 10

- Dry Land Training: Senior Circuit B
- 10' Mental: Three Types of Swimmers > See Mental Curriculum
- 10' Warm Up: FL Turns
- 10' Drill: FR > Speed 2 or Higher > 50s > 1st 25 Fast Kick/Slow Arms Drill > 2nd 25 Fast Kick/Fast Arms Drill
- 25' Challenge: FR > 100s > Speed 2 or Higher > MDPS > FFF
- 15' Kick: BK > 150s > Speed 2 or Higher > Odd 25s > 12 O'clock Kick Drill > RT Arm > Even 25s > 12 O'Clock Kick Drill > LT Arm > Odd 25s > Boil Water
- 20' Challenge: BK > 200s > Speed 2 or Higher > Odd 25s > 5" Rule > Even 25s > Breakout Timing
- 15' Pull: BR > 50s > Speed 2 or Higher > BR P With Hanging Legs Drill > Tennis Ball Breathing
- 15' Challenge: BR > 75s > Speed 2 or Higher > 7-Squeeze > 0" Glide

PRACTICE GLOSSARY

The following alphabetical and numerical list defines most of the terminology used in the sample novice-, junior-, and senior-level practices. Additional definitions may be found in the Technical Concepts section of Chapter 3.

Almost C/U Timing
Refers to a type of timing used in freestyle where the lead arm initiates the pull as the recovery arm passes the shoulder.

Boom Butt
Refers to a concept used to promote a more powerful butterfly kick. Swimmers are instructed to make a boom sound with the feet, while drawing the butt up through the surface.

Boil Water
Swimmers are challenged to make the water boil when performing backstroke or freestyle kick. Boiling water is different from splashing water. When boiling, the feet come up to the surface, and when splashing, the feet come down through the surface.

Body Whip
Swimmers travel underwater in a streamline position, kicking butterfly kick from the feet to the chest.

Breakout Timing
Refers to the coordination of the arm(s) and legs between the underwater portion of a start or turn to the above-water portion.

BR Pull With Hanging Legs Drill
Swimmers perform the breaststroke arm cycle allowing the legs to hang naturally with no kicking of any kind.

BR Pull With FR Kick

Swimmers perform the breaststroke arm cycle with continuous freestyle kick.

Build 25s
Swimmers progressively add speed as they travel down the pool.

Chest Press
Swimmers press the chest downward during the entry phase of the butterfly arm cycle. The chest press assists in elevating the hips and provides additional propulsion by sending the feet deeper during the downbeat phase of the first kick.

Cup Head
Swimmers perform backstroke as if balancing a cup of water on the forehead.

Equal Hip Rotation
Refers to equal or balanced hip rotation in backstroke and freestyle.

Even Speed
Each length is performed at the same speed.

Fast Kick/Fast Arms Drill
Swimmers perform fast backstroke kick together with fast backstroke arms or fast freestyle kick together with fast freestyle arms.

Fast Kick/Slow Arms Drill
Swimmers perform fast backstroke kick together with slow backstroke arms or fast freestyle kick together with slow freestyle arms.

FFF
Refers to a full fast finish in the butterfly, backstroke, and freestyle

arm cycles, and the breaststroke kick cycle

FL Arms With FR Kick Drill
Swimmers perform the butterfly arm cycle with continuous free-style kick.

FL Arms With No Kick Drill
Swimmers perform the butterfly arm cycle with no kick. The challenge is to create a horizontal body position at the end of each stroke cycle via a chest press.

Flat Back Finish
Refers to a type of backstroke finish where swimmers touch the wall flat on the back.

Flutter Not Sputter
Refers to a tight, symmetrical, continuous kick used in backstroke and freestyle.

Full Extension/Full Finish
Swimmers are challenged to extend the arms fully at the point of entry and finish in the butterfly, backstroke, and freestyle arm cycles.

Half Body Kick
Swimmers perform butterfly kick holding the top of a kickboard with the arms fully extended. As the name suggests, only the lower half of the body (hips down) is used.

> **Note:** *The half body kick represents the second kick in butterfly.*

High Heels
Refers to raising the heels as high as possible during the recovery

phase of the breaststroke kick cycle. The lesser the gap between the heels and butt, the greater the propulsive phase.

High Heel Drill
Swimmers perform breaststroke kick with the face out and the chin resting on the surface with the arms pressed against the sides of the body. The challenge is to touch the heels to the hands at the height of the recovery phase.

Horizontal Kick Drill
Swimmers perform freestyle kick holding the bottom of the kickboard with the arms fully extended and the face in the water. Breathing is to the front when needed.

I-Y-Elbows High
Refers to a method used to teach the first three steps of the breaststroke arm cycle. The letter I refers to the position of the arms when held in streamline; the letter Y refers to the position of the arms at the end of the outward sweep phase; the term *elbows high* refers to the ideal position of the elbows prior to the inward scull phase.

MDPS
Refers to maximum distance per stroke.

Max Distance U/W @ 25
Swimmers are challenged to travel the maximum distance underwater per 25.

> **Warning:** *Swimming underwater for an extended period of time can pose a health risk and in some instances lead to shallow water blackout, a loss of consciousness caused by cerebral hypoxia. It typically occurs toward the end of a breath-holding dive and/*

or swim in water no deeper than five meters. Shallow water blackout can be caused by taking several very deep breaths or hyperventilating (over-breathing) prior to diving into the pool or pushing off the wall. Victims are often established practitioners who have never experienced problems before. Coaches must be on guard, exercising strict supervision when the drill is performed. In addition swimmers must be cautioned on the dangers involved in breath holding prior to participating in a breath holding activity.

Minimal Kick
Refers to a tight, symmetrical, continuous backstroke or freestyle kick of minimal intensity.

Maximal Kick
Refers to a tight, symmetrical, continuous backstroke or freestyle kick of maximal intensity.

Nose Numbers
A method used to achieve the ideal head position in freestyle. Additional information may be found in the Technical Concepts section in Chapter 3.

Parallel Breathing
Refers to the ideal breathing position in freestyle. To achieve this position the entire side of the head must remain parallel to the surface throughout the inhalation phase of the breathing cycle. A parallel head position promotes a horizontal body position.

Parallel Breathing With Kickboard Drill
Swimmers perform freestyle kick holding a kickboard in the right hand with the right arm fully extended and the left arm pressed against the side of the body. From here breathing in parallel fashion is performed to the left. The drill is repeated on the

opposite side.

People Paddle Drill
Swimmers perform an exaggerated form of dog paddle with the face in the water. The arms extend fully forward of the shoulders and beyond the hips and recover under the water as opposed to over the water. Breathing is bilateral.

Power Triangle
Refers to the ideal push off position off the wall. To achieve the power triangle position, the feet land on the wall shoulder width apart with the knees bent ninety degrees. The upper body is held in a streamlined position with little or no arch in the back. In backstroke the feet land perpendicular to the surface, while in freestyle the feet land perpendicular or parallel to the surface depending upon the type of turn used.

> **Note:** *Swimmers depart the wall by pushing off on the balls of the feet.*

Roll In/Roll Out
Refers to the rotational timing in backstroke and freestyle. As the right arm enters, the right side of the body rolls into the water as one unit, and as the right arm exits, the right side of the body rolls out of the water as one unit. In addition, as the right arm enters, the ball of the left must be fully exposed, and as the right arm exits, the ball of the right shoulder must be fully exposed.

Seamless Swimming
Refers to the way in which each part of a stroke blends together to create ideal timing/flow.

Seamless Turns
Refers to the way in which each part of a turn blends together to create ideal timing/flow.

Side Kick Drill

Swimmers lie completely on the side (ninety degrees) with the lower arm extended forward of the shoulder, the upper arm pressed against the side of the body, and the face in the water. The top shoulder, hip, and foot must be positioned directly above the bottom shoulder, hip, and foot. The face is turned upward when a breath is needed, then returned immediately to the water.

Shoot Drill

Swimmers perform head-up breaststroke pull with freestyle kick while shooting the arms upward on a forty-five-degree angle. The arms must achieve full extension before returning to the water. The purpose of the drill is to energize the shoot phase of the breaststroke arm cycle.

Snap Butt

Refers to the finish in breaststroke kick. As the feet snap together, the butt draws upward through the surface. Finishing in this manner prolongs the kicking cycle, thus increasing muscle involvement.

Snap Finish

Refers to the finish in breaststroke kick. Finishing with a snap of the feet increases propulsion.

Streamline Kick on Back Drill

Swimmers lie on the back in a streamlined position when performing butterfly, backstroke, or breaststroke kick.

Streamline Stance

The following land-based drill is used to improve streamlining. Swimmers stand on the tiptoes with the fingertips pointing directly up. The hands are placed one behind the other with the thumb of the hand in back locked around the palm of the hand in front. The arms are placed behind the head with the elbows locked out. The head is held in a neutral position with the eyes facing forward. The legs and feet are squeezed tightly together.

Supersize
To supersize a stroke is to swim with the biggest reach, pull, and kick possible.

Tennis Ball Breathing
Swimmers imagine having a tennis ball tucked beneath the chin. The purpose of the drill is to achieve an ideal breaststroke head position and upper body angle.

Tick Tock Finish Drill
Swimmers place a kickboard between the upper legs and attempt to touch the side of the board against the surface of the water as the hand enters the water in backstroke or freestyle. As the right hand enters the water, the right side of the kickboard must touch the surface and vice versa. The purpose of the drill is to encourage full body rotation.

> **Note:** *The bottom portion of the kickboard must be flush with the upper legs so as not to increase drag as the body rotates from side to side.*

To, Not Through
To achieve maximal propulsion in backstroke or freestyle kick, the feet come to the surface without breaking through the surface. Feet that break the surface kick air, not water. Although kicking rates in freestyle may be improved by breaking the surface, the amount of propulsion generated by each foot is diminished.

W
At the end of the recovery phase of the breaststroke kick cycle, and prior to the propulsive phase, the legs and feet should

resemble the letter W, with the knees tilted inward and the feet rotated outward.

Water Height
Refers to a swimmer's potential height in the water with the arm(s) fully extended forward of the shoulder(s), the legs fully extended, and the toes pointed.

Whole-Body Kick Drill
Swimmers perform butterfly kick holding the bottom of a kickboard with the arms fully extended. As the name suggests, the entire body (minus the head) is used.

> **Note:** *The whole-body kick represents the first kick in butterfly.*

Windmill Arms
Refers to the most common form of arm timing used in backstroke. As one arm enters, the other arm exits.

> **Note:** *The same timing is also used in shoulder-driven freestyle.*

Zipper Drill
A drill used to promote a symmetrical high elbow freestyle recovery. Swimmers imagine zipping up the side of the body from the hip to the armpit during the first half of the recovery phase.

Zero to Three Nose Number
Swimmers imagine having a dial attached to the nose. Dialing the nose to zero creates a facedown head position while dialing the nose to ten creates a position with the head totally out of the water. A zero head position is considered ideal for backstroke while a zero to three head position is considered ideal for freestyle.

1A BK Drill
Swimmers perform one-arm backstroke with the other arm pressed against the side of the body.

1A FL Front/Front Drill
Swimmers perform one-arm butterfly breathing to the front with the other arm extended forward of the shoulder.

1A FL Front/Side Drill
Swimmers perform one-arm butterfly breathing to the front with the other arm pressed against the side of the body.

1A FL Side/Front Drill
Swimmers perform one-arm butterfly breathing to the side with the other arm extended forward of the shoulder.

1A FR With Other Arm at Side Drill
Swimmers perform one-arm freestyle with the other arm pressed against the side of the body.

½ Breathe
Swimmers perform one half of a 25 with breathing.

½ No Breathe
Swimmers perform one half of a 25 without breathing.

½ Shoot Drill
Swimmers perform the Breaststroke Shoot Drill for the first half of a 25.

½ Breast
Swimmers perform full stroke breaststroke for the second half of a 25.

1-2 BK Kick Cycle
The backstroke kick cycle consists of the downbeat phase and the upbeat phase.

1-2 BR Breathing Cycle
The breaststroke breathing cycle consists of the up-breath phase and the down-breath phase.

1-2 FL Breathing Cycle
The butterfly breathing cycle consists of the up-breath phase and the down- breath phase.

1-2 FL Kick Cycle
The butterfly kick cycle consists of the downbeat phase and the upbeat phase.

1-2 FR Breathing Cycle
The freestyle breathing cycle consists of the face out phase and the face in phase.

1-2 FR Kick Cycle
The freestyle kick cycle consists of the downbeat phase and the upbeat phase.

1-3 BK Turn Progression
The backstroke turn consists of three phases: 1) before the wall, 2) at the wall, and 3) after the wall.

1-3 BR Arm Cycle
The breaststroke arm cycle consists of three phases: 1) outward sweep, 2) inward scull, and 3) shoot.

1-3 BR Kick Cycle
The breaststroke kick cycle consists of three phases: 1) recovery, 2) catch, and 3) finish.

1-3 BR Turn Progression
The breaststroke turn consists of three phases: 1) before the wall, 2) at the wall, and 3) after the wall.

1-3 FL Turn Progression
The butterfly turn consists of three phases: 1) before the wall, 2) at the wall, and 3) after the wall.

1-4 BK Arm Cycle
The backstroke arm cycle consists of four phases: 1) entry, 2) catch, 3) finish, and 4) recovery.

1-4 BK Start Progression
The backstroke start consists of four phases: 1) launch pad, 2) blastoff, 3) splashdown, and 4) underwater travel/breakout.

1-4 FL Arm Cycle
The butterfly arm cycle consists of four phases: 1) entry, 2) catch, 3) finish, and 4) recovery.

1-4 FR Arm Cycle
The freestyle arm cycle consists of four phases: 1) entry, 2) catch, 3) finish, and 4) recovery.

1-4 Front Start Progression
The front start progression consists of four phases: 1) launch pad, 2) blastoff, 3) splashdown, and 4) underwater travel/breakout.

3-5 Knee Bend
Swimmers imagine having dials attached to the outside of the knee A locked out knee position equals zero on the dial while a fully flexed knee position equals ten. A three to five knee bend is considered ideal for maximum propulsion in backstroke and freestyle and the first kick in butterfly.

2+2+2 FL Drill

Swimmers perform two on-arm butterfly strokes with the right arm, two one-arm butterfly strokes with the left arm, followed by two full strokes butterfly. When performing one-arm butterfly, the non-pulling arm is extended forward of the shoulder.

3" Pause FR C/U Drill

Similar to a freestyle catch-up drill with three exceptions: 1) swimmers keep both arms extended forward of the shoulders without touching one hand to the other, 2) swimmers pause for three seconds between the entry of one hand and the initiation of the pull with the other arm, and 3) swimmers breathe to both sides. A constant kick must be maintained throughout.

> **Note:** *The hands never touch, remaining in line with the shoulders at the point of entry.*

3-S Pull

Refers to the three phases of breaststroke pull that begin with the letter S: sweep, scull, and shoot.

3-4 Knee Bend

Swimmers imagine having dials attached to the outsides of the knees. A locked out knee positionequals zero on the dial while a fully flexed knee postion equals ten. A three to four knee bend is considered ideal for maximum propulsion in the second kick of butterfly.

4-5 Knee Bend

Swimmers imagine having dials attached to the outsides of the knees. A locked out knee position equals zoro on the the dial while a fully flexed knee position equals ten. A four to five knee bend i scomsidered ideal for maximum proplsion in the second kick of butterfly

5" Rule (Five-Second Rule)

Swimmers perfrom body whip underwater for five seconds off a start or wall before surfacing. By the five-second mark, the desired racing speed must be achieved.

6-Kick FR Switch Drill

Swimmers kick freestyle lying directly on the side with the lower arm extended forward of the shoulder, and the other arm pressed against the side of the body. Upon completing six kicks, the lower arm pulls, while the arm at the side recovers. From here the body rotates to the other side and begins the process again. Breathing is performed while on the side.

7-Squeeze

Swimmers place the entire body in a breaststroke streamline position with the thumbs, arms, and head sqeezed tightly together. The eyes face directly downward. To complete the streamline, the shoulders, butt, leges, and feet sqeeze tightly together.

10-Knee Bend

Swimmers imagine having dials attached to the outsides of the knees. A locked out position equals zero on the dial while a fully flexed position equals ten. A ten knee bend is considered ideal for the recovery phase of the breaststroke kick cycle.

12 O'Clock Drill

Swimmers perform backstroke kick with the right arm directly above the right shoulder (similar to the hand of a clock pointing to twelve o'clock) while the other arm remains pressed against the side of the body. The drill is repeated with the left arm. Sculling is not permitted at any point within the drill.

Made in the USA
Columbia, SC
01 June 2018